Magical History Tour

3 in 1 1
Collecting "The Great Pyramid,"
"The Great Wall of China," and "Hidden Oil"

FABRICE ERRE
Writer

SYLVAIN SAVOIA
Artist

PAPERCUTZ

3 in 1 1
Collecting "The Great Pyramid,"
"The Great Wall of China," and "Hidden Oil"

By Fabrice Erre and Sylvain Savoia

Original series editors: Frédéric Niffle and Lewis Trondheim
Translation: Joseph Laredo
Lettering: Cromatik Ltd

Mark McNabb — *Production*
Ingrid Rios — *Original Editorial Intern*
Jeff Whitman — *Original Managing Editor*
Stephanie Brooks — *Editor*
Rex Ogle — *Editorial Director*

Papercutz was founded by Terry Nantier and Jim Salicrup.

November 2023

Printed in Turkey by Elma Basim
First Printing
ISBN 978-1-5458-1131-3

FABRICE ERRE SYLVAIN SAVOIA

Magical History Tour

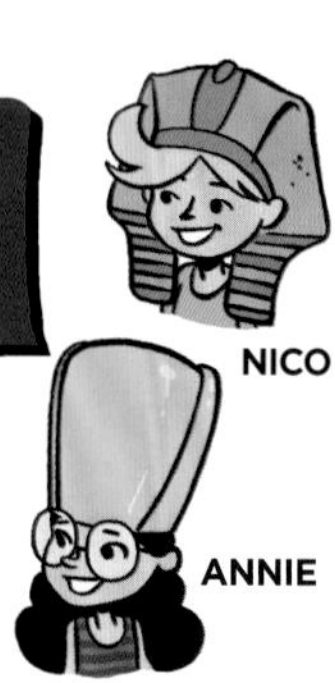
NICO
ANNIE

The Great Pyramid

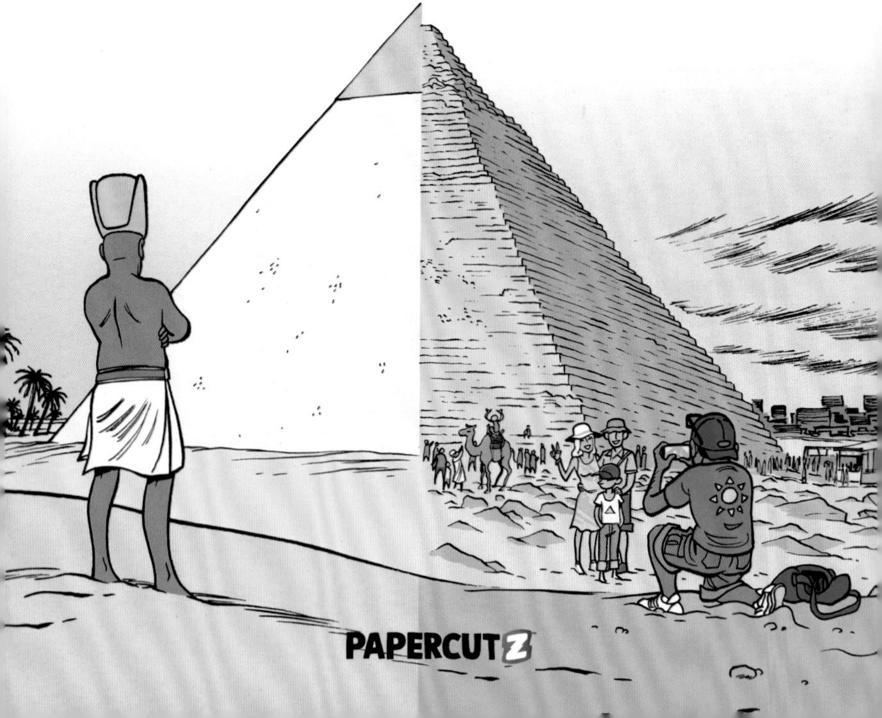

PAPERCUTZ

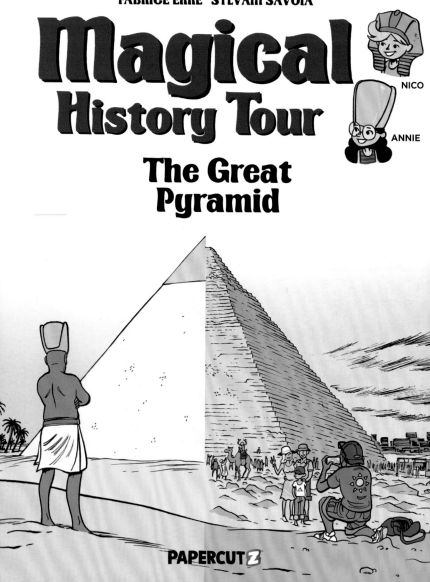

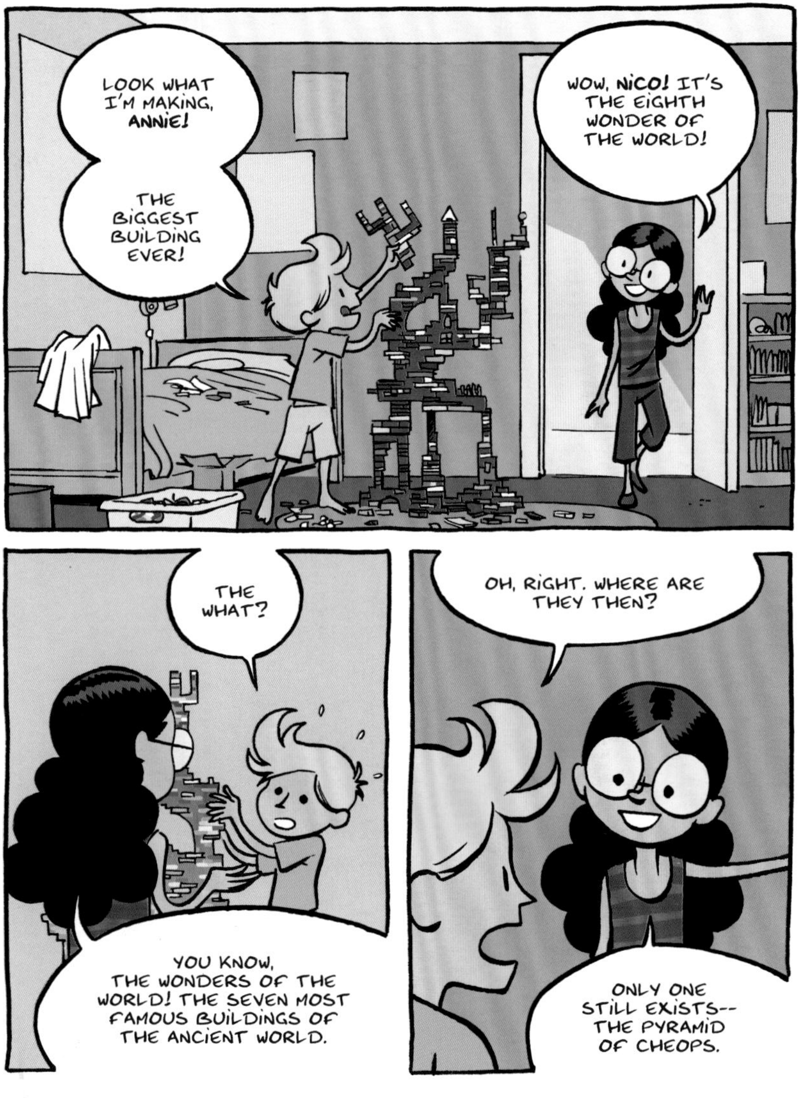
LOOK WHAT I'M MAKING, ANNIE!
THE BIGGEST BUILDING EVER!
WOW, NICO! IT'S THE EIGHTH WONDER OF THE WORLD!
THE WHAT?
YOU KNOW, THE WONDERS OF THE WORLD! THE SEVEN MOST FAMOUS BUILDINGS OF THE ANCIENT WORLD.
OH, RIGHT. WHERE ARE THEY THEN?
ONLY ONE STILL EXISTS-- THE PYRAMID OF CHEOPS.

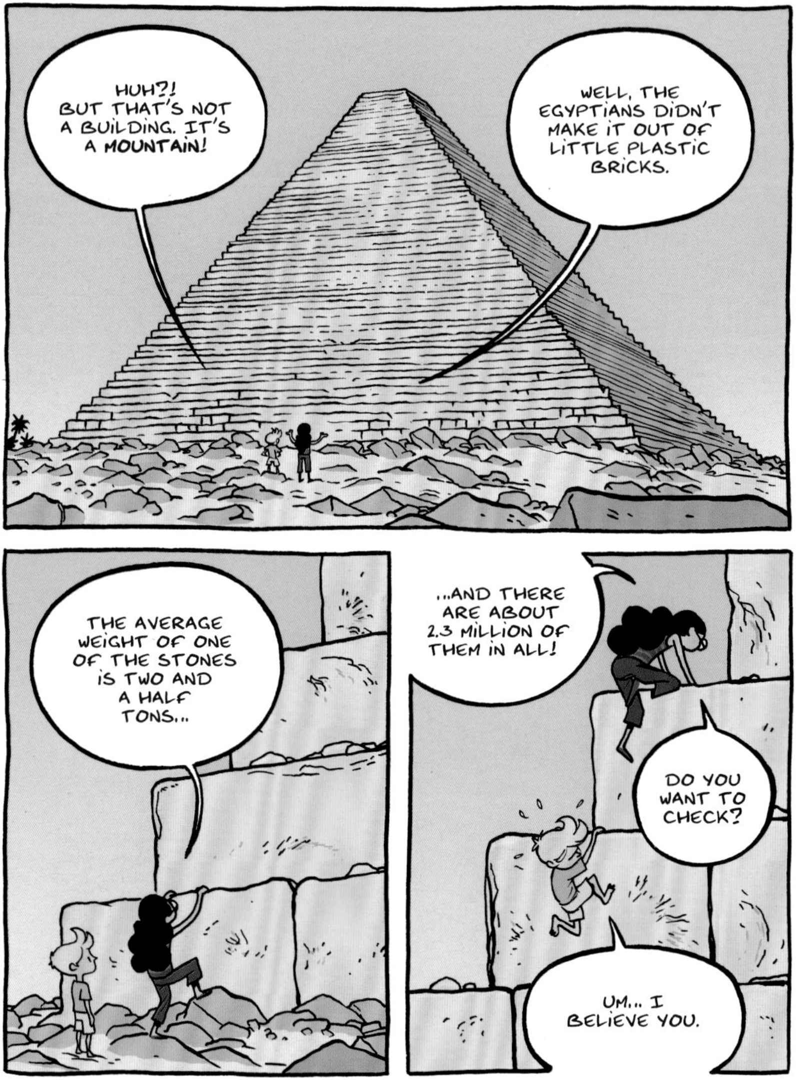
HUH?! BUT THAT'S NOT A BUILDING. IT'S A MOUNTAIN!
WELL, THE EGYPTIANS DIDN'T MAKE IT OUT OF LITTLE PLASTIC BRICKS.
THE AVERAGE WEIGHT OF ONE OF THE STONES IS TWO AND A HALF TONS...
...AND THERE ARE ABOUT 2.3 MILLION OF THEM IN ALL!
DO YOU WANT TO CHECK?
UM... I BELIEVE YOU.

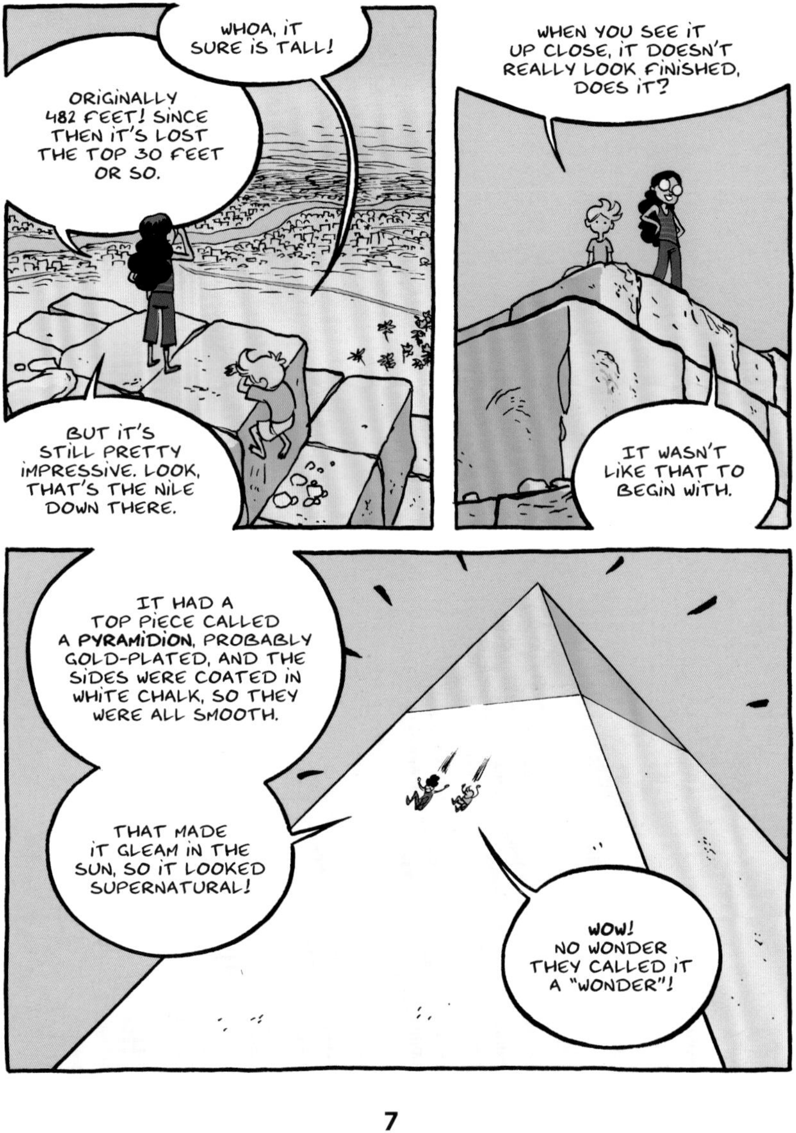
WHOA, IT SURE IS TALL!
ORIGINALLY 482 FEET! SINCE THEN IT'S LOST THE TOP 30 FEET OR SO.
BUT IT'S STILL PRETTY IMPRESSIVE. LOOK, THAT'S THE NILE DOWN THERE.
WHEN YOU SEE IT UP CLOSE, IT DOESN'T REALLY LOOK FINISHED, DOES IT?
IT WASN'T LIKE THAT TO BEGIN WITH.
IT HAD A TOP PIECE CALLED A **PYRAMIDION**, PROBABLY GOLD-PLATED, AND THE SIDES WERE COATED IN WHITE CHALK, SO THEY WERE ALL SMOOTH.
THAT MADE IT GLEAM IN THE SUN, SO IT LOOKED SUPERNATURAL!
WOW! NO WONDER THEY CALLED IT A "WONDER"!

SO WHY DOESN'T IT LOOK LIKE THAT ANYMORE?

IT'S VERY OLD, YOU KNOW. IT WAS BUILT IN 2550 B.C. THAT'S ABOUT 4,500 YEARS AGO!

IT'S HAD TO WITHSTAND SANDSTORMS, BOMBS, POLLUTION... NOT TO MENTION, RAIDERS, TREASURE-HUNTERS, AND TOURISTS...

SO STOP SCRATCHING IT!

FOR NEARLY 4,000 YEARS, IT WAS THE TALLEST BUILDING IN THE WORLD. IT WAS THE FIRST OF THE SEVEN WONDERS OF THE WORLD TO BE BUILT AND TODAY IT'S THE ONLY ONE STILL STANDING!

THE LAST ONE, THE LIGHTHOUSE OF ALEXANDRIA, FOR EXAMPLE, FELL DOWN 700 YEARS AGO.

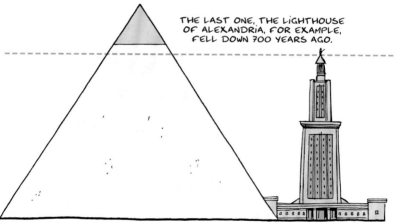

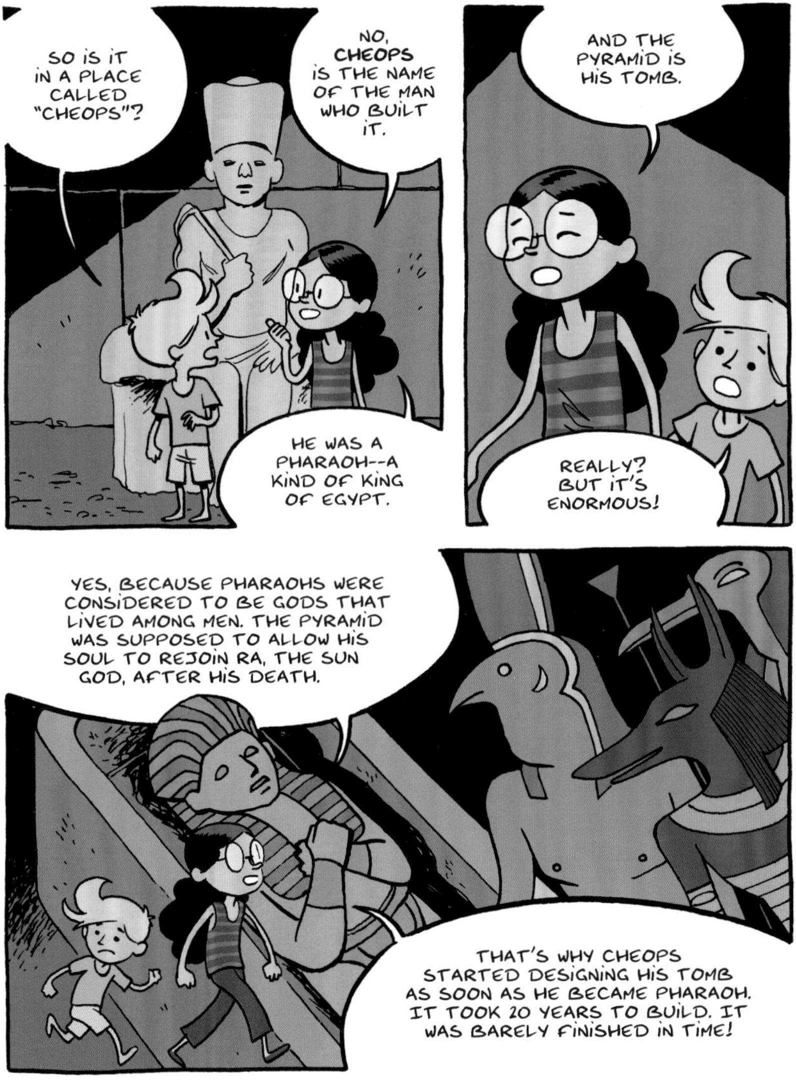
SO IS IT IN A PLACE CALLED "CHEOPS"?
NO, CHEOPS IS THE NAME OF THE MAN WHO BUILT IT.
HE WAS A PHARAOH--A KIND OF KING OF EGYPT.
AND THE PYRAMID IS HIS TOMB.
REALLY? BUT IT'S ENORMOUS!
YES, BECAUSE PHARAOHS WERE CONSIDERED TO BE GODS THAT LIVED AMONG MEN. THE PYRAMID WAS SUPPOSED TO ALLOW HIS SOUL TO REJOIN RA, THE SUN GOD, AFTER HIS DEATH.
THAT'S WHY CHEOPS STARTED DESIGNING HIS TOMB AS SOON AS HE BECAME PHARAOH. IT TOOK 20 YEARS TO BUILD. IT WAS BARELY FINISHED IN TIME!

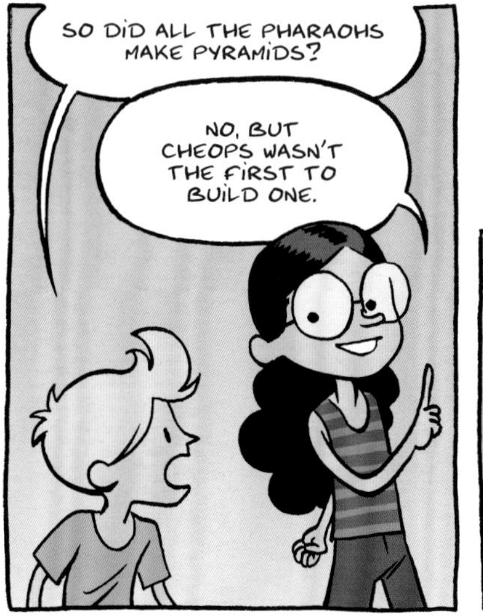
SO DID ALL THE PHARAOHS MAKE PYRAMIDS?
NO, BUT CHEOPS WASN'T THE FIRST TO BUILD ONE.

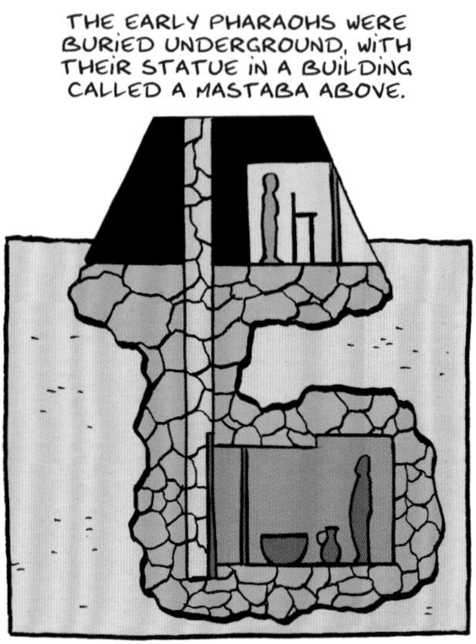
THE EARLY PHARAOHS WERE BURIED UNDERGROUND, WITH THEIR STATUE IN A BUILDING CALLED A MASTABA ABOVE.

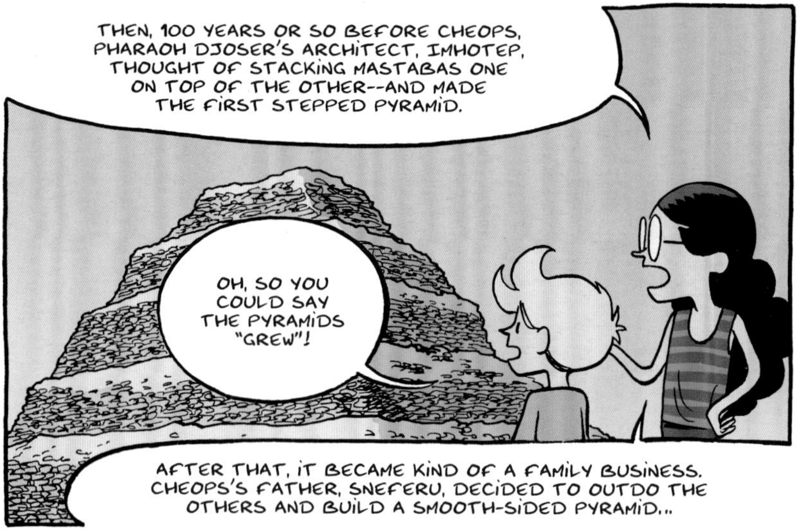
THEN, 100 YEARS OR SO BEFORE CHEOPS, PHARAOH DJOSER'S ARCHITECT, IMHOTEP, THOUGHT OF STACKING MASTABAS ONE ON TOP OF THE OTHER--AND MADE THE FIRST STEPPED PYRAMID.
OH, SO YOU COULD SAY THE PYRAMIDS "GREW"!
AFTER THAT, IT BECAME KIND OF A FAMILY BUSINESS. CHEOPS'S FATHER, SNEFERU, DECIDED TO OUTDO THE OTHERS AND BUILD A SMOOTH-SIDED PYRAMID...

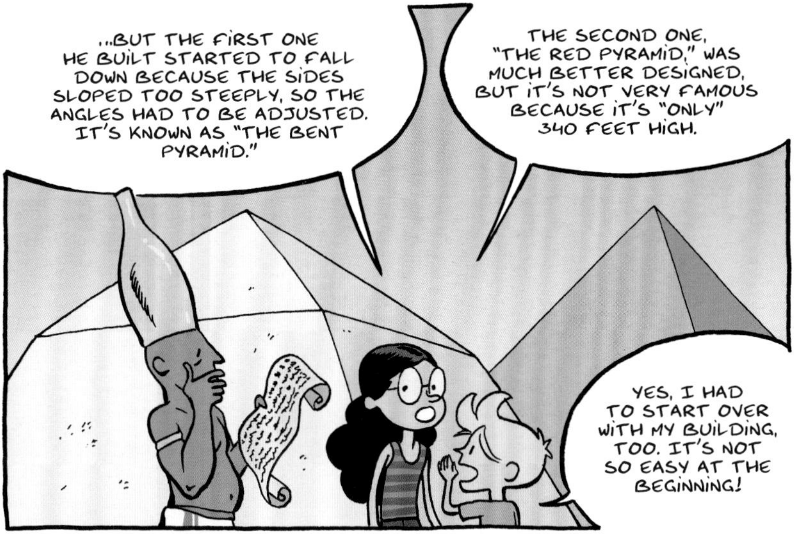
...BUT THE FIRST ONE HE BUILT STARTED TO FALL DOWN BECAUSE THE SIDES SLOPED TOO STEEPLY, SO THE ANGLES HAD TO BE ADJUSTED. IT'S KNOWN AS "THE BENT PYRAMID."
THE SECOND ONE, "THE RED PYRAMID," WAS MUCH BETTER DESIGNED, BUT IT'S NOT VERY FAMOUS BECAUSE IT'S "ONLY" 340 FEET HIGH.
YES, I HAD TO START OVER WITH MY BUILDING, TOO. IT'S NOT SO EASY AT THE BEGINNING!

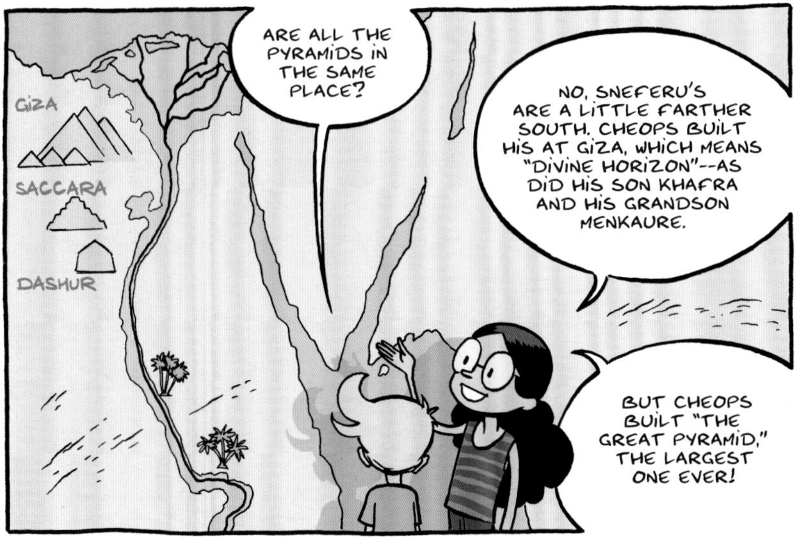
ARE ALL THE PYRAMIDS IN THE SAME PLACE?
GIZA
SACCARA
DASHUR
NO, SNEFERU'S ARE A LITTLE FARTHER SOUTH. CHEOPS BUILT HIS AT GIZA, WHICH MEANS "DIVINE HORIZON"--AS DID HIS SON KHAFRA AND HIS GRANDSON MENKAURE.
BUT CHEOPS BUILT "THE GREAT PYRAMID," THE LARGEST ONE EVER!

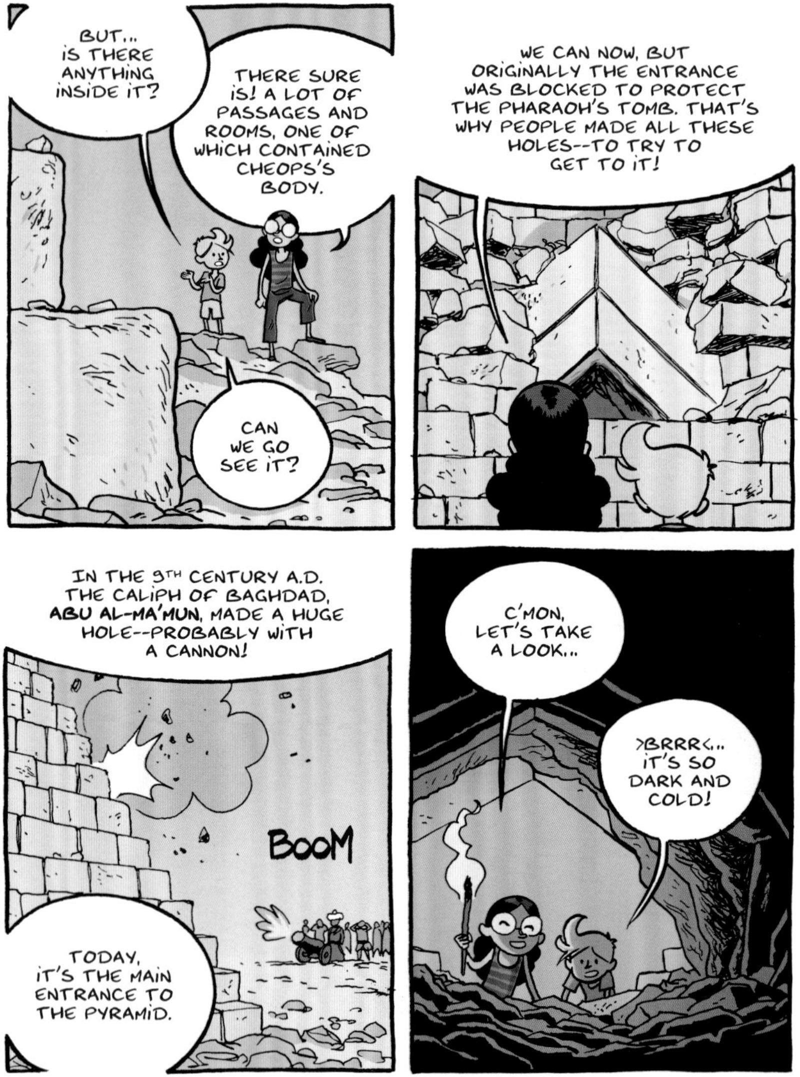
BUT... IS THERE ANYTHING INSIDE IT?
THERE SURE IS! A LOT OF PASSAGES AND ROOMS, ONE OF WHICH CONTAINED CHEOPS'S BODY.
CAN WE GO SEE IT?
WE CAN NOW, BUT ORIGINALLY THE ENTRANCE WAS BLOCKED TO PROTECT THE PHARAOH'S TOMB. THAT'S WHY PEOPLE MADE ALL THESE HOLES--TO TRY TO GET TO IT!
IN THE 9TH CENTURY A.D. THE CALIPH OF BAGHDAD, **ABU AL-MA'MUN**, MADE A HUGE HOLE--PROBABLY WITH A CANNON!
BOOM
TODAY, IT'S THE MAIN ENTRANCE TO THE PYRAMID.
C'MON, LET'S TAKE A LOOK...
>BRRR<... IT'S SO DARK AND COLD!

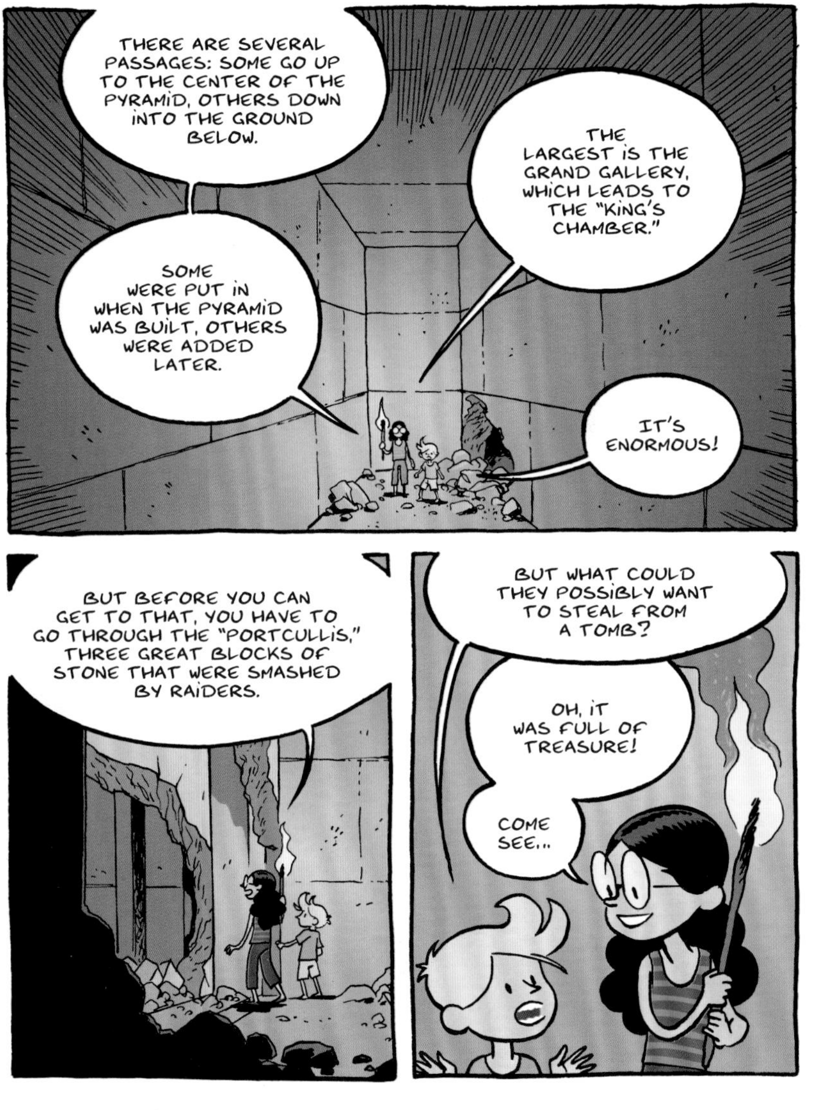
THERE ARE SEVERAL PASSAGES: SOME GO UP TO THE CENTER OF THE PYRAMID, OTHERS DOWN INTO THE GROUND BELOW.
SOME WERE PUT IN WHEN THE PYRAMID WAS BUILT, OTHERS WERE ADDED LATER.
THE LARGEST IS THE GRAND GALLERY, WHICH LEADS TO THE "KING'S CHAMBER."
IT'S ENORMOUS!
BUT BEFORE YOU CAN GET TO THAT, YOU HAVE TO GO THROUGH THE "PORTCULLIS," THREE GREAT BLOCKS OF STONE THAT WERE SMASHED BY RAIDERS.
BUT WHAT COULD THEY POSSIBLY WANT TO STEAL FROM A TOMB?
OH, IT WAS FULL OF TREASURE!
COME SEE...

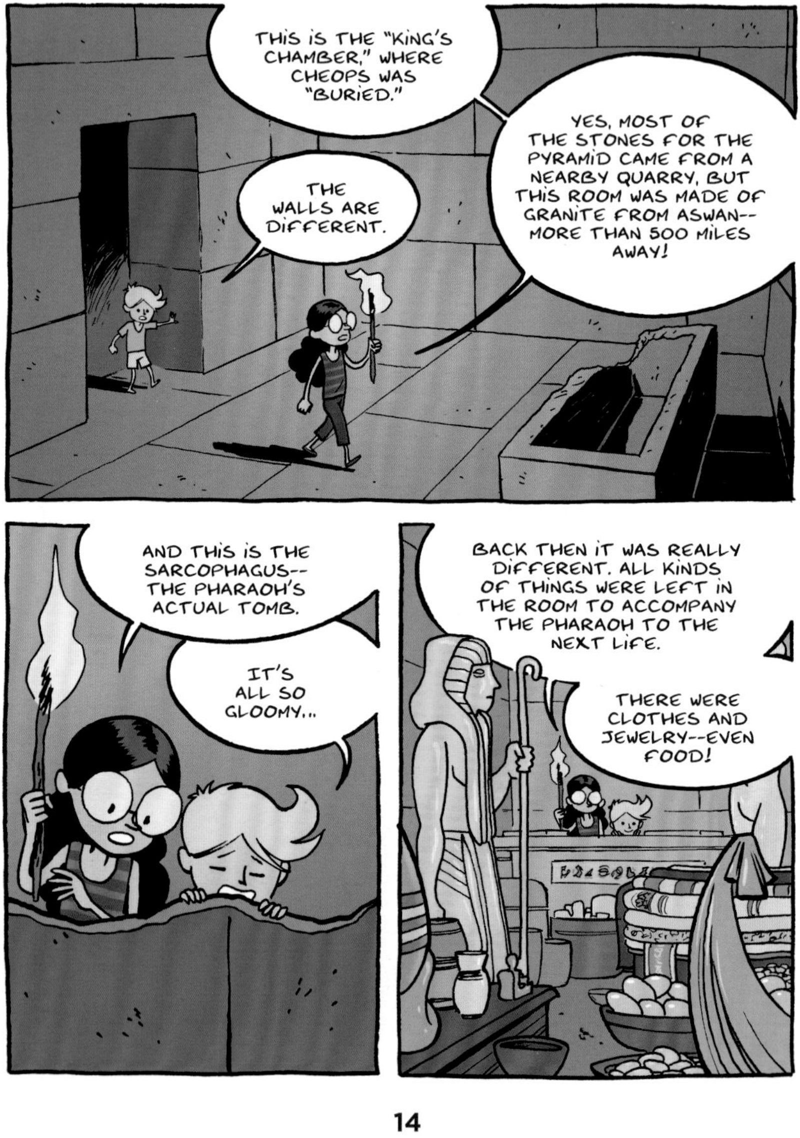
THIS IS THE "KING'S CHAMBER," WHERE CHEOPS WAS "BURIED."
THE WALLS ARE DIFFERENT.
YES, MOST OF THE STONES FOR THE PYRAMID CAME FROM A NEARBY QUARRY, BUT THIS ROOM WAS MADE OF GRANITE FROM ASWAN--MORE THAN 500 MILES AWAY!
AND THIS IS THE SARCOPHAGUS--THE PHARAOH'S ACTUAL TOMB.
IT'S ALL SO GLOOMY...
BACK THEN IT WAS REALLY DIFFERENT. ALL KINDS OF THINGS WERE LEFT IN THE ROOM TO ACCOMPANY THE PHARAOH TO THE NEXT LIFE.
THERE WERE CLOTHES AND JEWELRY--EVEN FOOD!

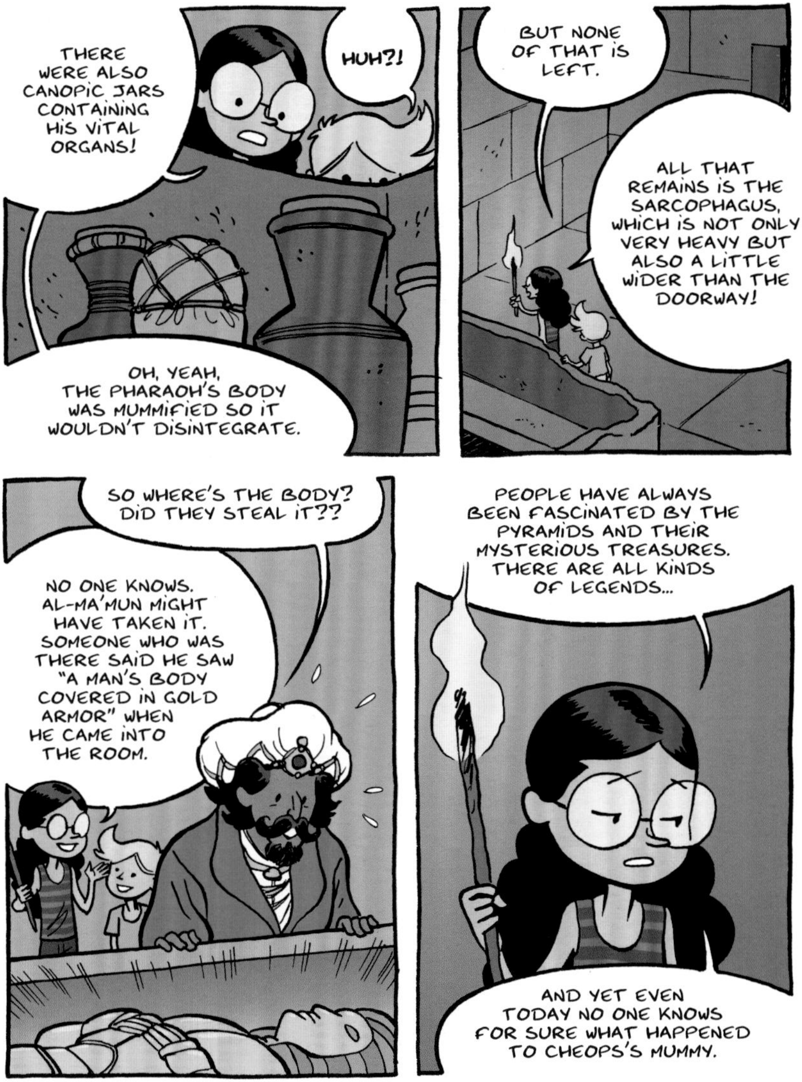
THERE WERE ALSO CANOPIC JARS CONTAINING HIS VITAL ORGANS!
HUH?!
OH, YEAH, THE PHARAOH'S BODY WAS MUMMIFIED SO IT WOULDN'T DISINTEGRATE.
BUT NONE OF THAT IS LEFT.
ALL THAT REMAINS IS THE SARCOPHAGUS, WHICH IS NOT ONLY VERY HEAVY BUT ALSO A LITTLE WIDER THAN THE DOORWAY!
SO WHERE'S THE BODY? DID THEY STEAL IT??
NO ONE KNOWS. AL-MA'MUN MIGHT HAVE TAKEN IT. SOMEONE WHO WAS THERE SAID HE SAW "A MAN'S BODY COVERED IN GOLD ARMOR" WHEN HE CAME INTO THE ROOM.
PEOPLE HAVE ALWAYS BEEN FASCINATED BY THE PYRAMIDS AND THEIR MYSTERIOUS TREASURES. THERE ARE ALL KINDS OF LEGENDS...
AND YET EVEN TODAY NO ONE KNOWS FOR SURE WHAT HAPPENED TO CHEOPS'S MUMMY.

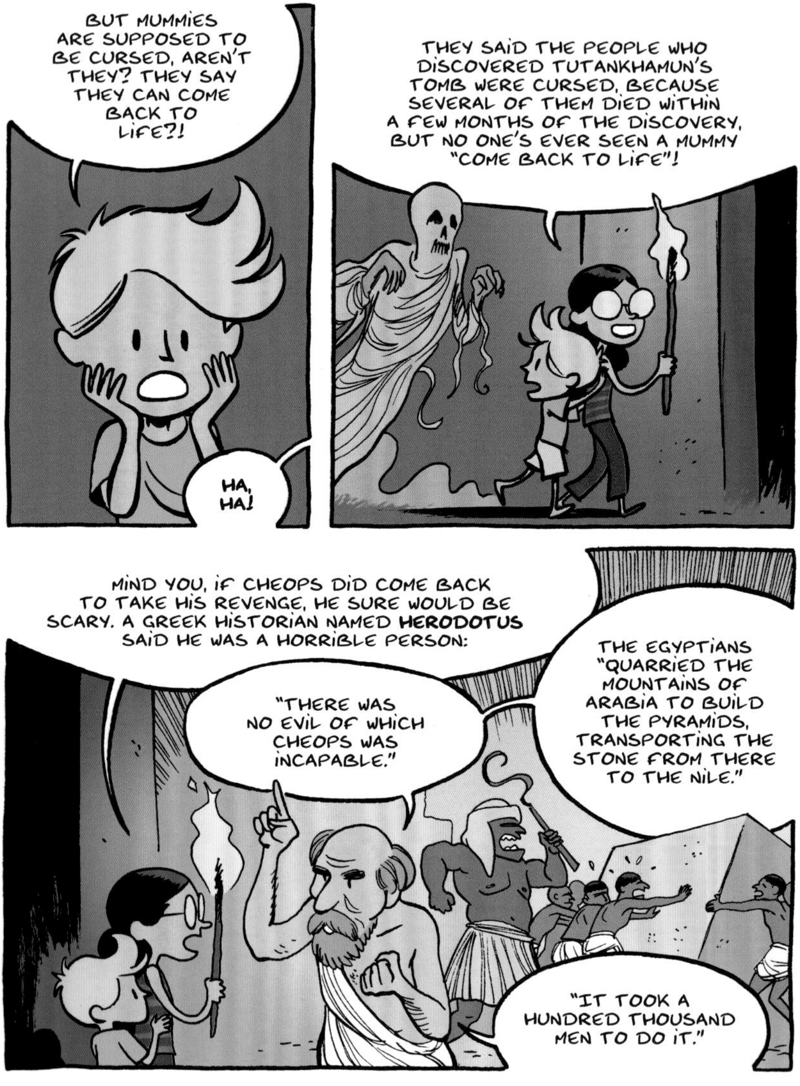

BUT MUMMIES ARE SUPPOSED TO BE CURSED, AREN'T THEY? THEY SAY THEY CAN COME BACK TO LIFE?!
HA, HA!
THEY SAID THE PEOPLE WHO DISCOVERED TUTANKHAMUN'S TOMB WERE CURSED, BECAUSE SEVERAL OF THEM DIED WITHIN A FEW MONTHS OF THE DISCOVERY, BUT NO ONE'S EVER SEEN A MUMMY "COME BACK TO LIFE"!
MIND YOU, IF CHEOPS DID COME BACK TO TAKE HIS REVENGE, HE SURE WOULD BE SCARY. A GREEK HISTORIAN NAMED **HERODOTUS** SAID HE WAS A HORRIBLE PERSON:
"THERE WAS NO EVIL OF WHICH CHEOPS WAS INCAPABLE."
THE EGYPTIANS "QUARRIED THE MOUNTAINS OF ARABIA TO BUILD THE PYRAMIDS, TRANSPORTING THE STONE FROM THERE TO THE NILE."
"IT TOOK A HUNDRED THOUSAND MEN TO DO IT."

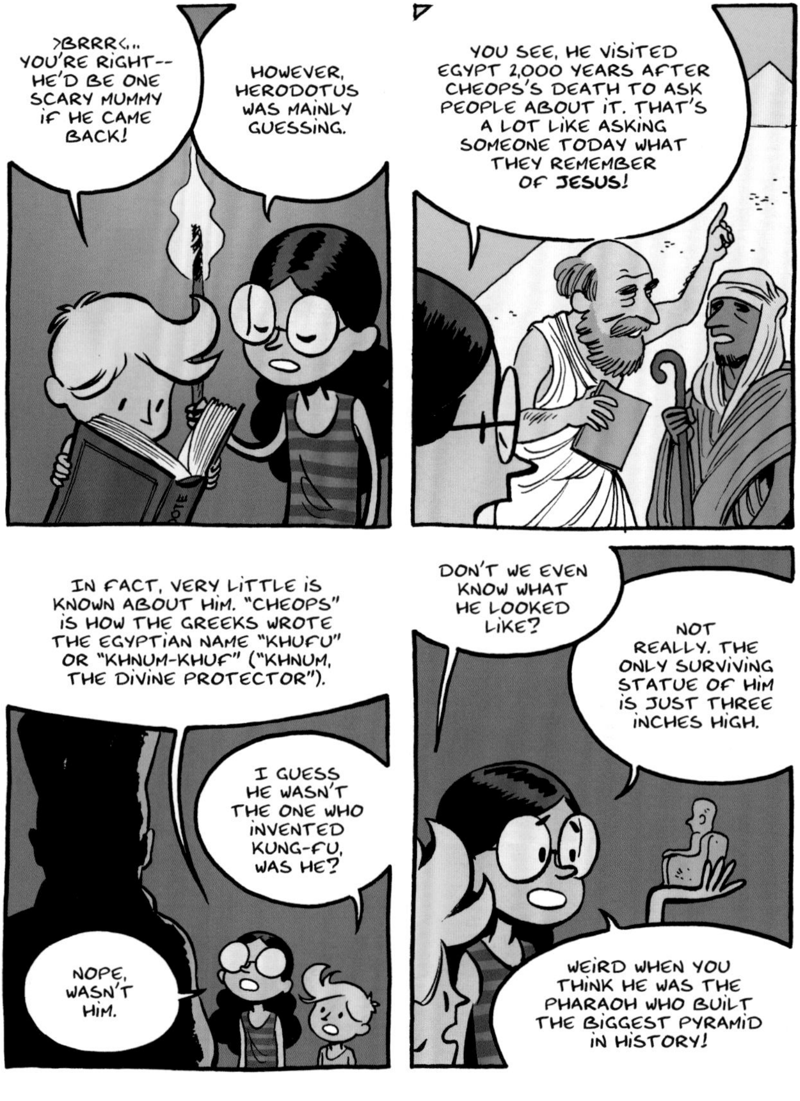

>BRRR<.. YOU'RE RIGHT-- HE'D BE ONE SCARY MUMMY IF HE CAME BACK!
HOWEVER, HERODOTUS WAS MAINLY GUESSING.
YOU SEE, HE VISITED EGYPT 2,000 YEARS AFTER CHEOPS'S DEATH TO ASK PEOPLE ABOUT IT. THAT'S A LOT LIKE ASKING SOMEONE TODAY WHAT THEY REMEMBER OF **JESUS**!
IN FACT, VERY LITTLE IS KNOWN ABOUT HIM. "CHEOPS" IS HOW THE GREEKS WROTE THE EGYPTIAN NAME "KHUFU" OR "KHNUM-KHUF" ("KHNUM, THE DIVINE PROTECTOR").
I GUESS HE WASN'T THE ONE WHO INVENTED KUNG-FU, WAS HE?
NOPE, WASN'T HIM.
DON'T WE EVEN KNOW WHAT HE LOOKED LIKE?
NOT REALLY. THE ONLY SURVIVING STATUE OF HIM IS JUST THREE INCHES HIGH.
WEIRD WHEN YOU THINK HE WAS THE PHARAOH WHO BUILT THE BIGGEST PYRAMID IN HISTORY!

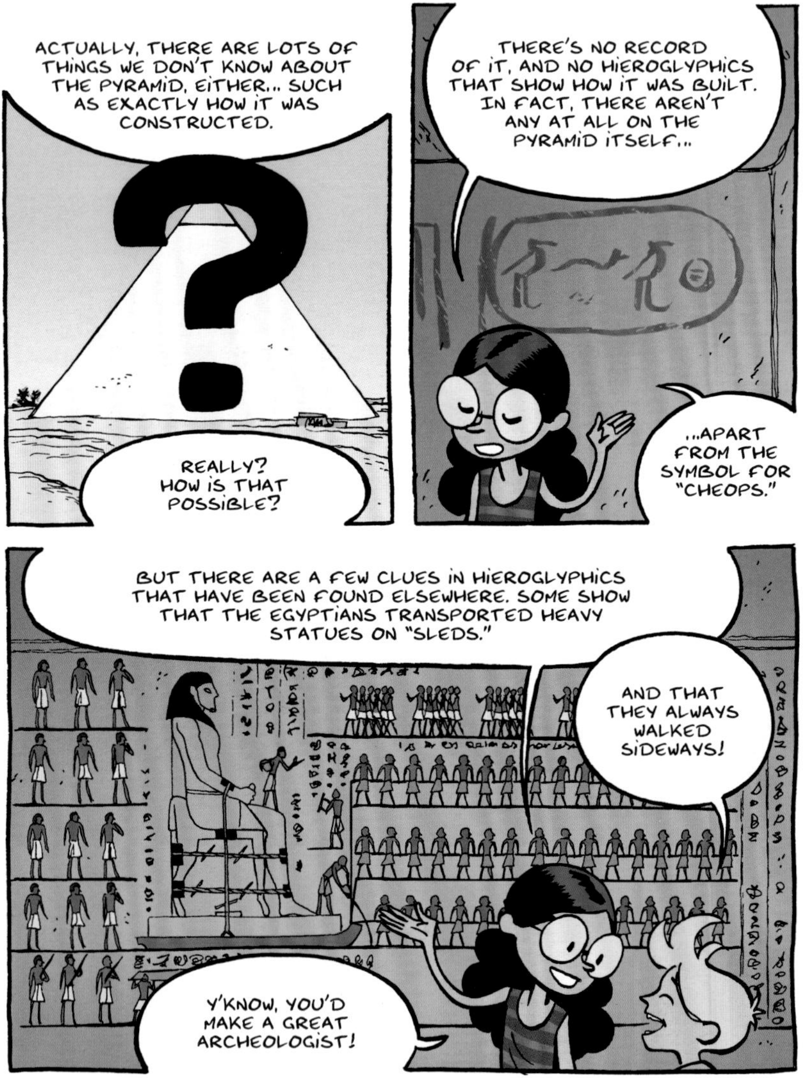
ACTUALLY, THERE ARE LOTS OF THINGS WE DON'T KNOW ABOUT THE PYRAMID, EITHER... SUCH AS EXACTLY HOW IT WAS CONSTRUCTED.
REALLY? HOW IS THAT POSSIBLE?
THERE'S NO RECORD OF IT, AND NO HIEROGLYPHICS THAT SHOW HOW IT WAS BUILT. IN FACT, THERE AREN'T ANY AT ALL ON THE PYRAMID ITSELF...
...APART FROM THE SYMBOL FOR "CHEOPS."
BUT THERE ARE A FEW CLUES IN HIEROGLYPHICS THAT HAVE BEEN FOUND ELSEWHERE. SOME SHOW THAT THE EGYPTIANS TRANSPORTED HEAVY STATUES ON "SLEDS."
AND THAT THEY ALWAYS WALKED SIDEWAYS!
Y'KNOW, YOU'D MAKE A GREAT ARCHEOLOGIST!

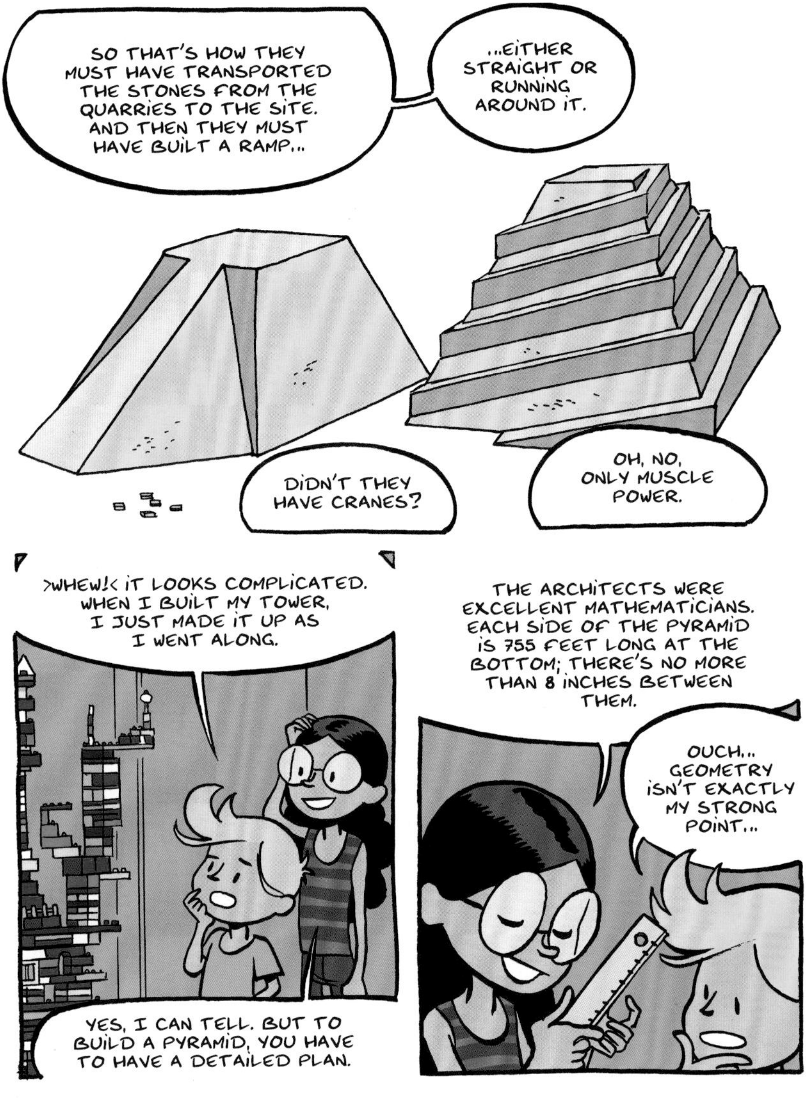
SO THAT'S HOW THEY MUST HAVE TRANSPORTED THE STONES FROM THE QUARRIES TO THE SITE. AND THEN THEY MUST HAVE BUILT A RAMP...
...EITHER STRAIGHT OR RUNNING AROUND IT.
DIDN'T THEY HAVE CRANES?
OH, NO, ONLY MUSCLE POWER.
>WHEW!< IT LOOKS COMPLICATED. WHEN I BUILT MY TOWER, I JUST MADE IT UP AS I WENT ALONG.
YES, I CAN TELL. BUT TO BUILD A PYRAMID, YOU HAVE TO HAVE A DETAILED PLAN.
THE ARCHITECTS WERE EXCELLENT MATHEMATICIANS. EACH SIDE OF THE PYRAMID IS 755 FEET LONG AT THE BOTTOM; THERE'S NO MORE THAN 8 INCHES BETWEEN THEM.
OUCH... GEOMETRY ISN'T EXACTLY MY STRONG POINT...

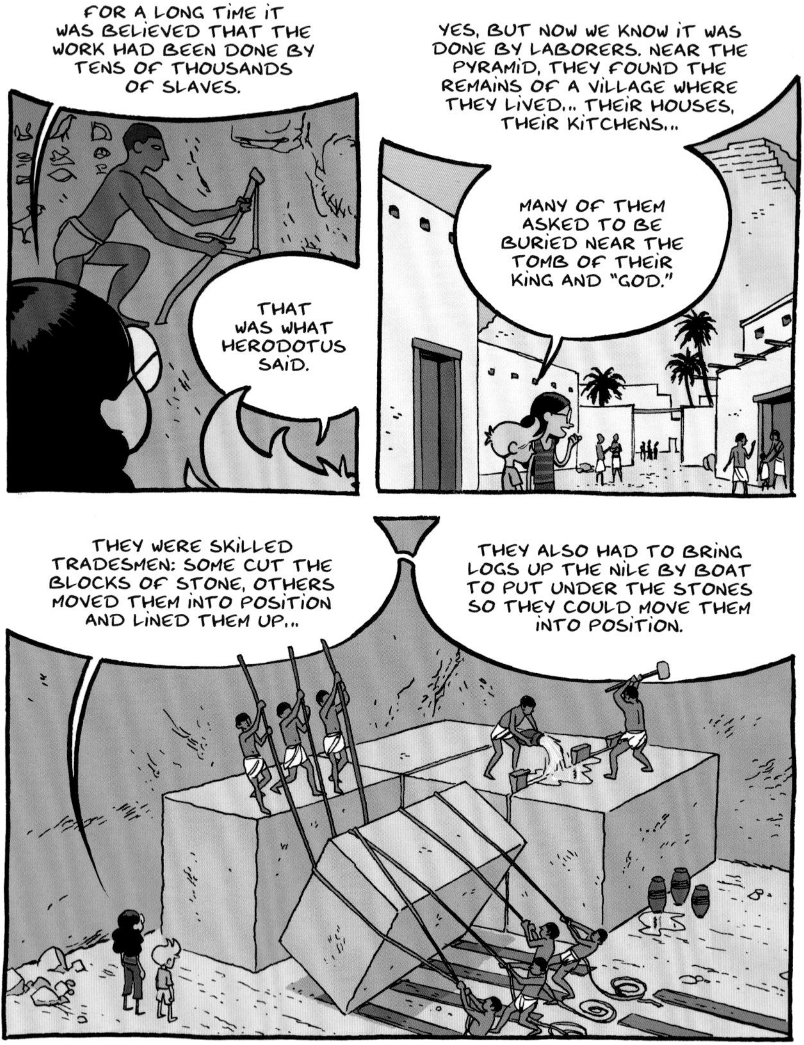
FOR A LONG TIME IT WAS BELIEVED THAT THE WORK HAD BEEN DONE BY TENS OF THOUSANDS OF SLAVES.
THAT WAS WHAT HERODOTUS SAID.
YES, BUT NOW WE KNOW IT WAS DONE BY LABORERS. NEAR THE PYRAMID, THEY FOUND THE REMAINS OF A VILLAGE WHERE THEY LIVED... THEIR HOUSES, THEIR KITCHENS...
MANY OF THEM ASKED TO BE BURIED NEAR THE TOMB OF THEIR KING AND "GOD."
THEY WERE SKILLED TRADESMEN: SOME CUT THE BLOCKS OF STONE, OTHERS MOVED THEM INTO POSITION AND LINED THEM UP...
THEY ALSO HAD TO BRING LOGS UP THE NILE BY BOAT TO PUT UNDER THE STONES SO THEY COULD MOVE THEM INTO POSITION.

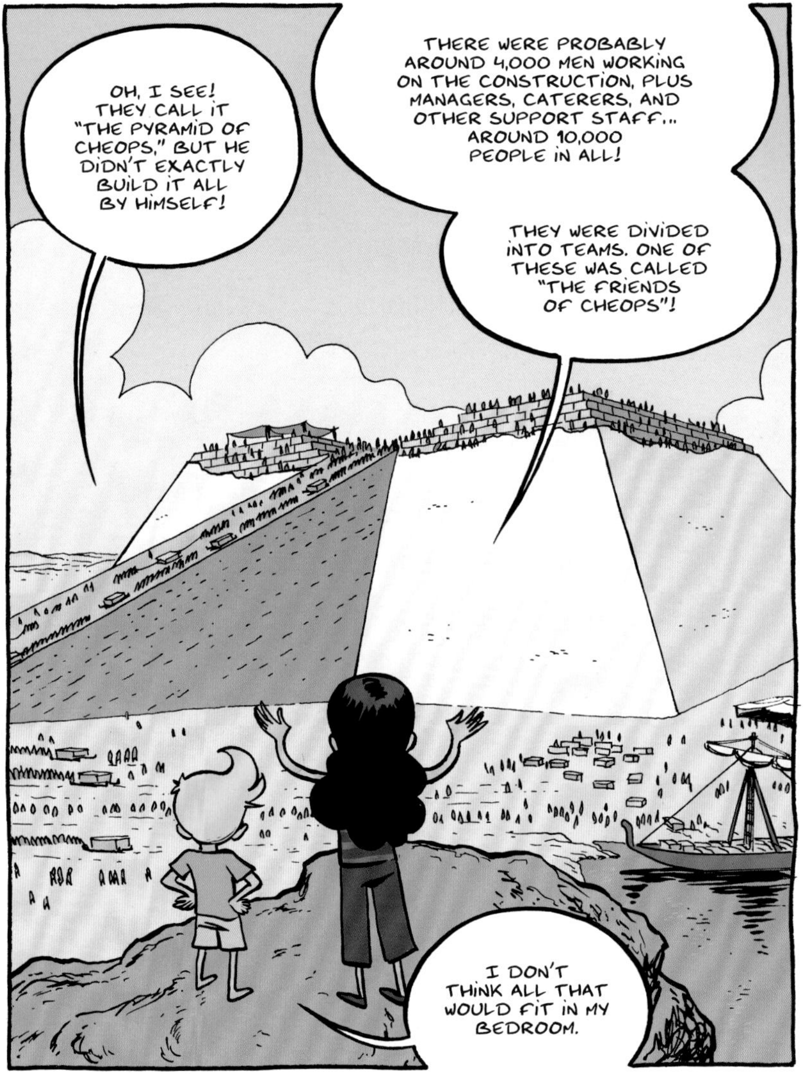
OH, I SEE! THEY CALL IT "THE PYRAMID OF CHEOPS," BUT HE DIDN'T EXACTLY BUILD IT ALL BY HIMSELF!
THERE WERE PROBABLY AROUND 4,000 MEN WORKING ON THE CONSTRUCTION, PLUS MANAGERS, CATERERS, AND OTHER SUPPORT STAFF... AROUND 10,000 PEOPLE IN ALL!
THEY WERE DIVIDED INTO TEAMS. ONE OF THESE WAS CALLED "THE FRIENDS OF CHEOPS"!
I DON'T THINK ALL THAT WOULD FIT IN MY BEDROOM.

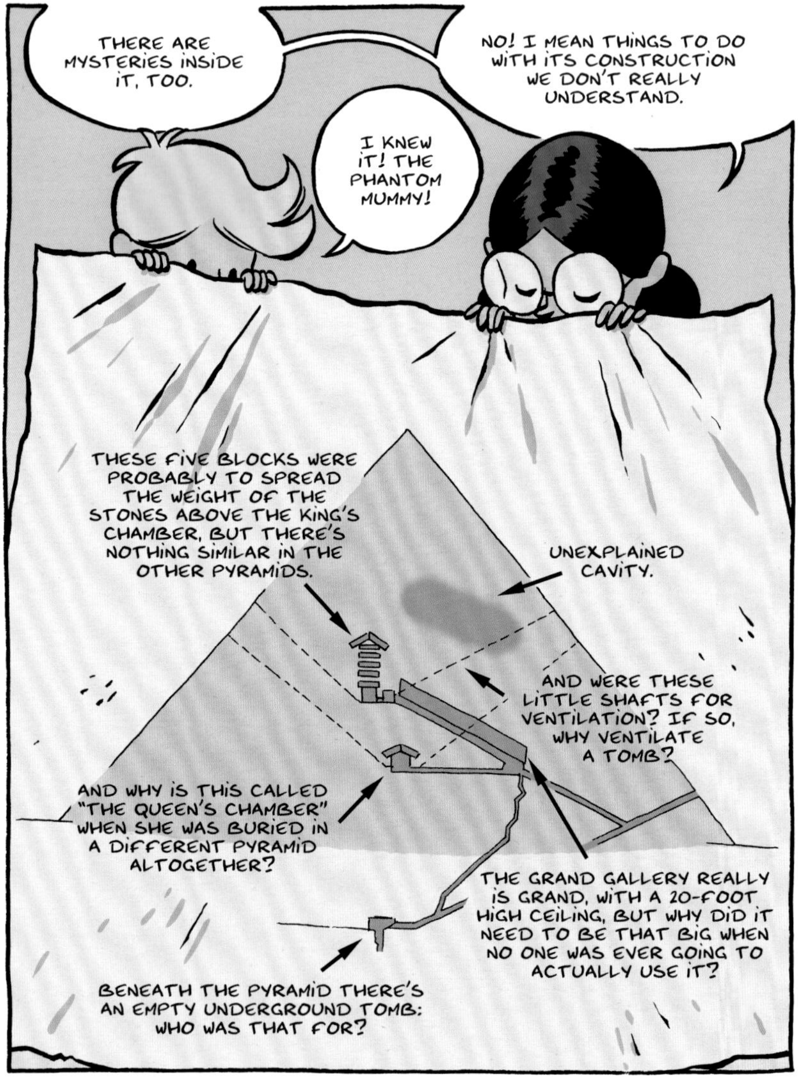
THERE ARE MYSTERIES INSIDE IT, TOO.
I KNEW IT! THE PHANTOM MUMMY!
NO! I MEAN THINGS TO DO WITH ITS CONSTRUCTION WE DON'T REALLY UNDERSTAND.
THESE FIVE BLOCKS WERE PROBABLY TO SPREAD THE WEIGHT OF THE STONES ABOVE THE KING'S CHAMBER, BUT THERE'S NOTHING SIMILAR IN THE OTHER PYRAMIDS.
UNEXPLAINED CAVITY.
AND WERE THESE LITTLE SHAFTS FOR VENTILATION? IF SO, WHY VENTILATE A TOMB?
AND WHY IS THIS CALLED "THE QUEEN'S CHAMBER" WHEN SHE WAS BURIED IN A DIFFERENT PYRAMID ALTOGETHER?
THE GRAND GALLERY REALLY IS GRAND, WITH A 20-FOOT HIGH CEILING, BUT WHY DID IT NEED TO BE THAT BIG WHEN NO ONE WAS EVER GOING TO ACTUALLY USE IT?
BENEATH THE PYRAMID THERE'S AN EMPTY UNDERGROUND TOMB: WHO WAS THAT FOR?

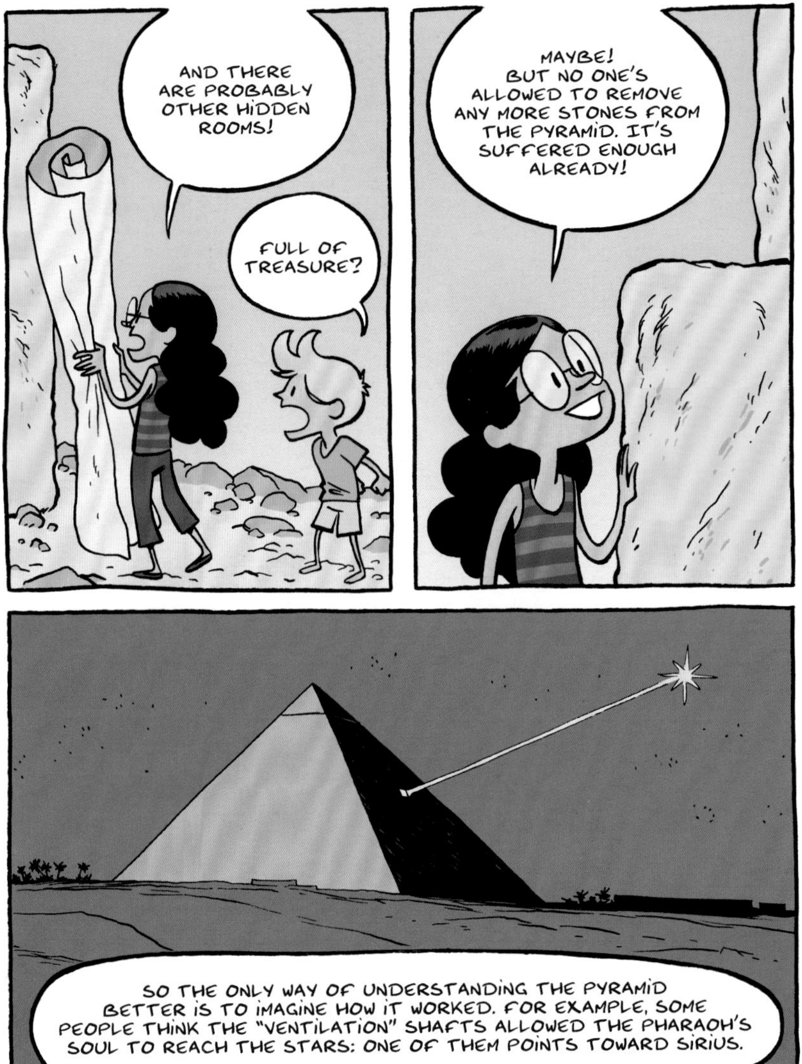
AND THERE ARE PROBABLY OTHER HIDDEN ROOMS!
FULL OF TREASURE?
MAYBE! BUT NO ONE'S ALLOWED TO REMOVE ANY MORE STONES FROM THE PYRAMID. IT'S SUFFERED ENOUGH ALREADY!
SO THE ONLY WAY OF UNDERSTANDING THE PYRAMID BETTER IS TO IMAGINE HOW IT WORKED. FOR EXAMPLE, SOME PEOPLE THINK THE "VENTILATION" SHAFTS ALLOWED THE PHARAOH'S SOUL TO REACH THE STARS: ONE OF THEM POINTS TOWARD SIRIUS.

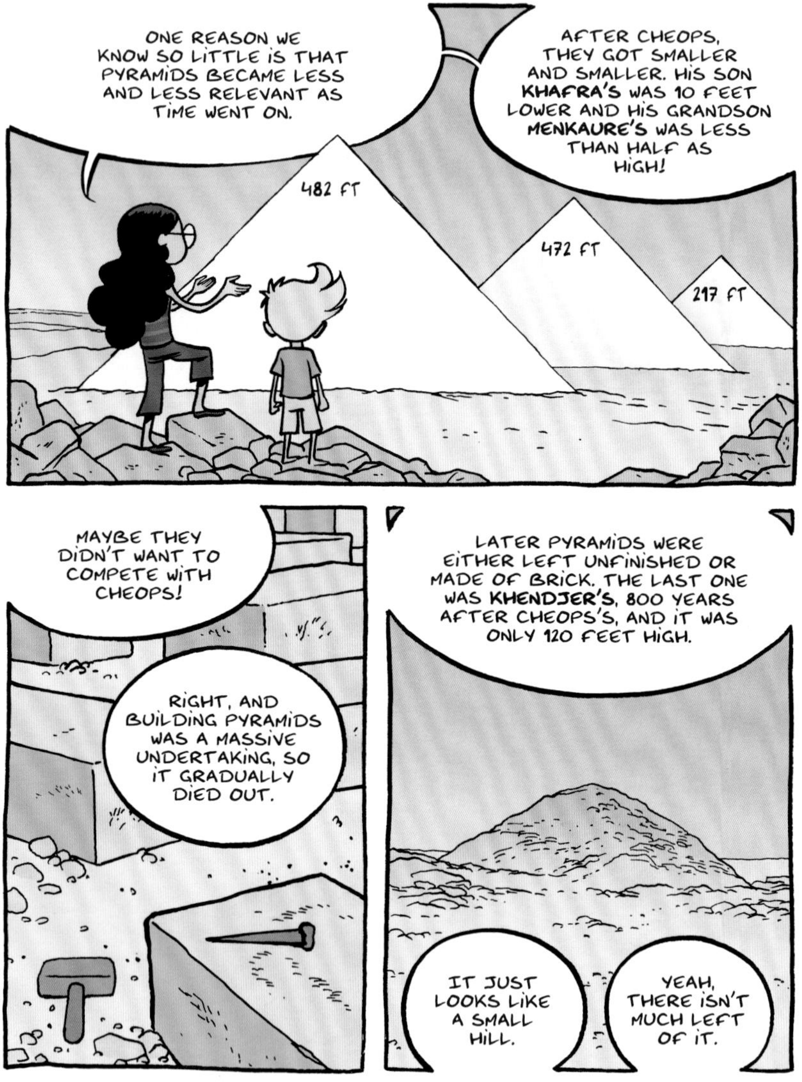
ONE REASON WE KNOW SO LITTLE IS THAT PYRAMIDS BECAME LESS AND LESS RELEVANT AS TIME WENT ON.
AFTER CHEOPS, THEY GOT SMALLER AND SMALLER. HIS SON **KHAFRA'S** WAS 10 FEET LOWER AND HIS GRANDSON **MENKAURE'S** WAS LESS THAN HALF AS HIGH!
482 FT
472 FT
217 FT
MAYBE THEY DIDN'T WANT TO COMPETE WITH CHEOPS!
RIGHT, AND BUILDING PYRAMIDS WAS A MASSIVE UNDERTAKING, SO IT GRADUALLY DIED OUT.
LATER PYRAMIDS WERE EITHER LEFT UNFINISHED OR MADE OF BRICK. THE LAST ONE WAS **KHENDJER'S**, 800 YEARS AFTER CHEOPS'S, AND IT WAS ONLY 120 FEET HIGH.
IT JUST LOOKS LIKE A SMALL HILL.
YEAH, THERE ISN'T MUCH LEFT OF IT.

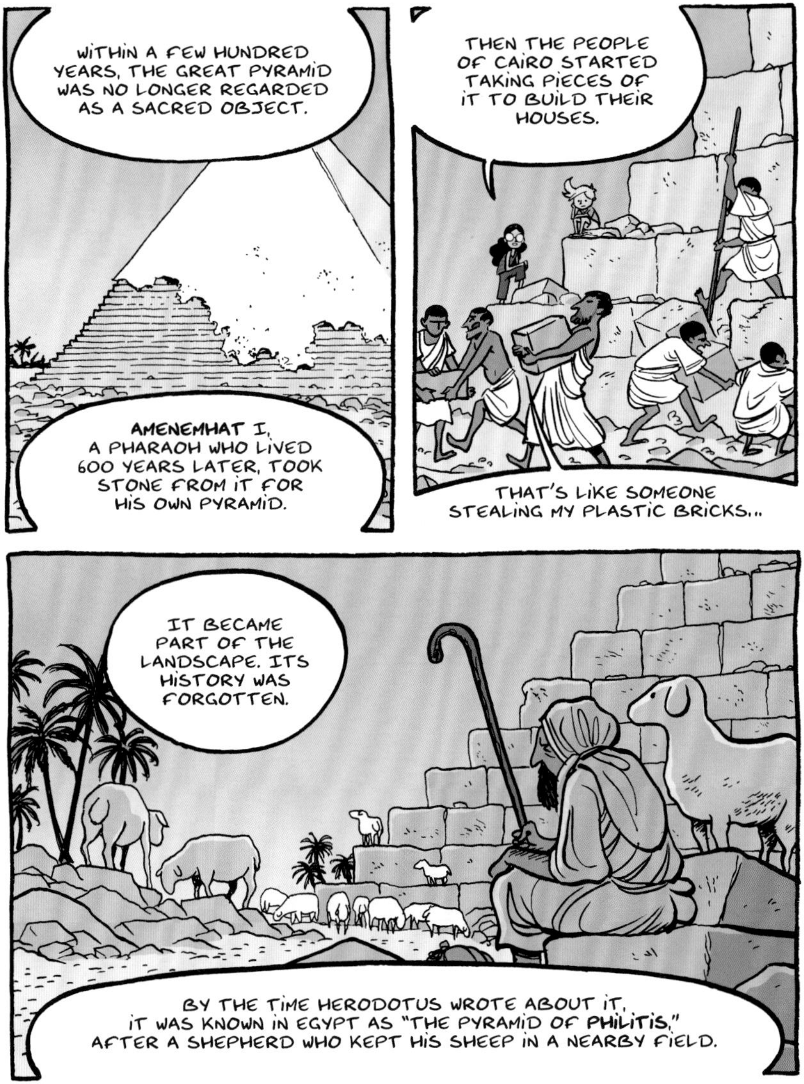
WITHIN A FEW HUNDRED YEARS, THE GREAT PYRAMID WAS NO LONGER REGARDED AS A SACRED OBJECT.
AMENEMHAT I, A PHARAOH WHO LIVED 600 YEARS LATER, TOOK STONE FROM IT FOR HIS OWN PYRAMID.
THEN THE PEOPLE OF CAIRO STARTED TAKING PIECES OF IT TO BUILD THEIR HOUSES.
THAT'S LIKE SOMEONE STEALING MY PLASTIC BRICKS...
IT BECAME PART OF THE LANDSCAPE. ITS HISTORY WAS FORGOTTEN.
BY THE TIME HERODOTUS WROTE ABOUT IT, IT WAS KNOWN IN EGYPT AS "THE PYRAMID OF PHILITIS," AFTER A SHEPHERD WHO KEPT HIS SHEEP IN A NEARBY FIELD.

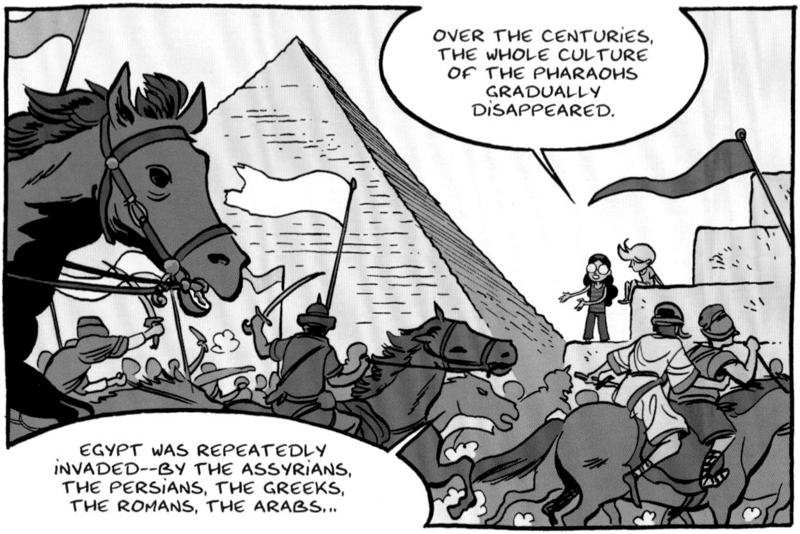
OVER THE CENTURIES, THE WHOLE CULTURE OF THE PHARAOHS GRADUALLY DISAPPEARED.
EGYPT WAS REPEATEDLY INVADED--BY THE ASSYRIANS, THE PERSIANS, THE GREEKS, THE ROMANS, THE ARABS...

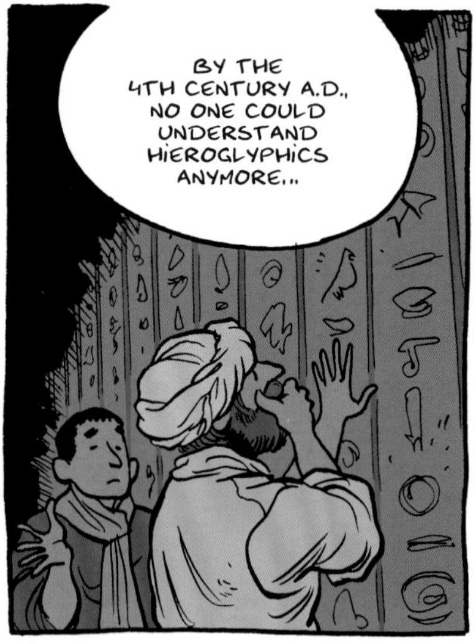
BY THE 4TH CENTURY A.D., NO ONE COULD UNDERSTAND HIEROGLYPHICS ANYMORE...

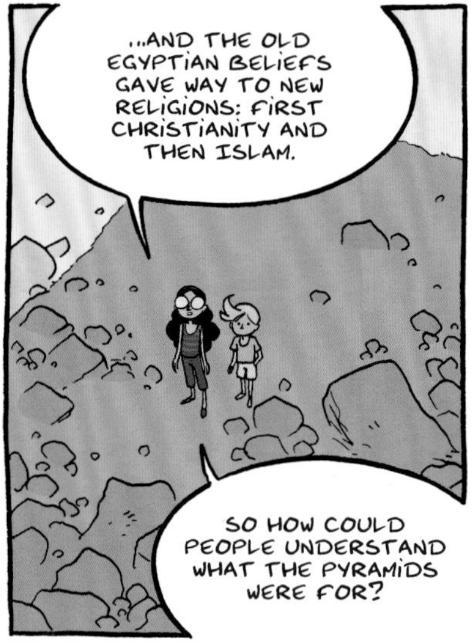
...AND THE OLD EGYPTIAN BELIEFS GAVE WAY TO NEW RELIGIONS: FIRST CHRISTIANITY AND THEN ISLAM.
SO HOW COULD PEOPLE UNDERSTAND WHAT THE PYRAMIDS WERE FOR?

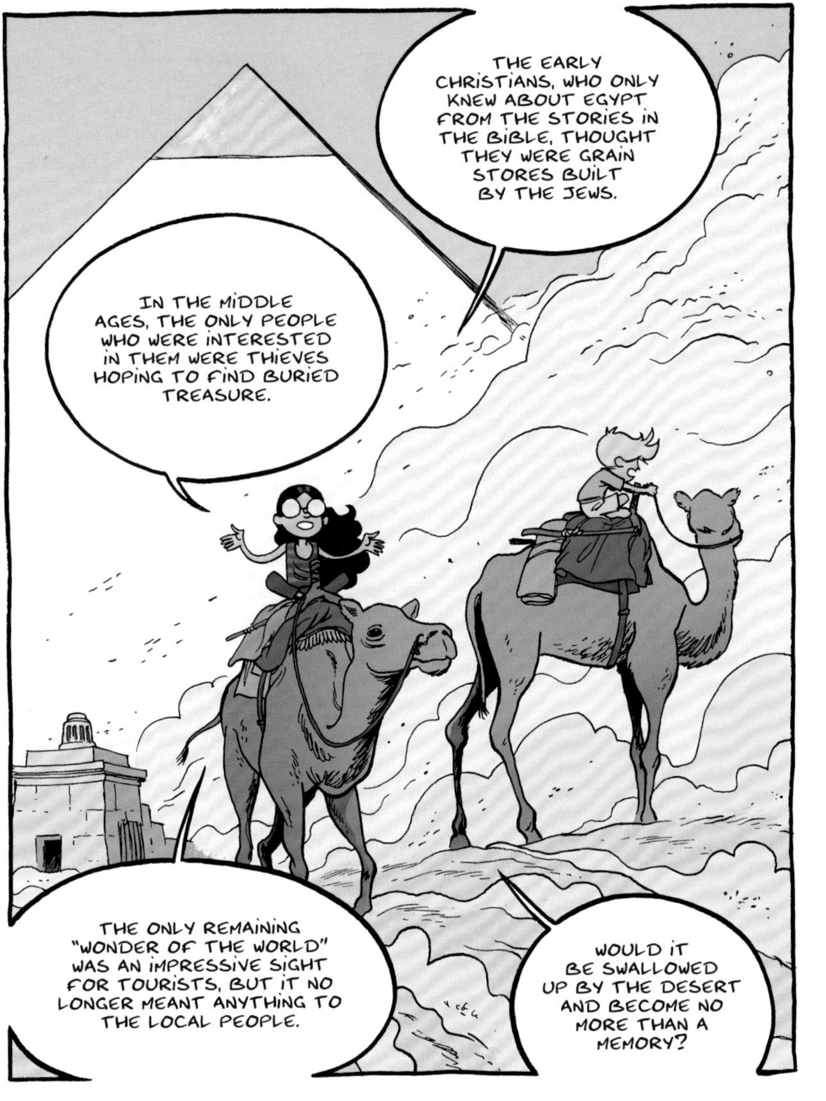
THE EARLY CHRISTIANS, WHO ONLY KNEW ABOUT EGYPT FROM THE STORIES IN THE BIBLE, THOUGHT THEY WERE GRAIN STORES BUILT BY THE JEWS.
IN THE MIDDLE AGES, THE ONLY PEOPLE WHO WERE INTERESTED IN THEM WERE THIEVES HOPING TO FIND BURIED TREASURE.
THE ONLY REMAINING "WONDER OF THE WORLD" WAS AN IMPRESSIVE SIGHT FOR TOURISTS, BUT IT NO LONGER MEANT ANYTHING TO THE LOCAL PEOPLE.
WOULD IT BE SWALLOWED UP BY THE DESERT AND BECOME NO MORE THAN A MEMORY?

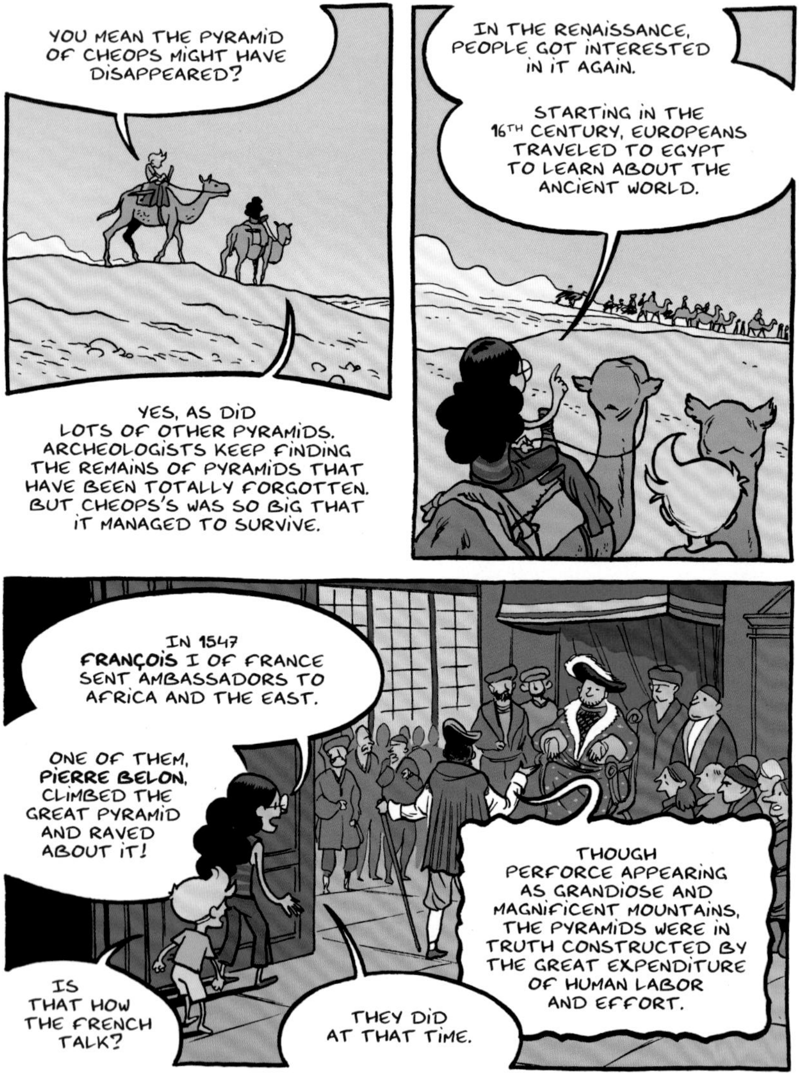
YOU MEAN THE PYRAMID OF CHEOPS MIGHT HAVE DISAPPEARED?
YES, AS DID LOTS OF OTHER PYRAMIDS. ARCHEOLOGISTS KEEP FINDING THE REMAINS OF PYRAMIDS THAT HAVE BEEN TOTALLY FORGOTTEN. BUT CHEOPS'S WAS SO BIG THAT IT MANAGED TO SURVIVE.
IN THE RENAISSANCE, PEOPLE GOT INTERESTED IN IT AGAIN.
STARTING IN THE 16TH CENTURY, EUROPEANS TRAVELED TO EGYPT TO LEARN ABOUT THE ANCIENT WORLD.
IN 1547 FRANÇOIS I OF FRANCE SENT AMBASSADORS TO AFRICA AND THE EAST.
ONE OF THEM, PIERRE BELON, CLIMBED THE GREAT PYRAMID AND RAVED ABOUT IT!
THOUGH PERFORCE APPEARING AS GRANDIOSE AND MAGNIFICENT MOUNTAINS, THE PYRAMIDS WERE IN TRUTH CONSTRUCTED BY THE GREAT EXPENDITURE OF HUMAN LABOR AND EFFORT.
IS THAT HOW THE FRENCH TALK?
THEY DID AT THAT TIME.

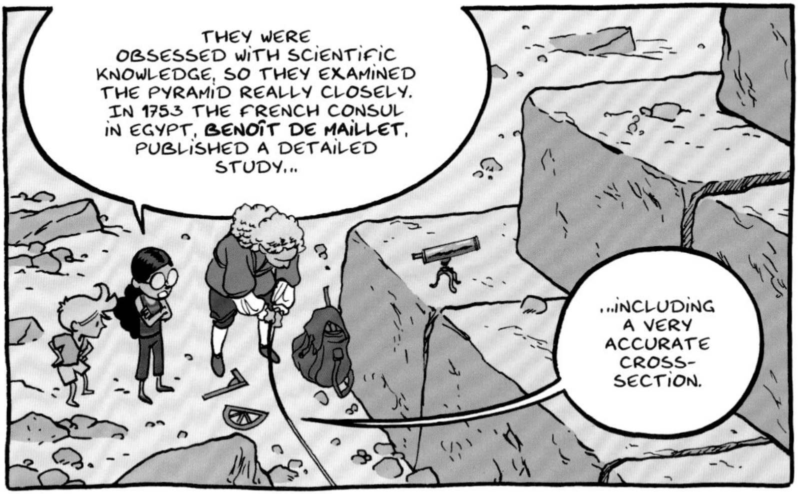
THEY WERE OBSESSED WITH SCIENTIFIC KNOWLEDGE, SO THEY EXAMINED THE PYRAMID REALLY CLOSELY. IN 1753 THE FRENCH CONSUL IN EGYPT, **BENOÎT DE MAILLET**, PUBLISHED A DETAILED STUDY...
...INCLUDING A VERY ACCURATE CROSS-SECTION.

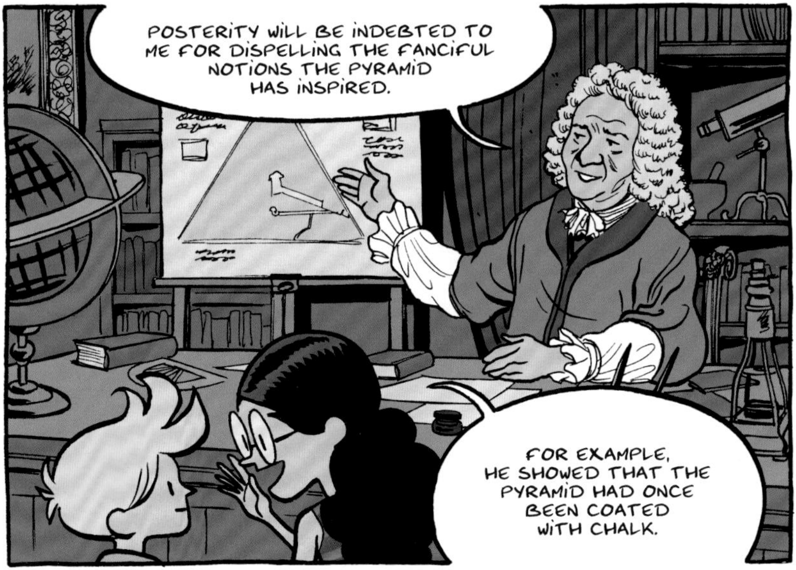
POSTERITY WILL BE INDEBTED TO ME FOR DISPELLING THE FANCIFUL NOTIONS THE PYRAMID HAS INSPIRED.
FOR EXAMPLE, HE SHOWED THAT THE PYRAMID HAD ONCE BEEN COATED WITH CHALK.

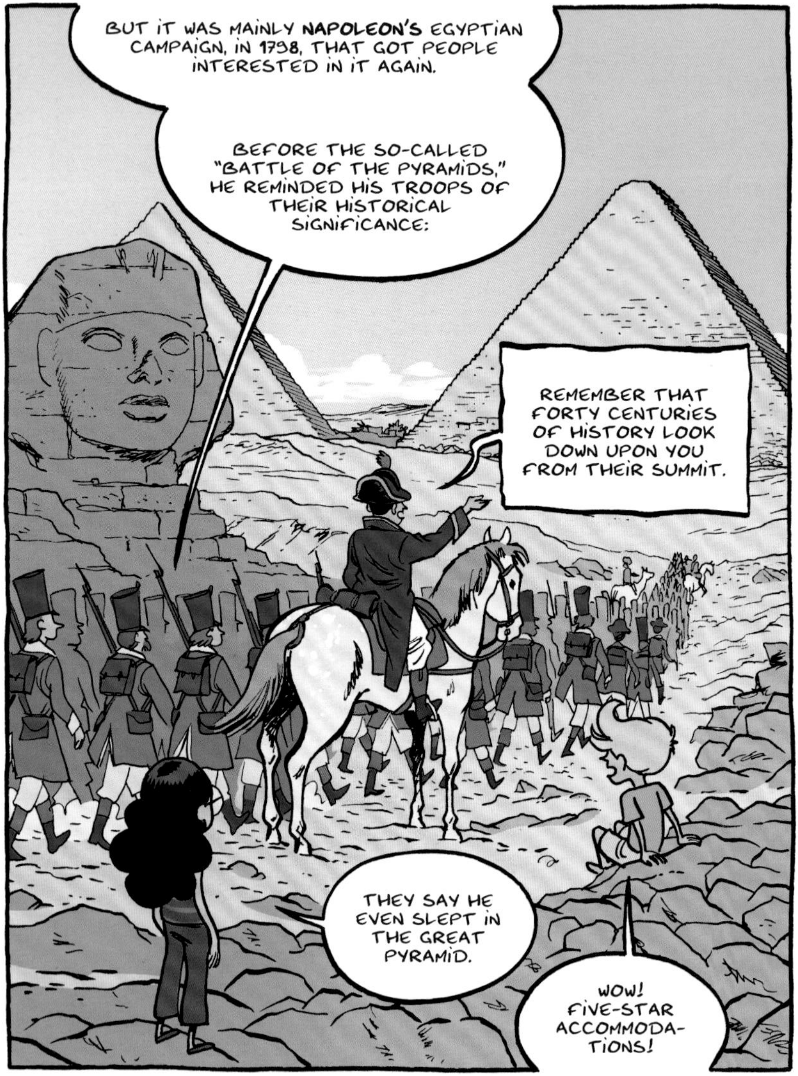
BUT IT WAS MAINLY **NAPOLEON'S** EGYPTIAN CAMPAIGN, IN 1798, THAT GOT PEOPLE INTERESTED IN IT AGAIN.
BEFORE THE SO-CALLED "BATTLE OF THE PYRAMIDS," HE REMINDED HIS TROOPS OF THEIR HISTORICAL SIGNIFICANCE:
REMEMBER THAT FORTY CENTURIES OF HISTORY LOOK DOWN UPON YOU FROM THEIR SUMMIT.
THEY SAY HE EVEN SLEPT IN THE GREAT PYRAMID.
WOW! FIVE-STAR ACCOMMODATIONS!

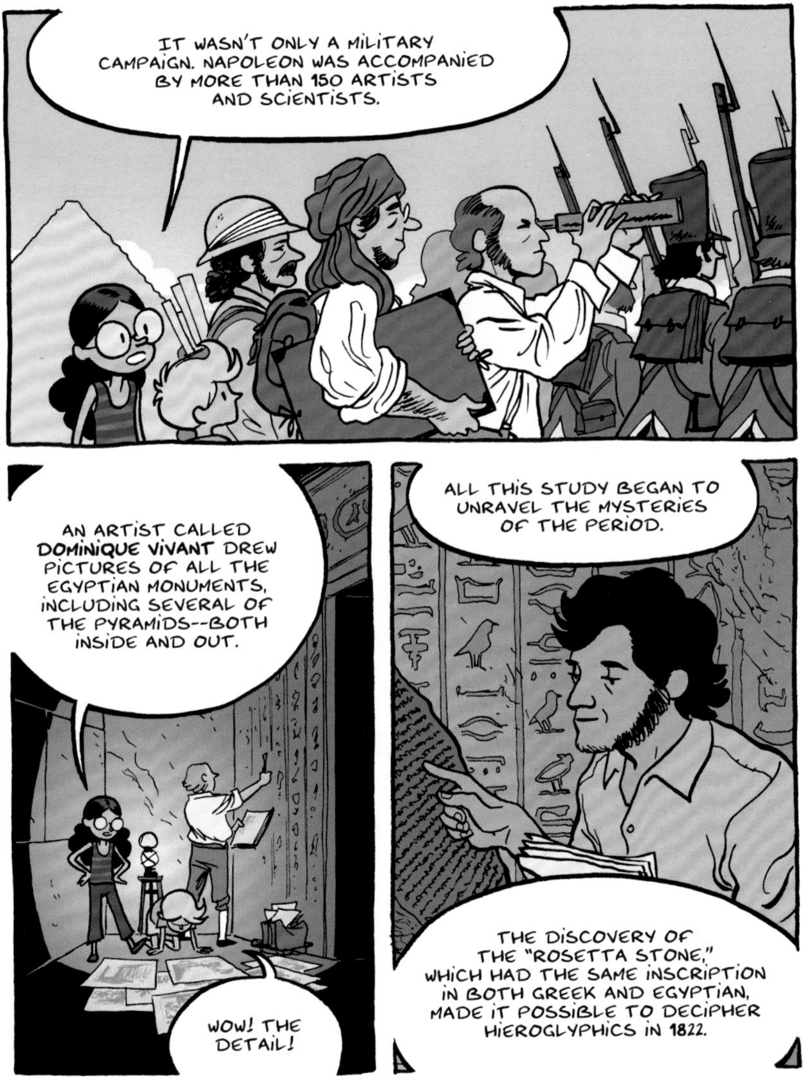
IT WASN'T ONLY A MILITARY CAMPAIGN. NAPOLEON WAS ACCOMPANIED BY MORE THAN 150 ARTISTS AND SCIENTISTS.
AN ARTIST CALLED **DOMINIQUE VIVANT** DREW PICTURES OF ALL THE EGYPTIAN MONUMENTS, INCLUDING SEVERAL OF THE PYRAMIDS--BOTH INSIDE AND OUT.
WOW! THE DETAIL!
ALL THIS STUDY BEGAN TO UNRAVEL THE MYSTERIES OF THE PERIOD.
THE DISCOVERY OF THE "ROSETTA STONE," WHICH HAD THE SAME INSCRIPTION IN BOTH GREEK AND EGYPTIAN, MADE IT POSSIBLE TO DECIPHER HIEROGLYPHICS IN 1822.

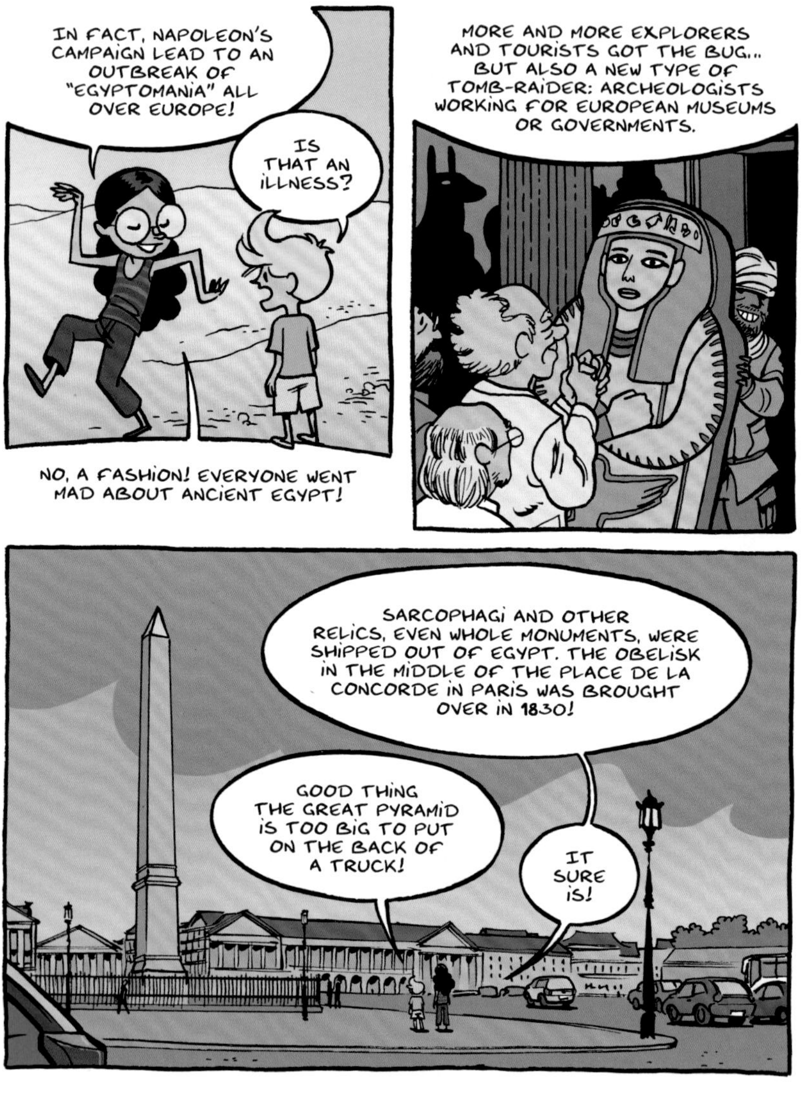
IN FACT, NAPOLEON'S CAMPAIGN LEAD TO AN OUTBREAK OF "EGYPTOMANIA" ALL OVER EUROPE!
IS THAT AN ILLNESS?
NO, A FASHION! EVERYONE WENT MAD ABOUT ANCIENT EGYPT!
MORE AND MORE EXPLORERS AND TOURISTS GOT THE BUG... BUT ALSO A NEW TYPE OF TOMB-RAIDER: ARCHEOLOGISTS WORKING FOR EUROPEAN MUSEUMS OR GOVERNMENTS.
SARCOPHAGI AND OTHER RELICS, EVEN WHOLE MONUMENTS, WERE SHIPPED OUT OF EGYPT. THE OBELISK IN THE MIDDLE OF THE PLACE DE LA CONCORDE IN PARIS WAS BROUGHT OVER IN 1830!
GOOD THING THE GREAT PYRAMID IS TOO BIG TO PUT ON THE BACK OF A TRUCK!
IT SURE IS!

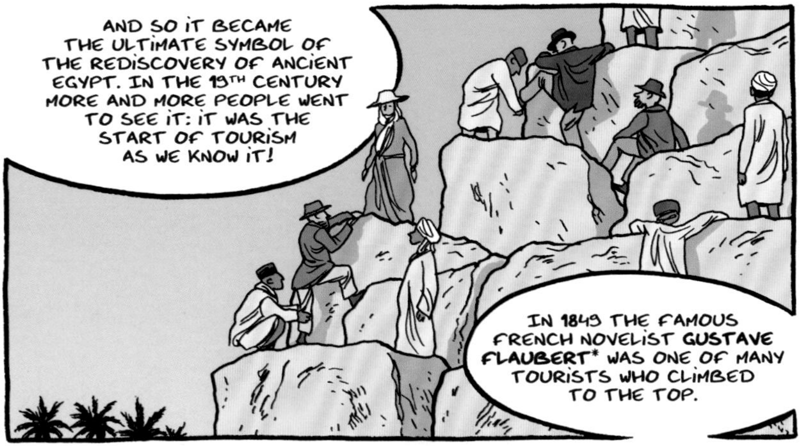
AND SO IT BECAME THE ULTIMATE SYMBOL OF THE REDISCOVERY OF ANCIENT EGYPT. IN THE 19TH CENTURY MORE AND MORE PEOPLE WENT TO SEE IT: IT WAS THE START OF TOURISM AS WE KNOW IT!
IN 1849 THE FAMOUS FRENCH NOVELIST **GUSTAVE FLAUBERT*** WAS ONE OF MANY TOURISTS WHO CLIMBED TO THE TOP.

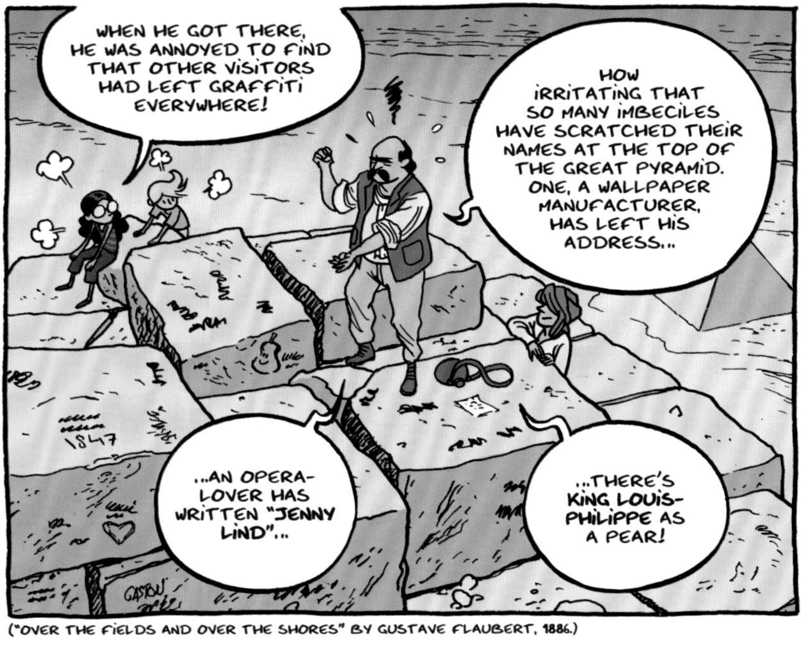
WHEN HE GOT THERE, HE WAS ANNOYED TO FIND THAT OTHER VISITORS HAD LEFT GRAFFITI EVERYWHERE!
HOW IRRITATING THAT SO MANY IMBECILES HAVE SCRATCHED THEIR NAMES AT THE TOP OF THE GREAT PYRAMID. ONE, A WALLPAPER MANUFACTURER, HAS LEFT HIS ADDRESS...
1847
...AN OPERA-LOVER HAS WRITTEN "JENNY LIND"...
...THERE'S **KING LOUIS-PHILIPPE** AS A PEAR!

("OVER THE FIELDS AND OVER THE SHORES" BY GUSTAVE FLAUBERT, 1886.)

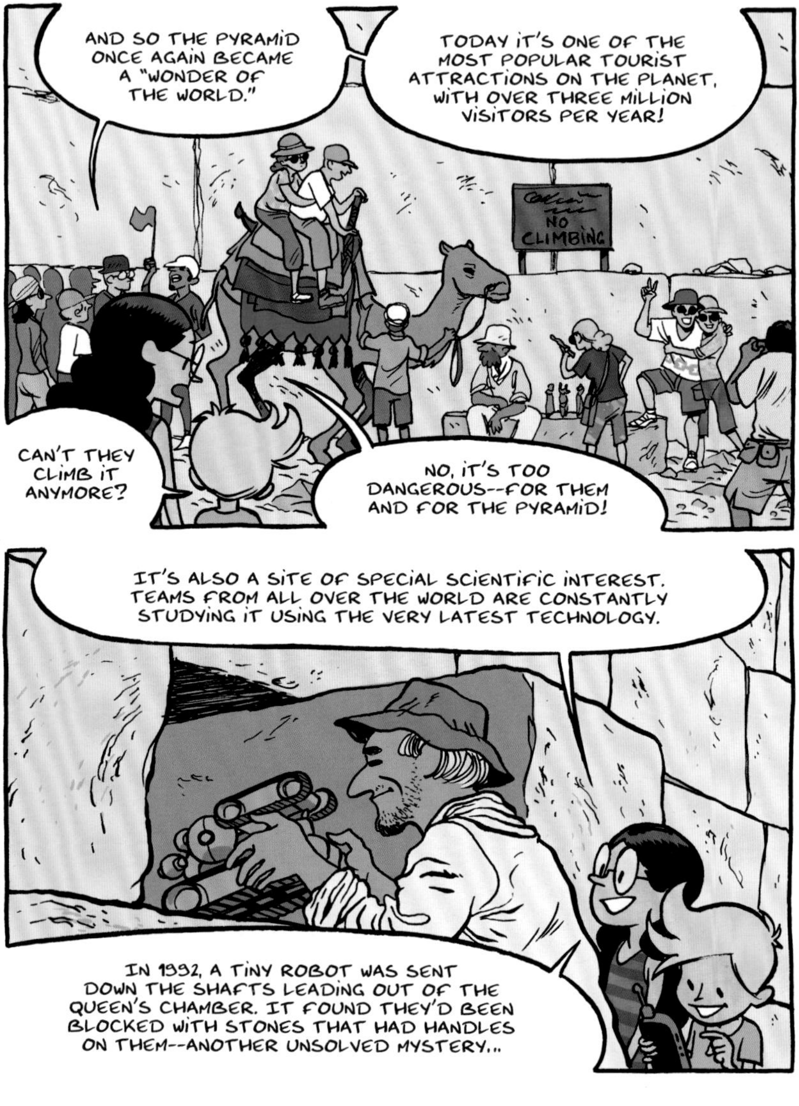
AND SO THE PYRAMID ONCE AGAIN BECAME A "WONDER OF THE WORLD."
TODAY IT'S ONE OF THE MOST POPULAR TOURIST ATTRACTIONS ON THE PLANET, WITH OVER THREE MILLION VISITORS PER YEAR!
NO CLIMBING
CAN'T THEY CLIMB IT ANYMORE?
NO, IT'S TOO DANGEROUS--FOR THEM AND FOR THE PYRAMID!
IT'S ALSO A SITE OF SPECIAL SCIENTIFIC INTEREST. TEAMS FROM ALL OVER THE WORLD ARE CONSTANTLY STUDYING IT USING THE VERY LATEST TECHNOLOGY.
IN 1992, A TINY ROBOT WAS SENT DOWN THE SHAFTS LEADING OUT OF THE QUEEN'S CHAMBER. IT FOUND THEY'D BEEN BLOCKED WITH STONES THAT HAD HANDLES ON THEM--ANOTHER UNSOLVED MYSTERY...

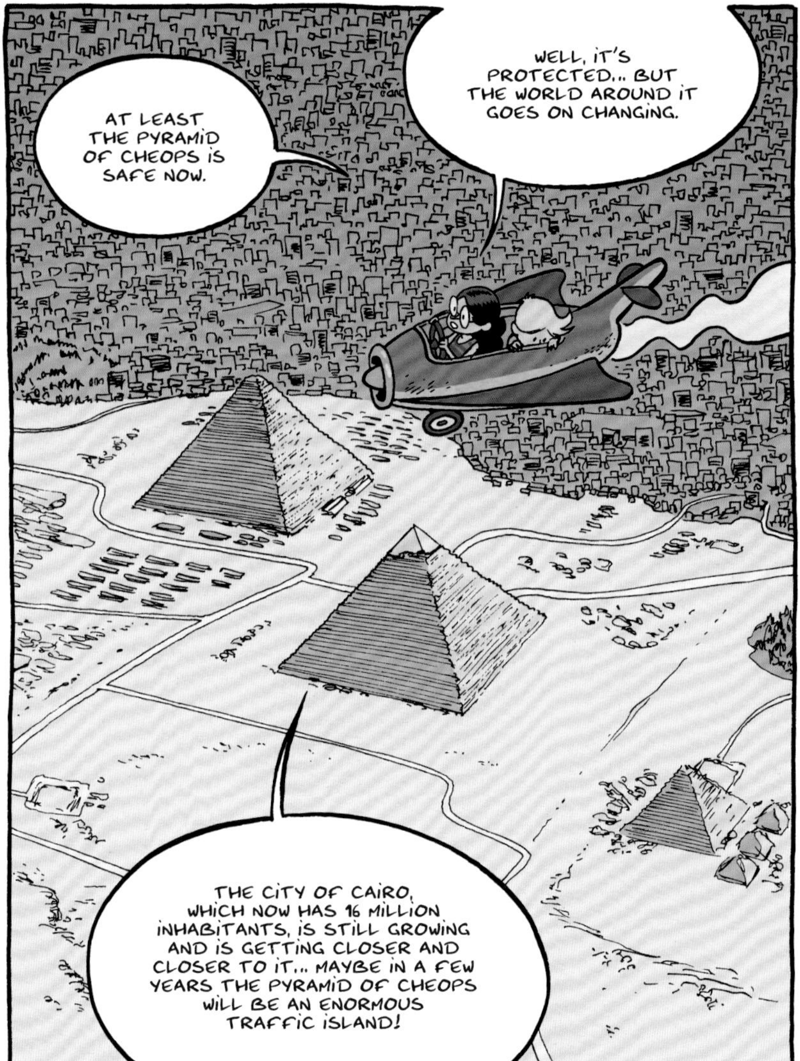
AT LEAST THE PYRAMID OF CHEOPS IS SAFE NOW.
WELL, IT'S PROTECTED... BUT THE WORLD AROUND IT GOES ON CHANGING.
THE CITY OF CAIRO, WHICH NOW HAS 16 MILLION INHABITANTS, IS STILL GROWING AND IS GETTING CLOSER AND CLOSER TO IT... MAYBE IN A FEW YEARS THE PYRAMID OF CHEOPS WILL BE AN ENORMOUS TRAFFIC ISLAND!

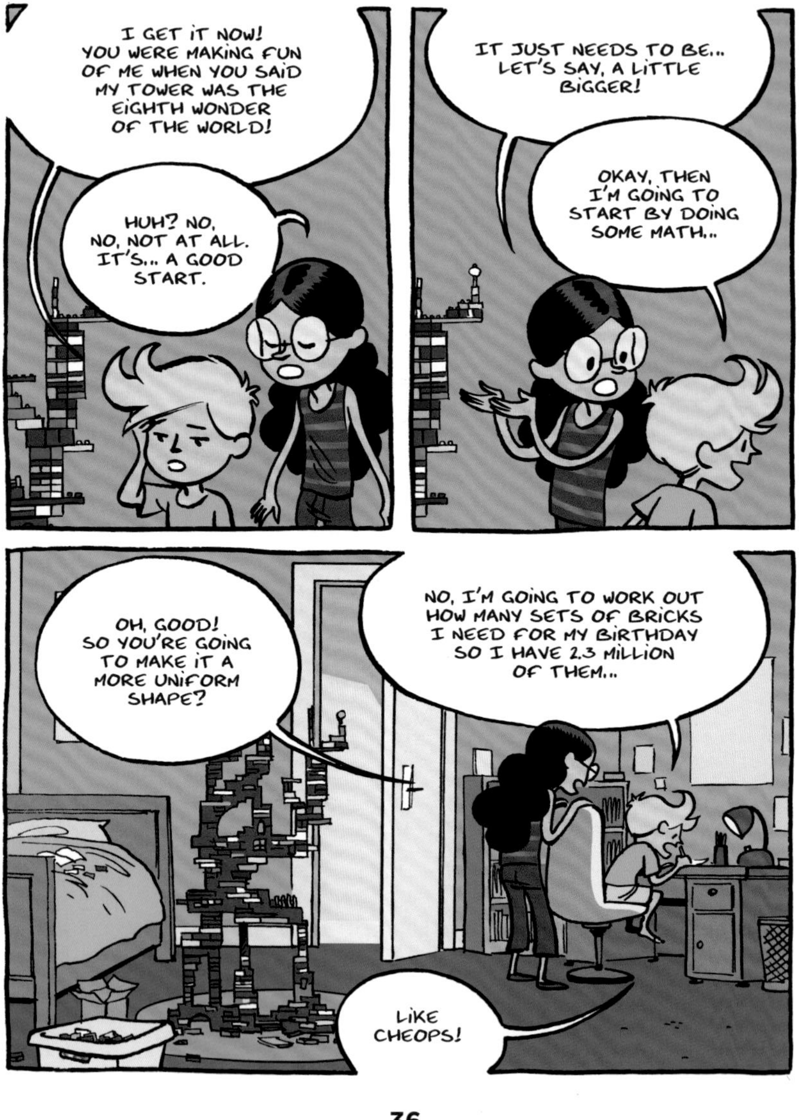
I GET IT NOW! YOU WERE MAKING FUN OF ME WHEN YOU SAID MY TOWER WAS THE EIGHTH WONDER OF THE WORLD!
HUH? NO, NO, NOT AT ALL. IT'S... A GOOD START.
IT JUST NEEDS TO BE... LET'S SAY, A LITTLE BIGGER!
OKAY, THEN I'M GOING TO START BY DOING SOME MATH...
OH, GOOD! SO YOU'RE GOING TO MAKE IT A MORE UNIFORM SHAPE?
NO, I'M GOING TO WORK OUT HOW MANY SETS OF BRICKS I NEED FOR MY BIRTHDAY SO I HAVE 2.3 MILLION OF THEM...
LIKE CHEOPS!

And there's more...

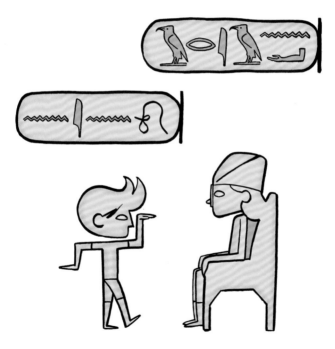

Some people who made history

Cheops
(c. 2500 B.C.)

Cheops was one of the 4th Dynasty of pharaohs. Despite his legacy of vast buildings, very little is known about him. He probably ruled for 22 to 40 years in the early 17th century B.C. Cheops (or Khêops) was his Greek name, and he's also known by his Egyptian name Khufu, and as Súphis, Sofe, Saurid, and Salhuk.

Imhotep
(c. 3000 B.C.)

Imhotep was a doctor, architect, and philosopher, and he was Pharaoh Djoser's vizier (personal advisor). He designed the pharaoh's tomb as a stepped pyramid, which was the first type of pyramid to be built. He was made a god after his death.

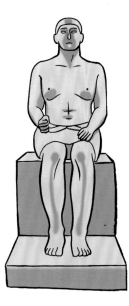

Hemiunu
(c. 2500 B.C.)

A grandson of Pharaoh Sneferu, Hemiunu was Cheops's vizir and the designer of the Great Pyramid. He also built himself a mastaba (tomb), which was discovered by archeologists in the early 20th century, along with an almost perfectly preserved statue of him.

Herodotus
(born 480 B.C., died c. 425 B.C.)

A Greek explorer known as "The Father of History," Herodotus talked to people living around the Mediterranean and wrote about them in *The Histories,* a work that became a key source of information about the ancient world—and about Cheops and the pyramids—right up until modern times.

The Giza Plateau

The Giza Pyramids stand on a chalk plateau that was leveled for the purpose. They each have one side facing north, one facing south, one facing east and one facing west.

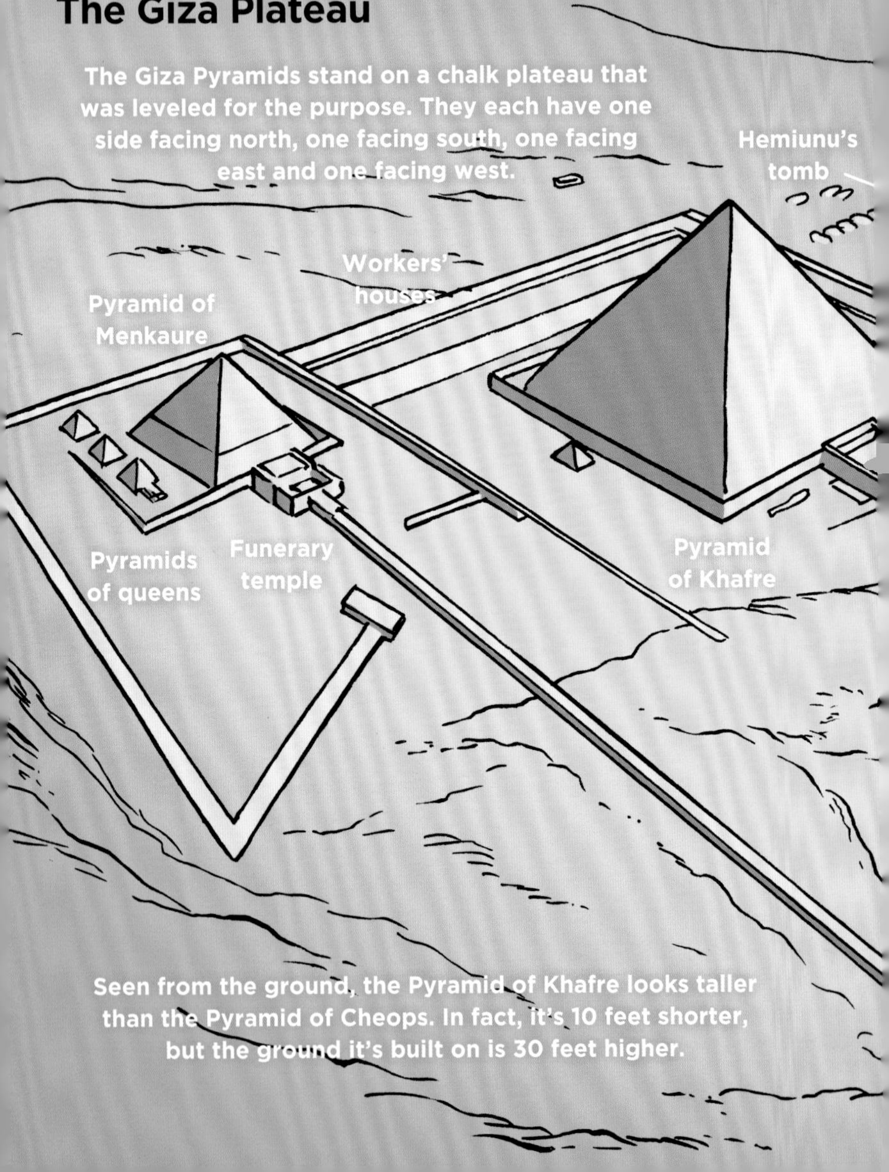
Hemiunu's tomb
Workers' houses
Pyramid of Menkaure
Pyramids of queens
Funerary temple
Pyramid of Khafre

Seen from the ground, the Pyramid of Khafre looks taller than the Pyramid of Cheops. In fact, it's 10 feet shorter, but the ground it's built on is 30 feet higher.

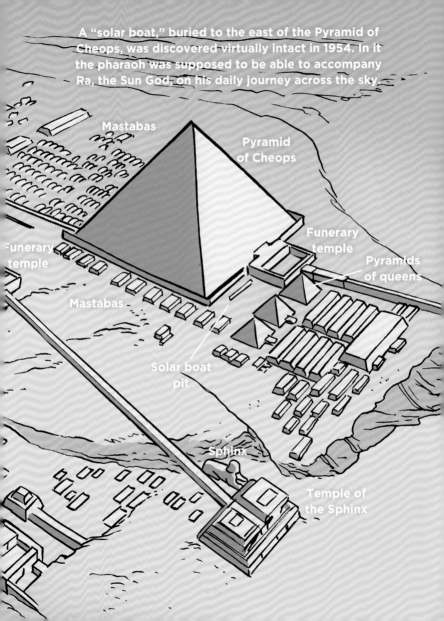

A "solar boat," buried to the east of the Pyramid of Cheops, was discovered virtually intact in 1954. In it the pharaoh was supposed to be able to accompany Ra, the Sun God, on his daily journey across the sky.

Mastabas

Pyramid of Cheops

Funerary temple

Funerary temple

Pyramids of queens

Mastabas

Solar boat pit

Sphinx

Temple of the Sphinx

The six other Wonders of the World

The Hanging Gardens of Babylon

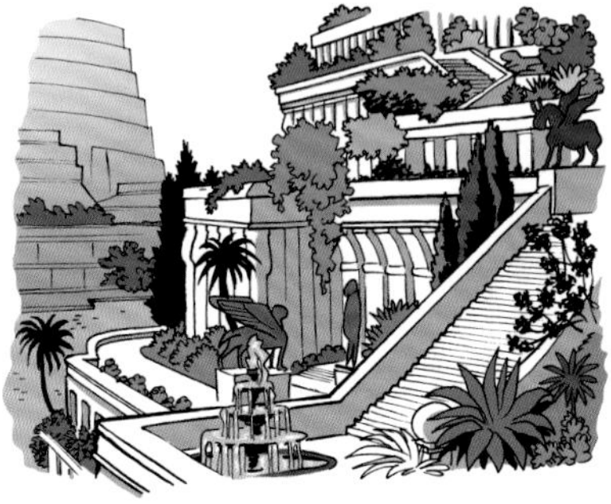

According to legend, King Nebuchadnezzar II had magnificent terraced gardens built around 600 B.C. in the city of Babylon, in what is now part of Iraq, but archeologists have found no trace of their existence.

The Statue of Zeus at Olympia

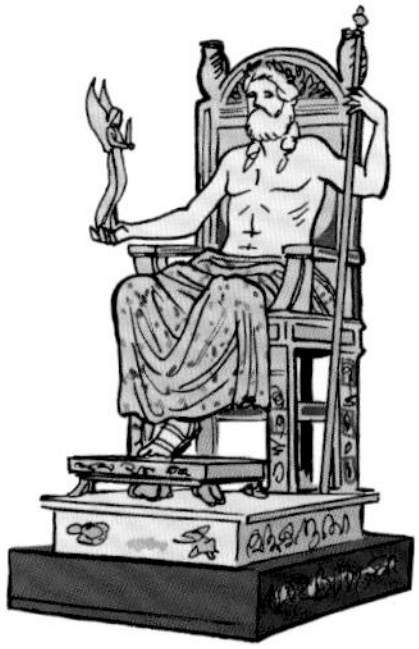

An ivory and gold statue of the King of the Gods was carved by Phidias around 436 B.C. It was moved from Olympia (in Greece) to Constantinople (now Istanbul) 800 years later and was destroyed by fire.

The Temple of Artemis at Ephesus

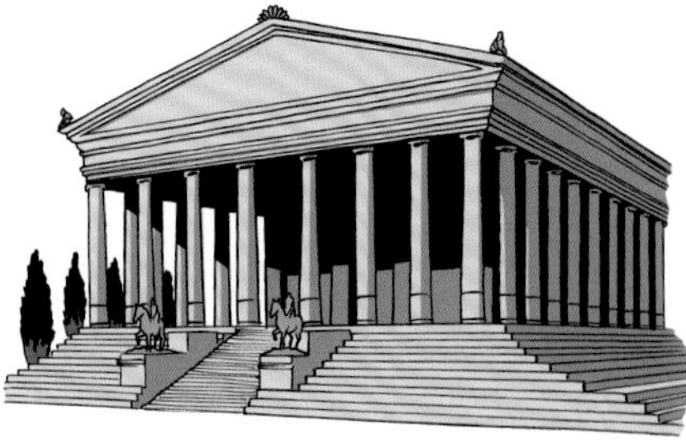

The Greek king Croesus had this vast temple (over 425 feet long) built at Ephesus in 560 B.C., but it was burned to the ground in 356 B.C. by a man who hoped this would make him famous.

The Mausoleum at Halicarnassus

A giant tomb, more than 160 feet high, built for Mausolus, a Persian King, in 353 B.C. at Halicarnassus—now Bodrum in Turkey. It collapsed in the Middle Ages and is now a ruin.

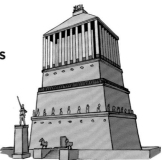

The Colossus of Rhodes

An enormous bronze statue (over 100 feet high) of Helios, the Sun God, was built around 292 B.C. at the entrance to the Greek port of Rhodes. It was destroyed by an earthquake 65 years later.

The Lighthouse of Alexandria

Built around 290 B.C., the lighthouse, which was visible from a distance of 30 miles, was used by sailors for 1,700 years. It was destroyed by a succession of earthquakes.

Timeline

Imhotep designs the
first pyramid for
Pharaoh Djoser.

▼

Pharaoh Sneferu, Cheops's father,
makes several attempts at
building a smooth pyramid,
finally succeeding with
"The Red Pyramid."

▼

2650 B.C.

2590–2560 B.C.

0

450 B.C.

1550 B.C.

▲

▲

The Greek historian
Herodotus visits Egypt
and collects information
about Cheops.

Ahmose builds the
last pyramid.

820 A.D.

1500–1700 A.D.

▲

▲

Khalif Al-Ma'mun breaks
open the north face of the
Pyramid of Cheops.

European explorers rediscover
the Egyptian pyramids.

ANTIQUITY | MIDDLE AGES | RENAISSANCE | MODERN TIMES

Cheops builds the Great Pyramid on the Giza Plateau, 15 miles from Cairo.

2580–2560 B.C.

The Pyramids of Khafre and Menkaure complete the Giza site.

2570–2510 B.C.

2500–2300 B.C.

Pharaohs build their pyramids at another site, Abusir.

1991–1962 B.C.

During his reign, Amenemhat I uses stones from the Pyramid of Cheops to build his own memorial complex.

1798 A.D.

Napoleon Bonaparte wins "The Battle of the Pyramids," part of his Egyptian campaign.

1979 A.D.

The Pyramids of Giza become a UNESCO World Heritage Site.

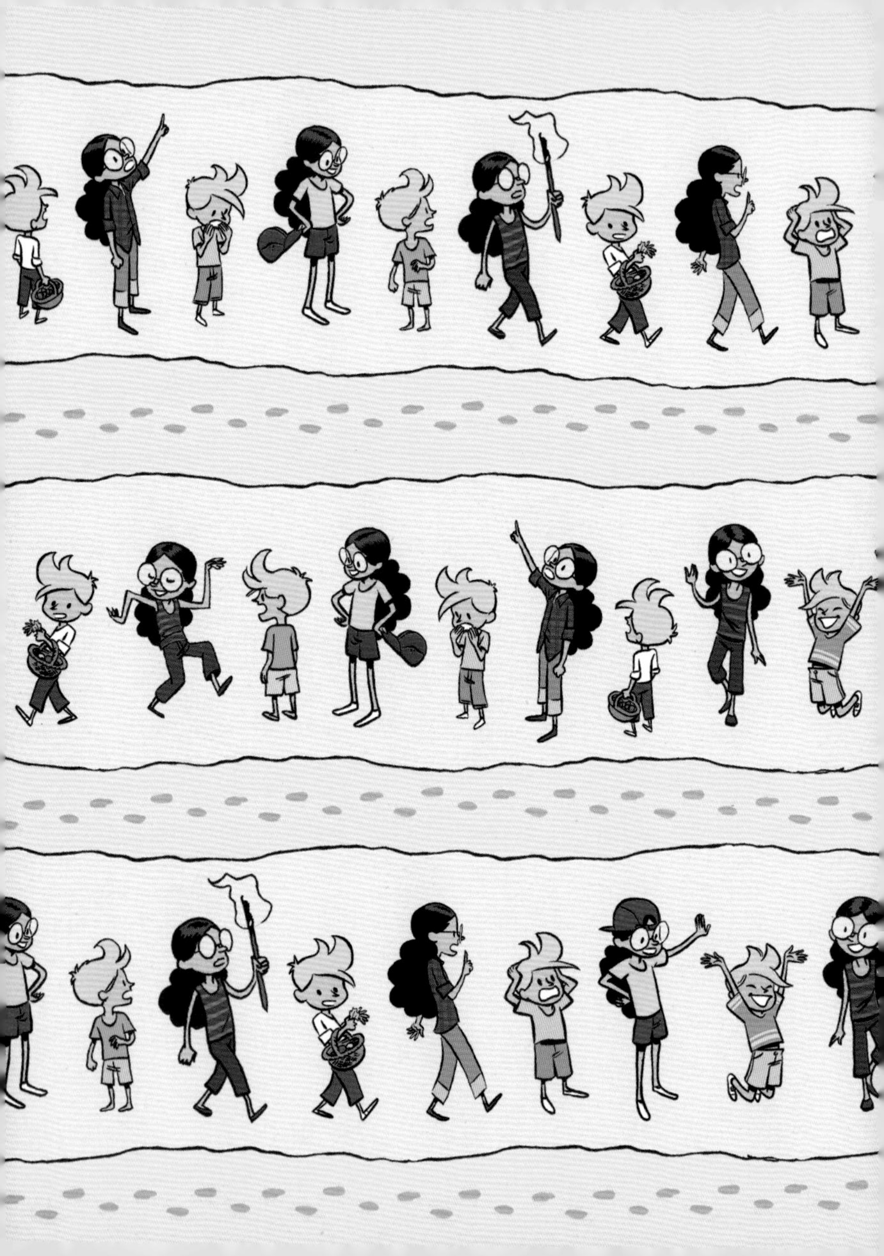

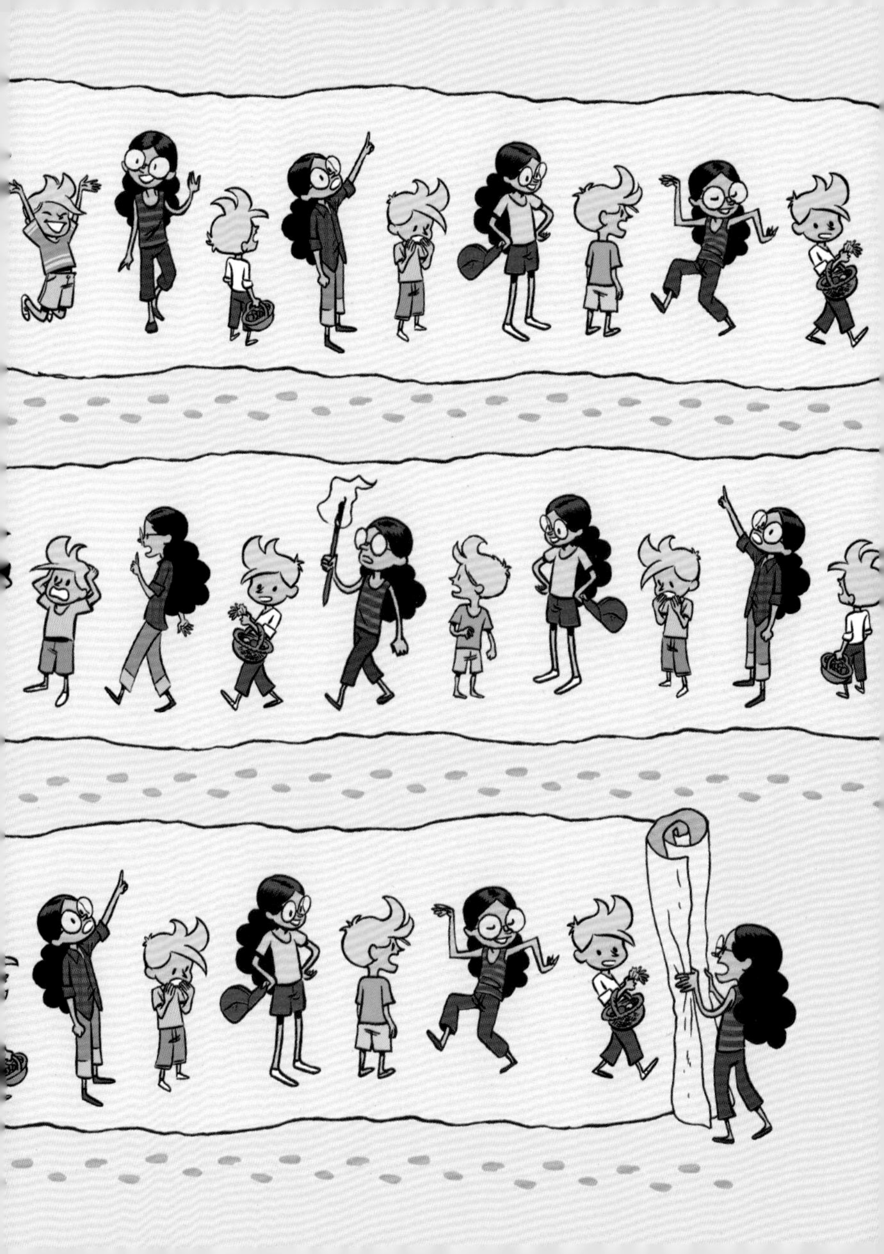

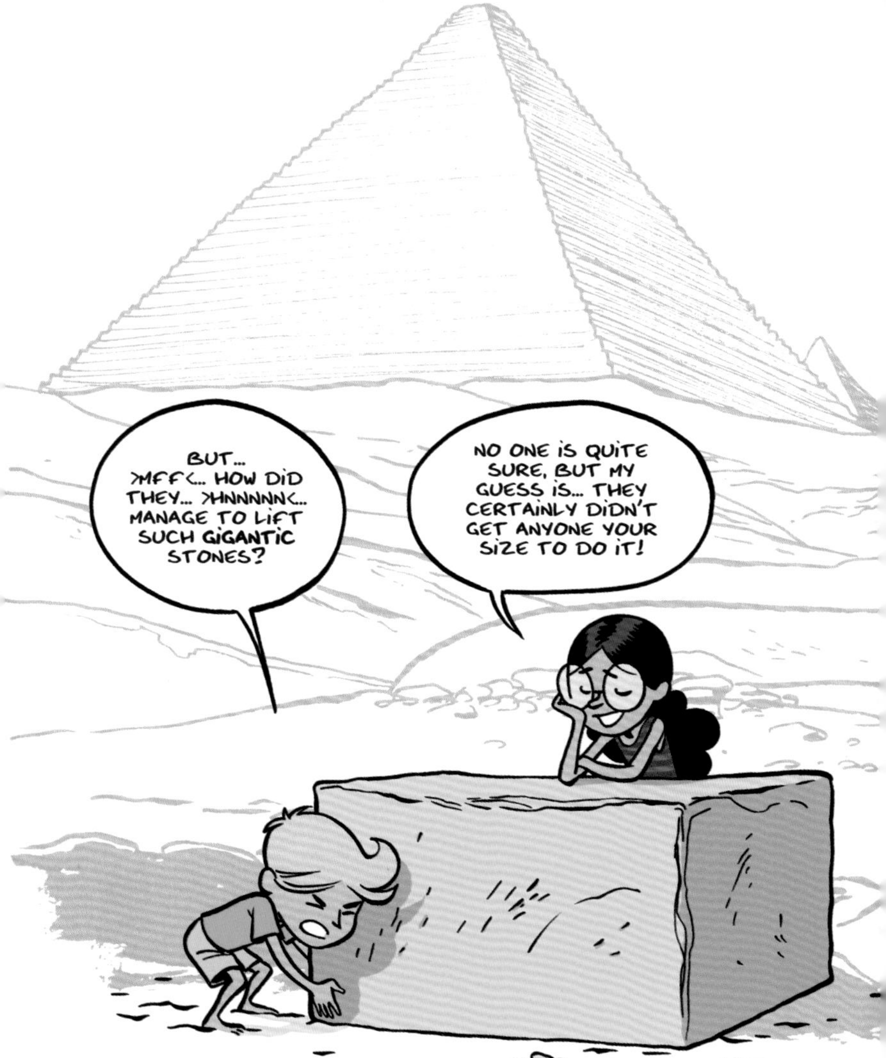
BUT... >MFF<... HOW DID THEY... >HNNNNN<... MANAGE TO LIFT SUCH GIGANTIC STONES?
NO ONE IS QUITE SURE, BUT MY GUESS IS... THEY CERTAINLY DIDN'T GET ANYONE YOUR SIZE TO DO IT!

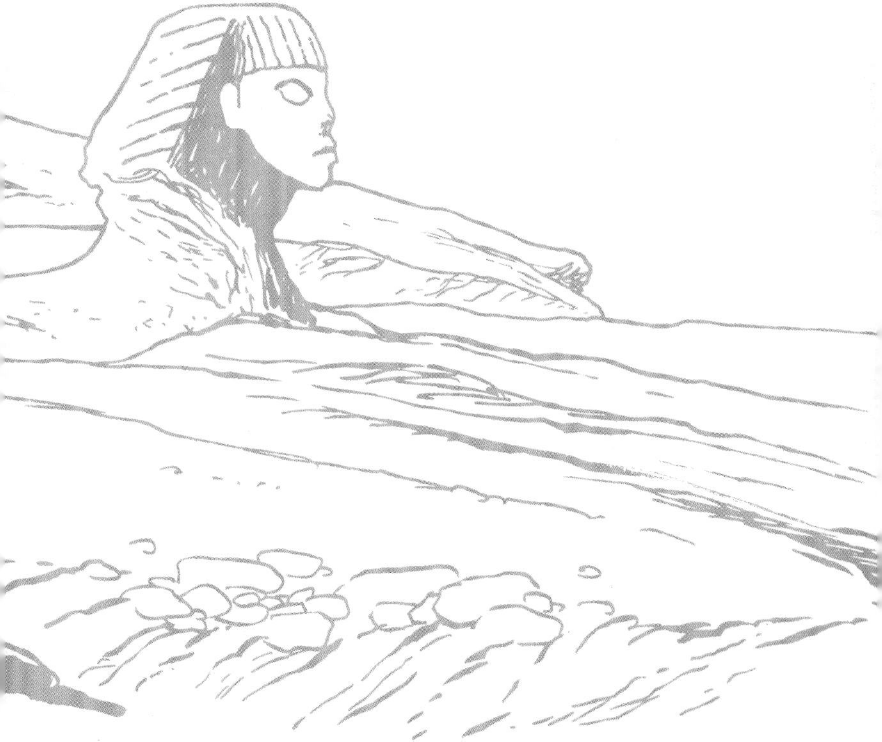

FABRICE ERRE SYLVAIN SAVOIA

Magical History Tour

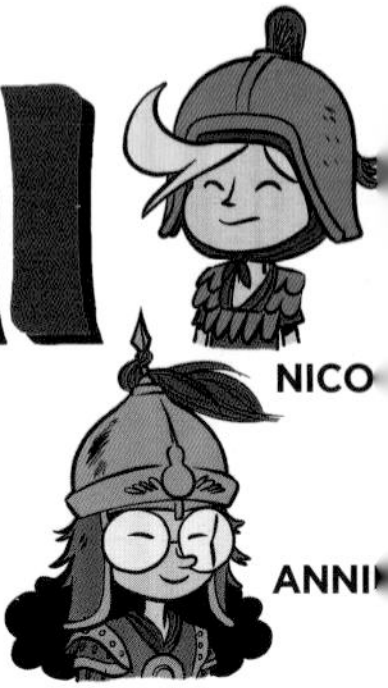
NICO
ANNI

The Great Wall of China

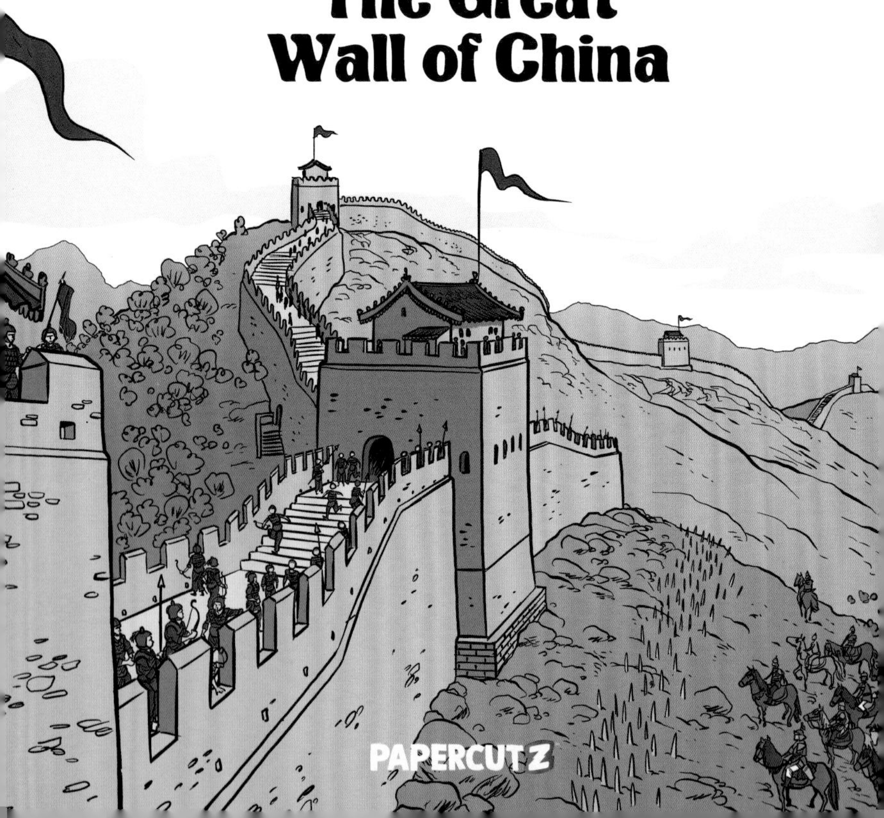

PAPERCUTZ

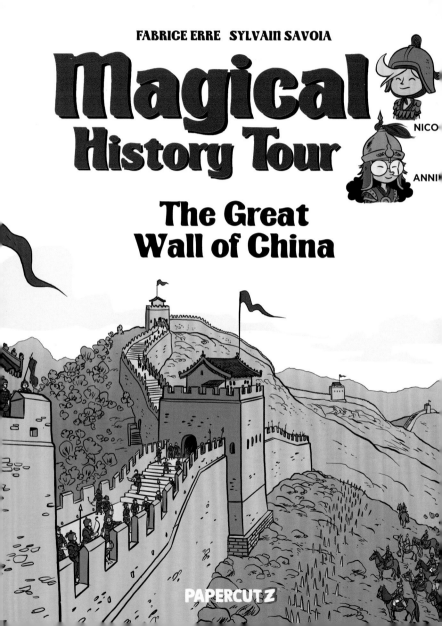

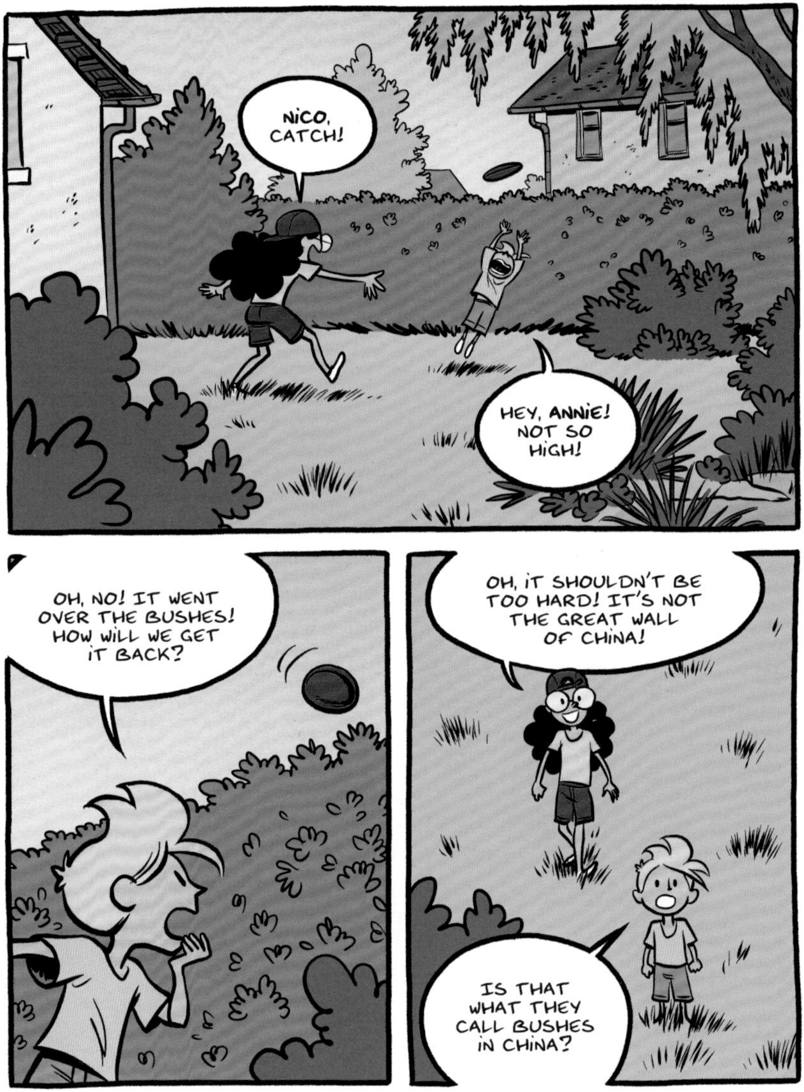
NICO, CATCH!
HEY, ANNIE! NOT SO HIGH!
OH, NO! IT WENT OVER THE BUSHES! HOW WILL WE GET IT BACK?
OH, IT SHOULDN'T BE TOO HARD! IT'S NOT THE GREAT WALL OF CHINA!
IS THAT WHAT THEY CALL BUSHES IN CHINA?

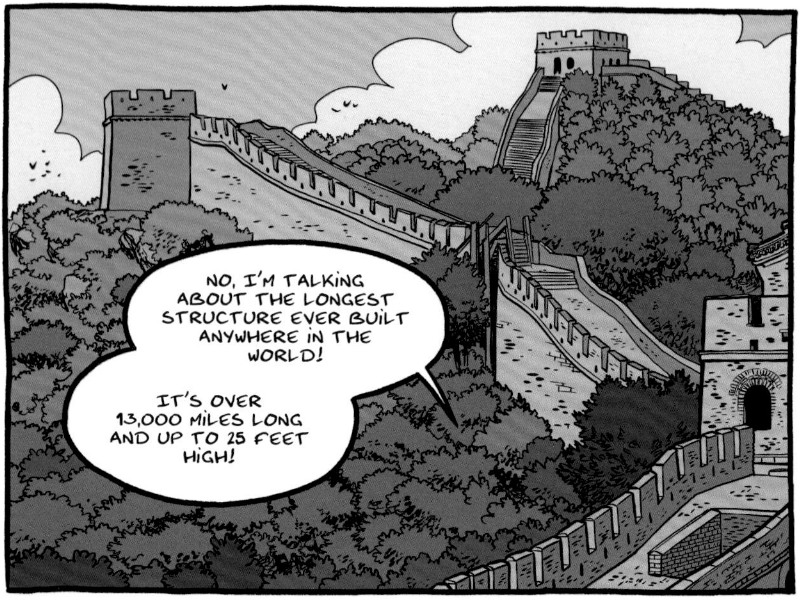
NO, I'M TALKING ABOUT THE LONGEST STRUCTURE EVER BUILT ANYWHERE IN THE WORLD!
IT'S OVER 13,000 MILES LONG AND UP TO 25 FEET HIGH!

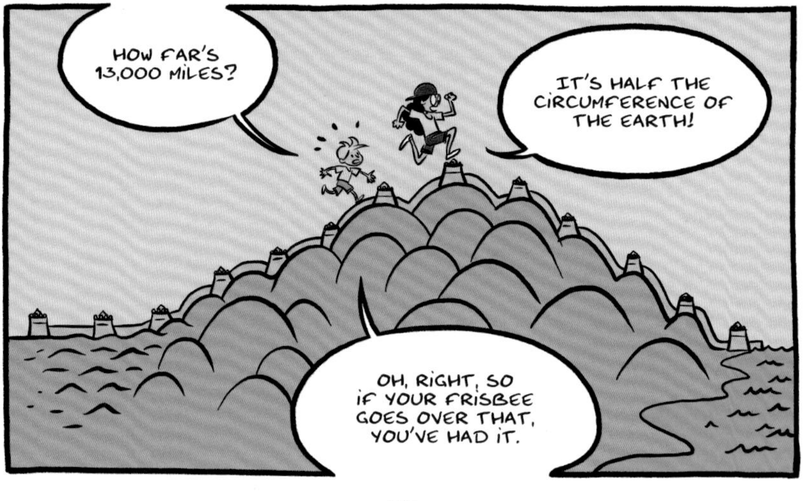
HOW FAR'S 13,000 MILES?
IT'S HALF THE CIRCUMFERENCE OF THE EARTH!
OH, RIGHT, SO IF YOUR FRISBEE GOES OVER THAT, YOU'VE HAD IT.

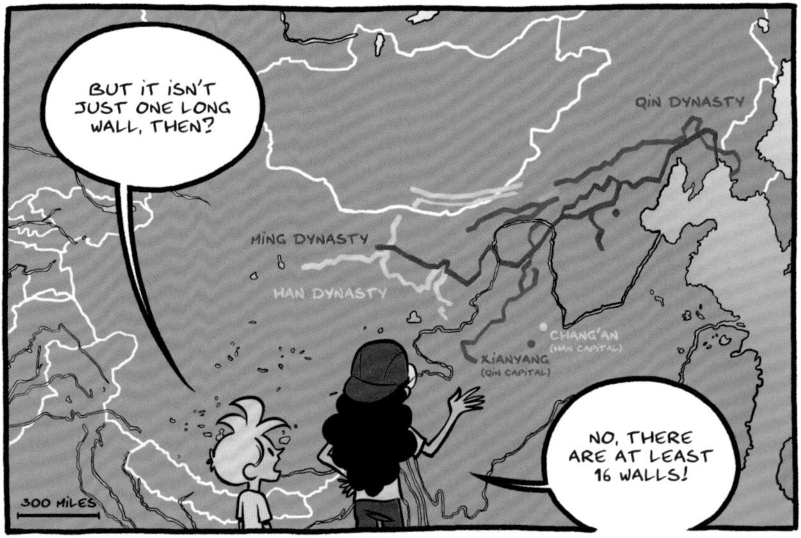
BUT IT ISN'T JUST ONE LONG WALL, THEN?
QIN DYNASTY
MING DYNASTY
HAN DYNASTY
CHANG'AN (HAN CAPITAL)
XIANYANG (QIN CAPITAL)
300 MILES
NO, THERE ARE AT LEAST 16 WALLS!

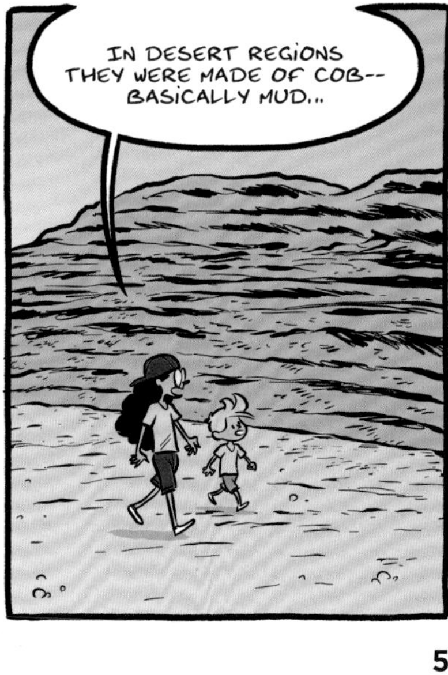
IN DESERT REGIONS THEY WERE MADE OF COB-- BASICALLY MUD...

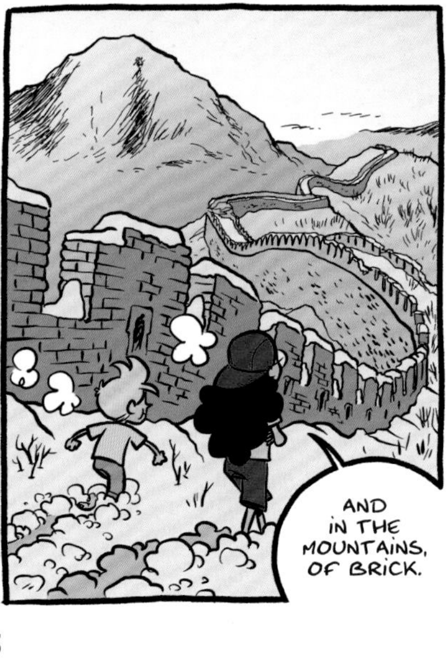
AND IN THE MOUNTAINS, OF BRICK.

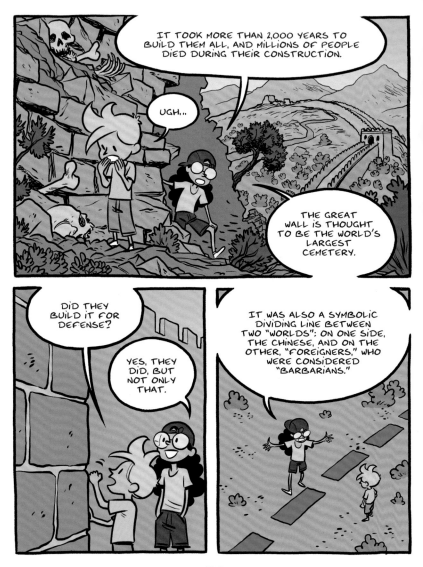

IT TOOK MORE THAN 2,000 YEARS TO BUILD THEM ALL, AND MILLIONS OF PEOPLE DIED DURING THEIR CONSTRUCTION.

UGH...

THE GREAT WALL IS THOUGHT TO BE THE WORLD'S LARGEST CEMETERY.

DID THEY BUILD IT FOR DEFENSE?

YES, THEY DID, BUT NOT ONLY THAT.

IT WAS ALSO A SYMBOLIC DIVIDING LINE BETWEEN TWO "WORLDS": ON ONE SIDE, THE CHINESE, AND ON THE OTHER, "FOREIGNERS," WHO WERE CONSIDERED "BARBARIANS."

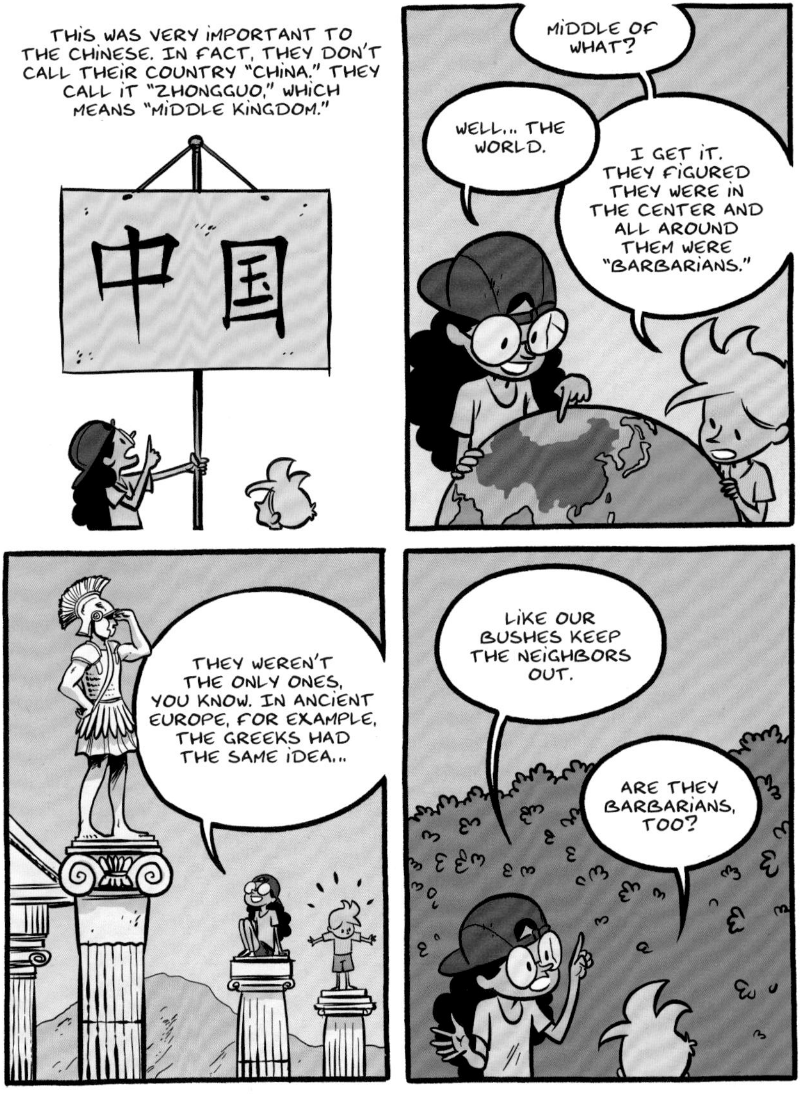
THIS WAS VERY IMPORTANT TO THE CHINESE. IN FACT, THEY DON'T CALL THEIR COUNTRY "CHINA." THEY CALL IT "ZHONGGUO," WHICH MEANS "MIDDLE KINGDOM."
中国
MIDDLE OF WHAT?
WELL... THE WORLD.
I GET IT. THEY FIGURED THEY WERE IN THE CENTER AND ALL AROUND THEM WERE "BARBARIANS."
THEY WEREN'T THE ONLY ONES, YOU KNOW. IN ANCIENT EUROPE, FOR EXAMPLE, THE GREEKS HAD THE SAME IDEA...
LIKE OUR BUSHES KEEP THE NEIGHBORS OUT.
ARE THEY BARBARIANS, TOO?

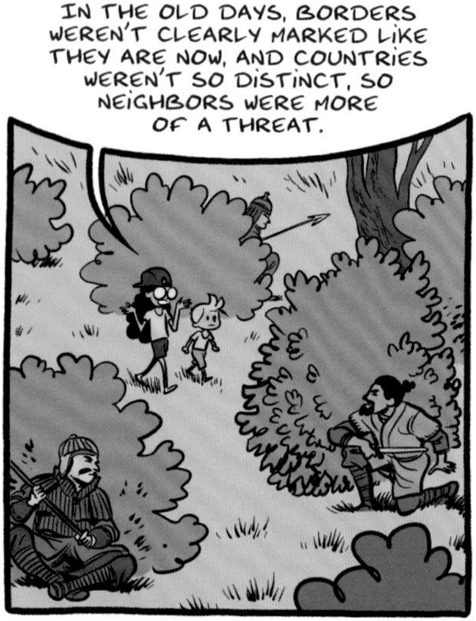
IN THE OLD DAYS, BORDERS WEREN'T CLEARLY MARKED LIKE THEY ARE NOW, AND COUNTRIES WEREN'T SO DISTINCT, SO NEIGHBORS WERE MORE OF A THREAT.

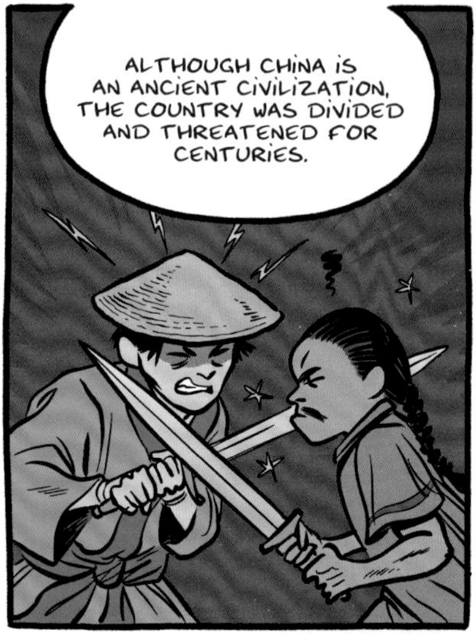
ALTHOUGH CHINA IS AN ANCIENT CIVILIZATION, THE COUNTRY WAS DIVIDED AND THREATENED FOR CENTURIES.

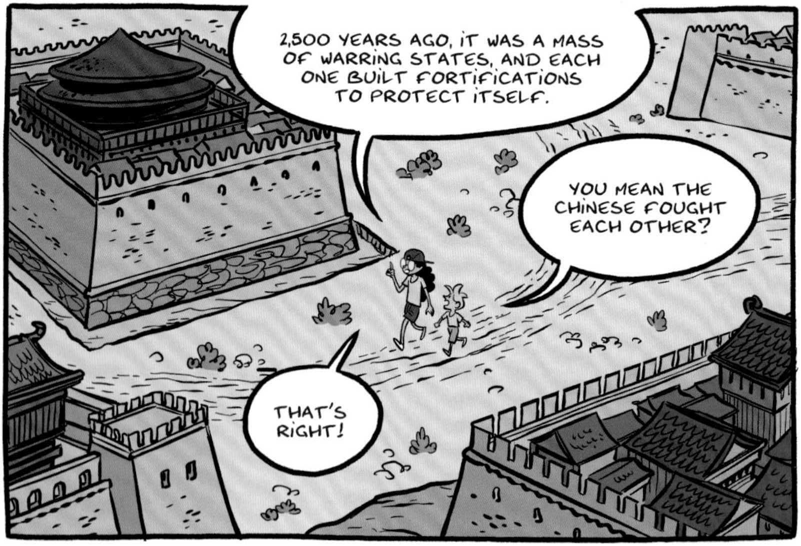
2,500 YEARS AGO, IT WAS A MASS OF WARRING STATES, AND EACH ONE BUILT FORTIFICATIONS TO PROTECT ITSELF.
YOU MEAN THE CHINESE FOUGHT EACH OTHER?
THAT'S RIGHT!

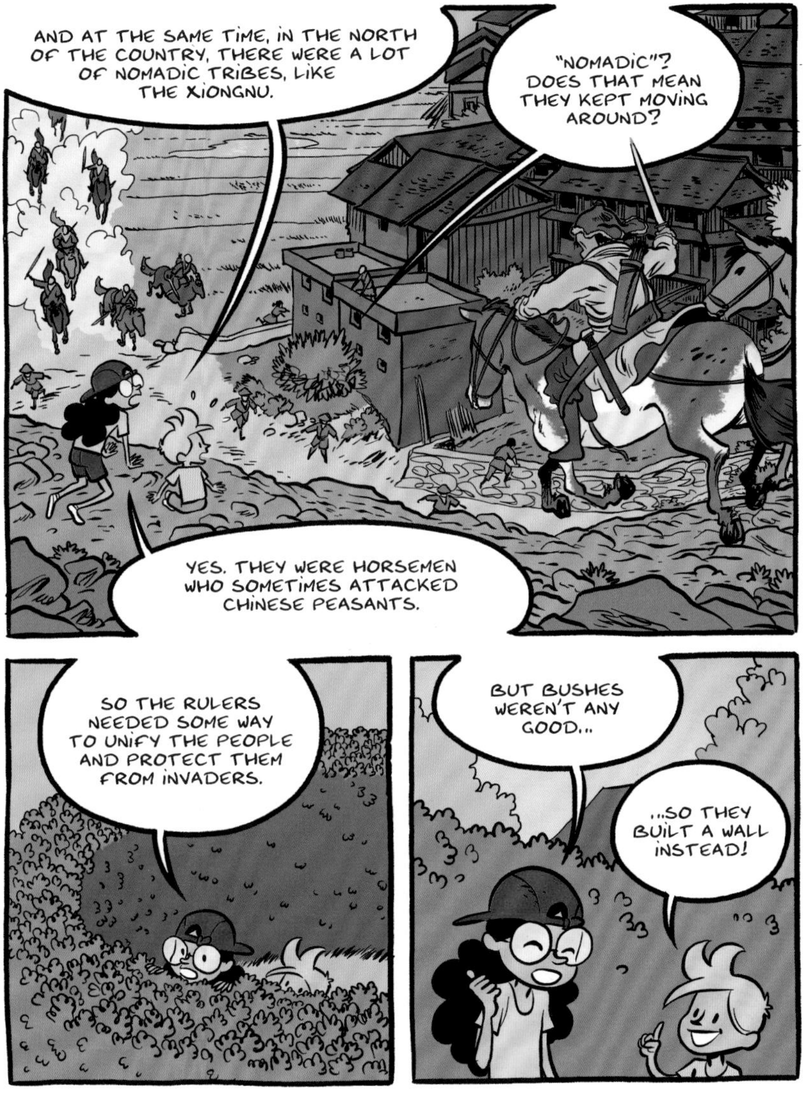
AND AT THE SAME TIME, IN THE NORTH OF THE COUNTRY, THERE WERE A LOT OF NOMADIC TRIBES, LIKE THE XIONGNU.
"NOMADIC"? DOES THAT MEAN THEY KEPT MOVING AROUND?
YES. THEY WERE HORSEMEN WHO SOMETIMES ATTACKED CHINESE PEASANTS.
SO THE RULERS NEEDED SOME WAY TO UNIFY THE PEOPLE AND PROTECT THEM FROM INVADERS.
BUT BUSHES WEREN'T ANY GOOD...
...SO THEY BUILT A WALL INSTEAD!

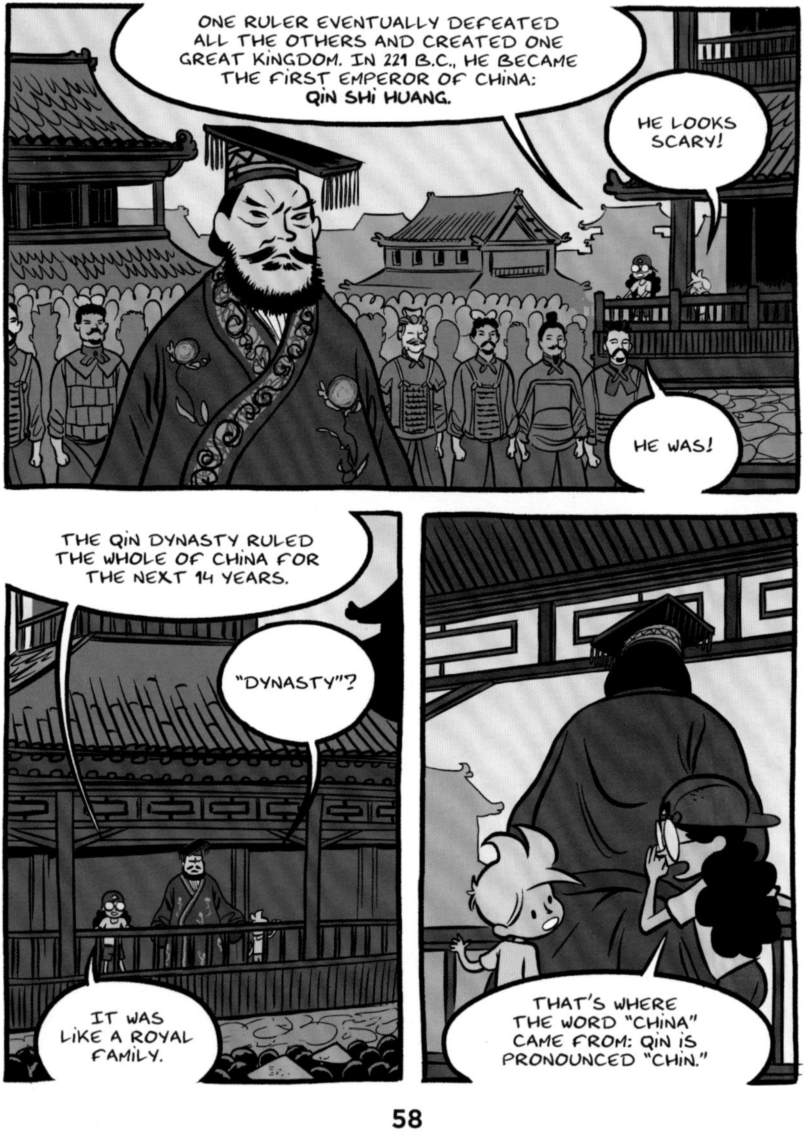
ONE RULER EVENTUALLY DEFEATED ALL THE OTHERS AND CREATED ONE GREAT KINGDOM. IN 221 B.C., HE BECAME THE FIRST EMPEROR OF CHINA: **QIN SHI HUANG.**
HE LOOKS SCARY!
HE WAS!
THE QIN DYNASTY RULED THE WHOLE OF CHINA FOR THE NEXT 14 YEARS.
"DYNASTY"?
IT WAS LIKE A ROYAL FAMILY.
THAT'S WHERE THE WORD "CHINA" CAME FROM: QIN IS PRONOUNCED "CHIN."

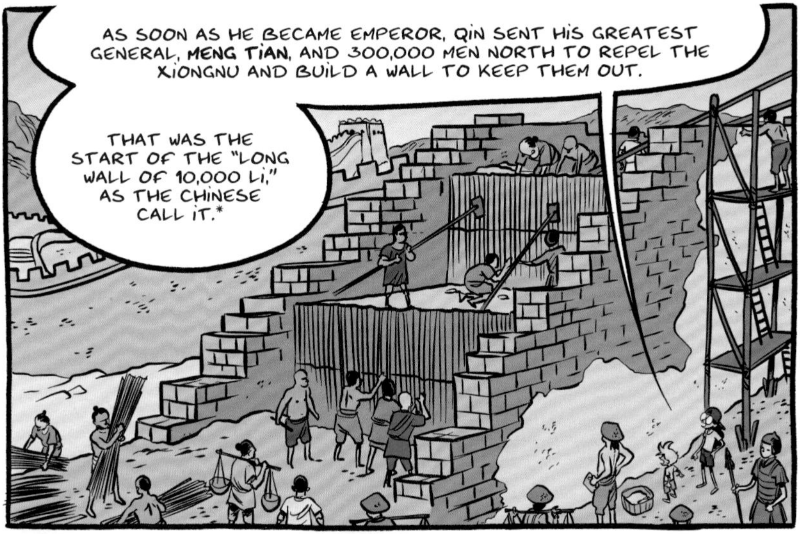
AS SOON AS HE BECAME EMPEROR, QIN SENT HIS GREATEST GENERAL, MENG TIAN, AND 300,000 MEN NORTH TO REPEL THE XIONGNU AND BUILD A WALL TO KEEP THEM OUT.
THAT WAS THE START OF THE "LONG WALL OF 10,000 LI," AS THE CHINESE CALL IT.*

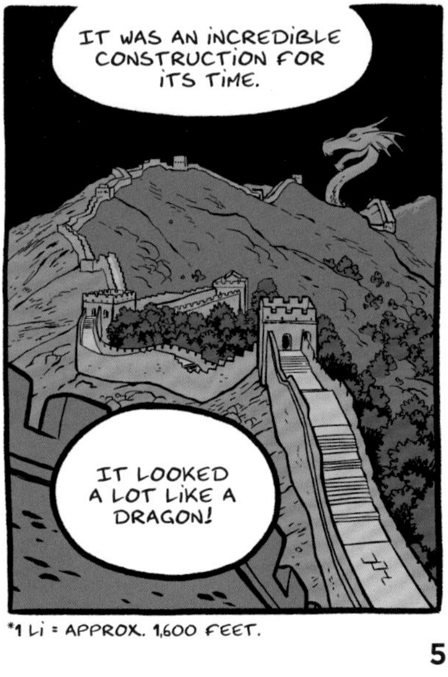
IT WAS AN INCREDIBLE CONSTRUCTION FOR ITS TIME.
IT LOOKED A LOT LIKE A DRAGON!

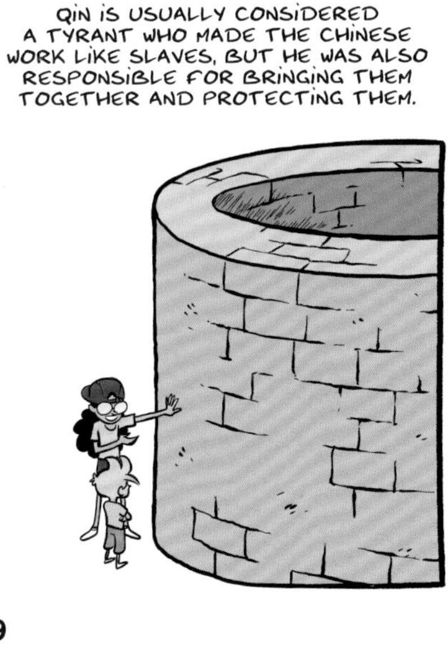
QIN IS USUALLY CONSIDERED A TYRANT WHO MADE THE CHINESE WORK LIKE SLAVES, BUT HE WAS ALSO RESPONSIBLE FOR BRINGING THEM TOGETHER AND PROTECTING THEM.

*1 LI = APPROX. 1,600 FEET.

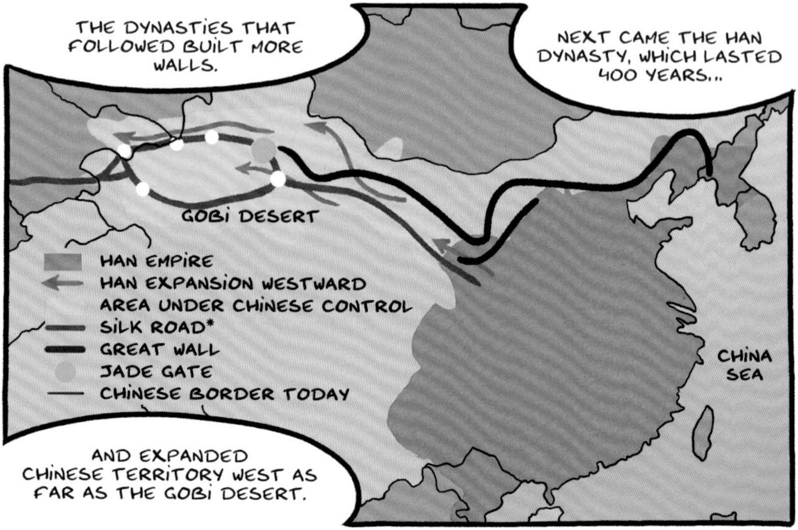
THE DYNASTIES THAT FOLLOWED BUILT MORE WALLS.
NEXT CAME THE HAN DYNASTY, WHICH LASTED 400 YEARS...
GOBI DESERT
HAN EMPIRE
HAN EXPANSION WESTWARD
AREA UNDER CHINESE CONTROL
SILK ROAD*
GREAT WALL
JADE GATE
CHINESE BORDER TODAY
CHINA SEA
AND EXPANDED CHINESE TERRITORY WEST AS FAR AS THE GOBI DESERT.

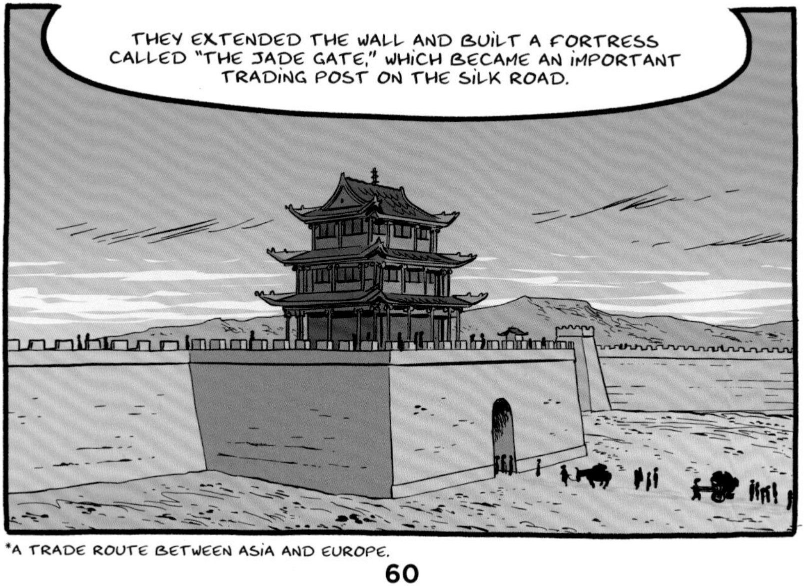
THEY EXTENDED THE WALL AND BUILT A FORTRESS CALLED "THE JADE GATE," WHICH BECAME AN IMPORTANT TRADING POST ON THE SILK ROAD.

*A TRADE ROUTE BETWEEN ASIA AND EUROPE.

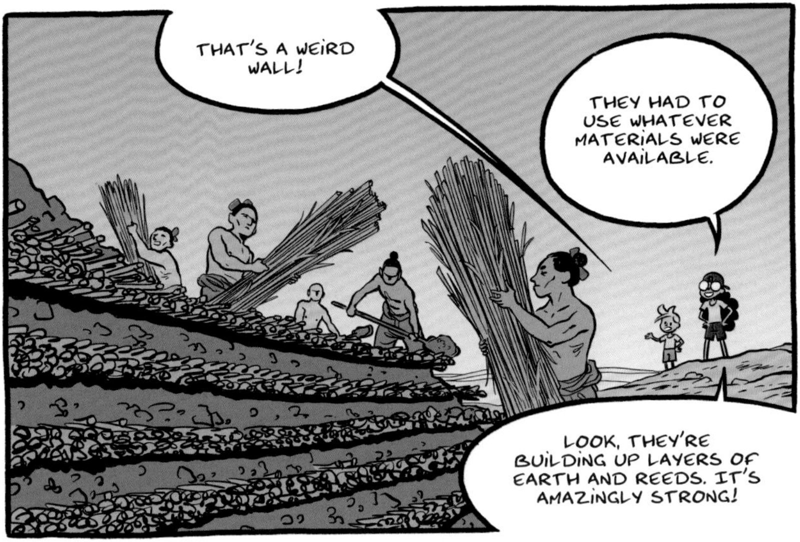
THAT'S A WEIRD WALL!
THEY HAD TO USE WHATEVER MATERIALS WERE AVAILABLE.
LOOK, THEY'RE BUILDING UP LAYERS OF EARTH AND REEDS. IT'S AMAZINGLY STRONG!

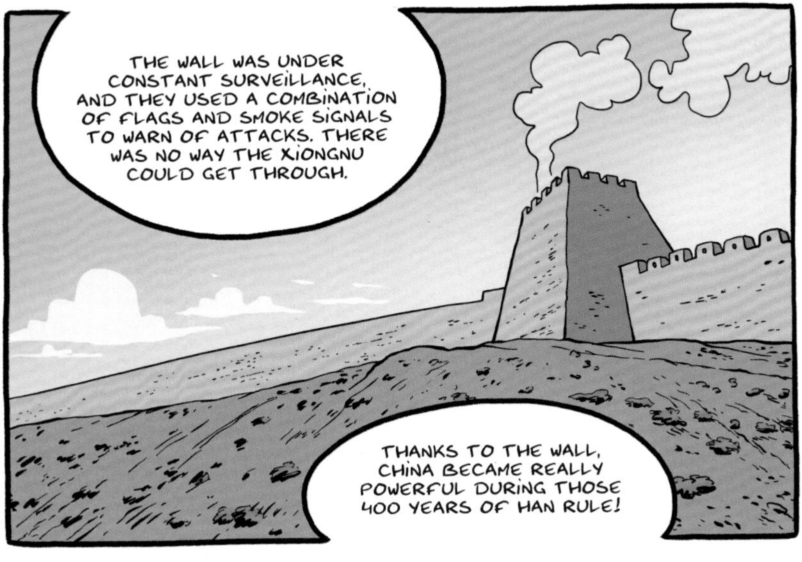
THE WALL WAS UNDER CONSTANT SURVEILLANCE, AND THEY USED A COMBINATION OF FLAGS AND SMOKE SIGNALS TO WARN OF ATTACKS. THERE WAS NO WAY THE XIONGNU COULD GET THROUGH.
THANKS TO THE WALL, CHINA BECAME REALLY POWERFUL DURING THOSE 400 YEARS OF HAN RULE!

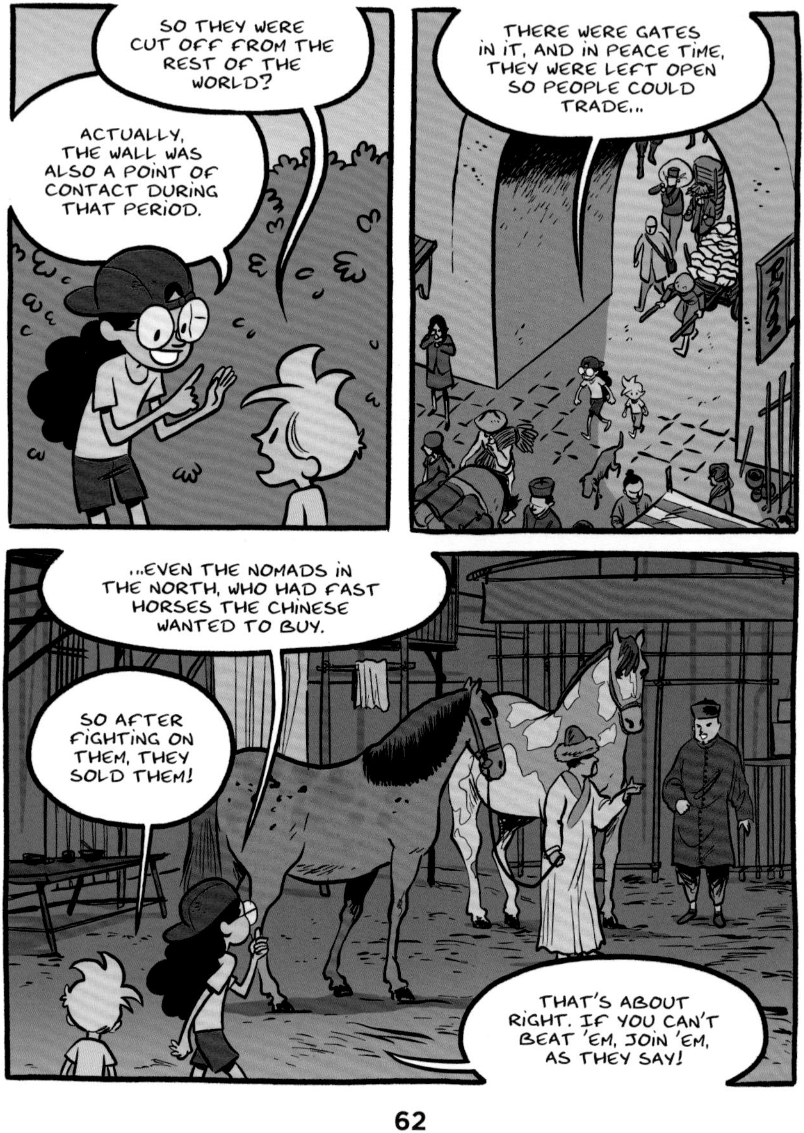
SO THEY WERE CUT OFF FROM THE REST OF THE WORLD?
ACTUALLY, THE WALL WAS ALSO A POINT OF CONTACT DURING THAT PERIOD.
THERE WERE GATES IN IT, AND IN PEACE TIME, THEY WERE LEFT OPEN SO PEOPLE COULD TRADE...
...EVEN THE NOMADS IN THE NORTH, WHO HAD FAST HORSES THE CHINESE WANTED TO BUY.
SO AFTER FIGHTING ON THEM, THEY SOLD THEM!
THAT'S ABOUT RIGHT. IF YOU CAN'T BEAT 'EM, JOIN 'EM, AS THEY SAY!

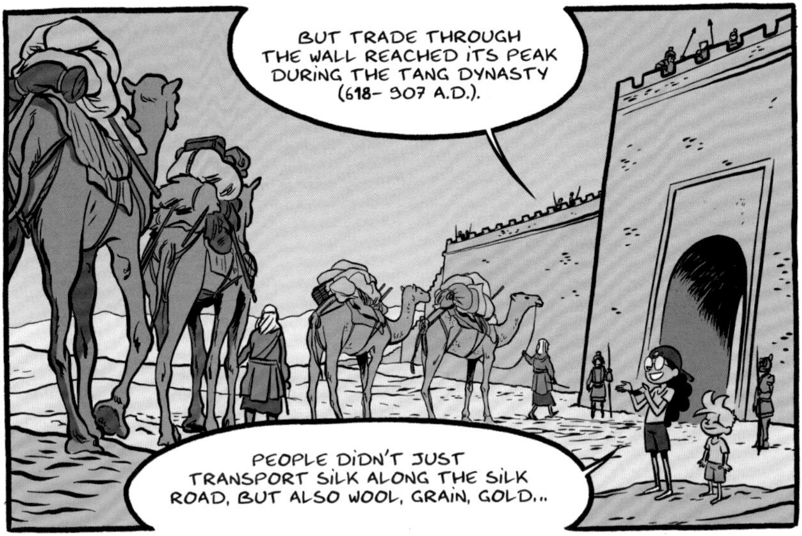
BUT TRADE THROUGH THE WALL REACHED ITS PEAK DURING THE TANG DYNASTY (618- 907 A.D.).
PEOPLE DIDN'T JUST TRANSPORT SILK ALONG THE SILK ROAD, BUT ALSO WOOL, GRAIN, GOLD...

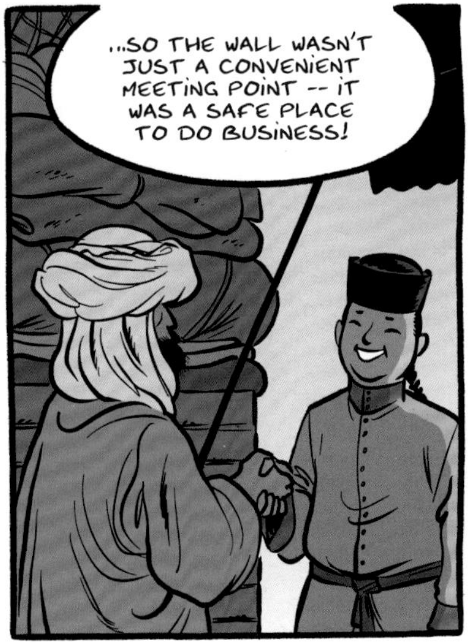
...SO THE WALL WASN'T JUST A CONVENIENT MEETING POINT -- IT WAS A SAFE PLACE TO DO BUSINESS!

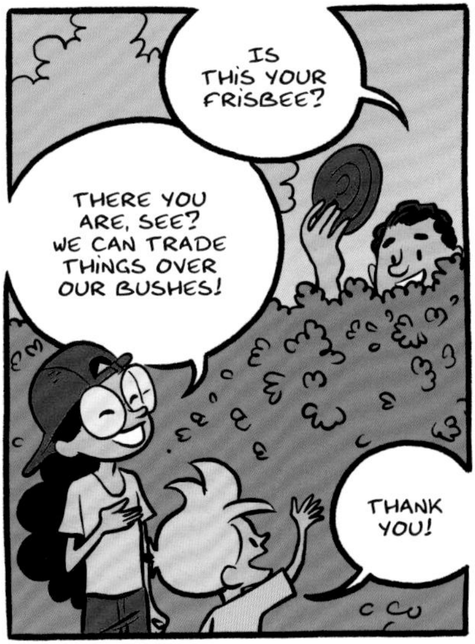
IS THIS YOUR FRISBEE?
THERE YOU ARE, SEE? WE CAN TRADE THINGS OVER OUR BUSHES!
THANK YOU!

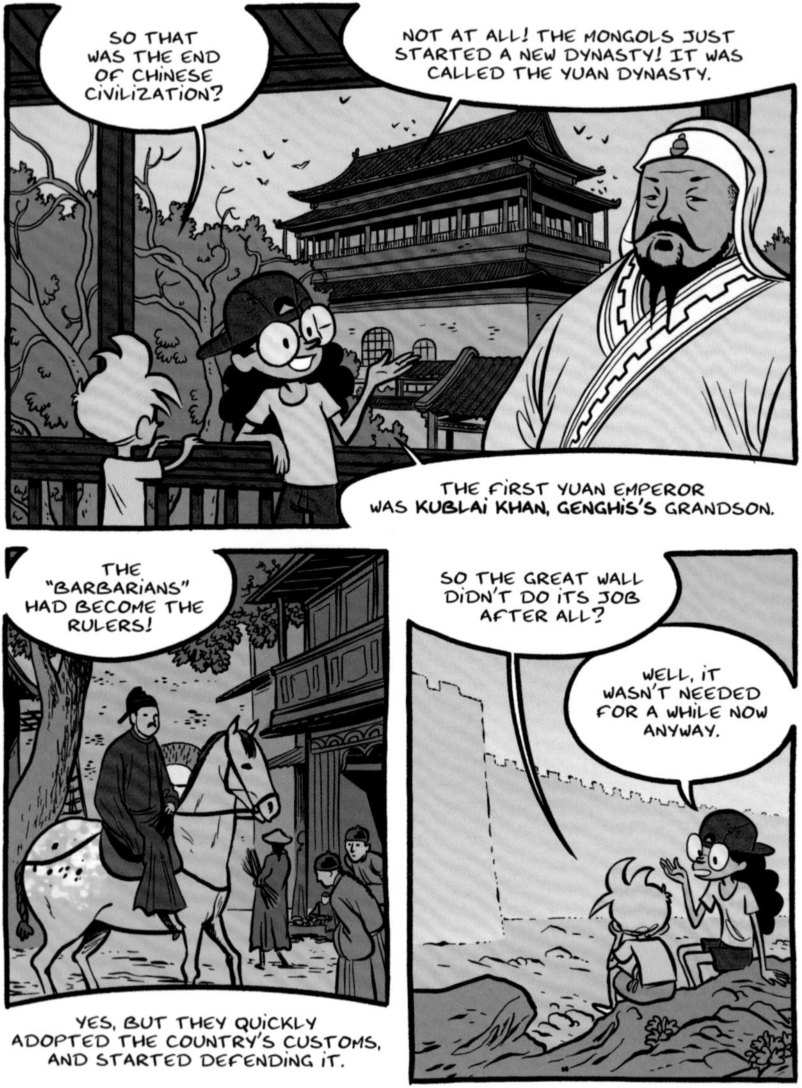
SO THAT WAS THE END OF CHINESE CIVILIZATION?
NOT AT ALL! THE MONGOLS JUST STARTED A NEW DYNASTY! IT WAS CALLED THE YUAN DYNASTY.
THE FIRST YUAN EMPEROR WAS KUBLAI KHAN, GENGHIS'S GRANDSON.
THE "BARBARIANS" HAD BECOME THE RULERS!
YES, BUT THEY QUICKLY ADOPTED THE COUNTRY'S CUSTOMS, AND STARTED DEFENDING IT.
SO THE GREAT WALL DIDN'T DO ITS JOB AFTER ALL?
WELL, IT WASN'T NEEDED FOR A WHILE NOW ANYWAY.

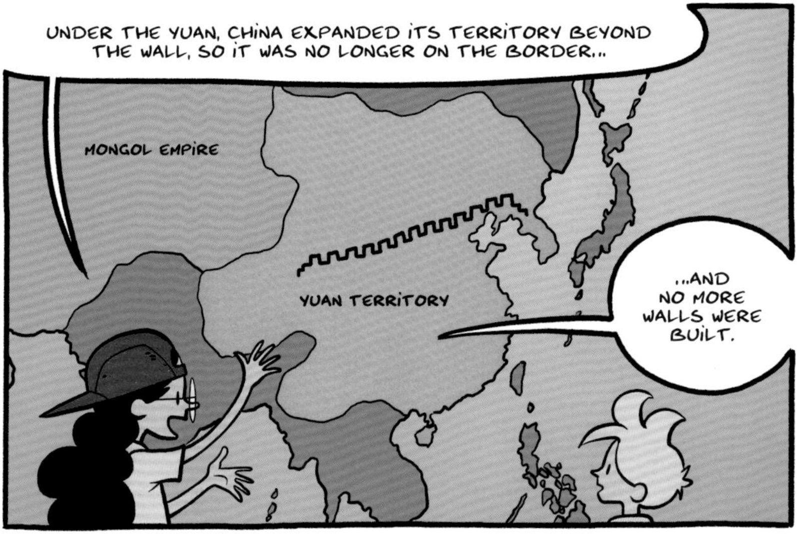
UNDER THE YUAN, CHINA EXPANDED ITS TERRITORY BEYOND THE WALL, SO IT WAS NO LONGER ON THE BORDER...
MONGOL EMPIRE
YUAN TERRITORY
...AND NO MORE WALLS WERE BUILT.

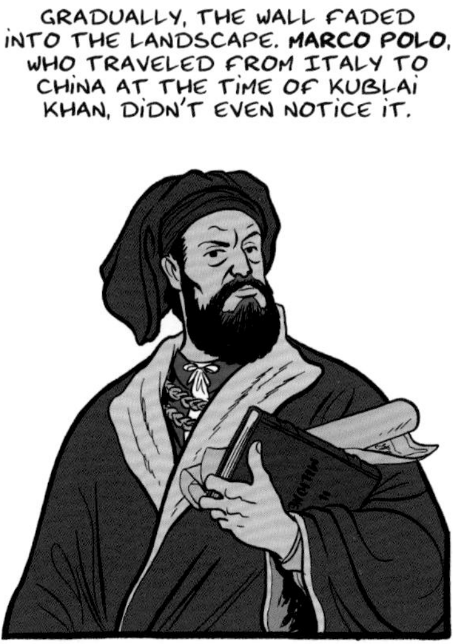
GRADUALLY, THE WALL FADED INTO THE LANDSCAPE. **MARCO POLO**, WHO TRAVELED FROM ITALY TO CHINA AT THE TIME OF KUBLAI KHAN, DIDN'T EVEN NOTICE IT.

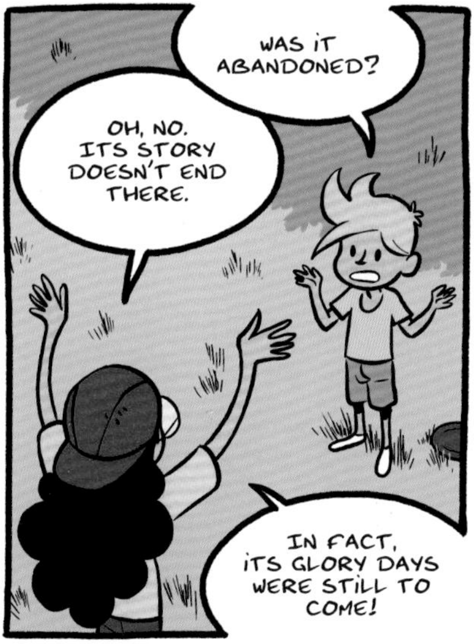
WAS IT ABANDONED?
OH, NO. ITS STORY DOESN'T END THERE.
IN FACT, ITS GLORY DAYS WERE STILL TO COME!

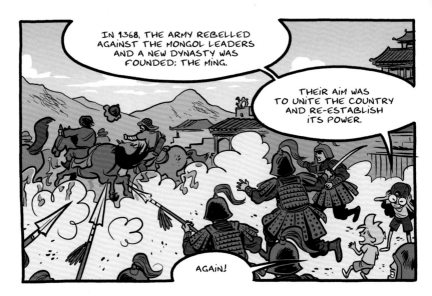

IN 1368, THE ARMY REBELLED AGAINST THE MONGOL LEADERS AND A NEW DYNASTY WAS FOUNDED: THE MING.

THEIR AIM WAS TO UNITE THE COUNTRY AND RE-ESTABLISH ITS POWER.

AGAIN!

THE YONGLE EMPEROR (1402-1424) MOUNTED SEVERAL EXPEDITIONS AGAINST THE MONGOLS, WHO WERE STILL A THREAT...

AND HIS SUCCESSORS DECIDED TO MAKE THE WALL MUCH STRONGER. THEY'RE THE ONES WHO BUILT THE SECTIONS THAT ARE BEST KNOWN TODAY.

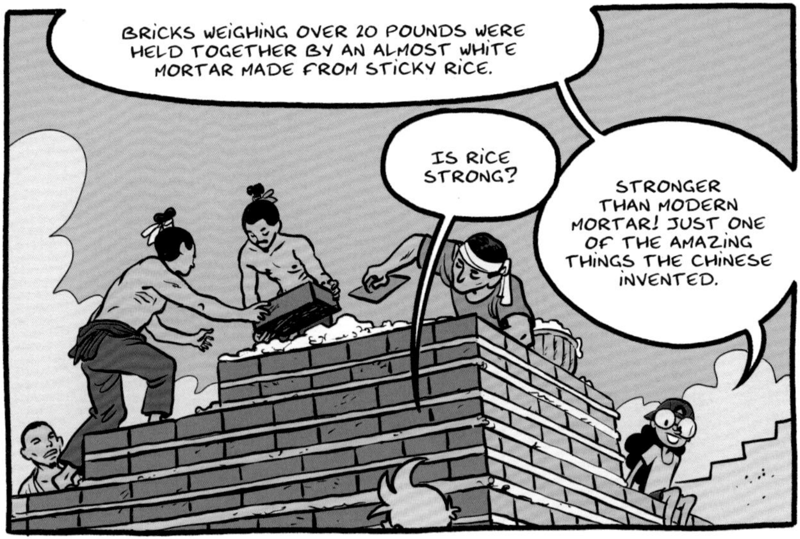
BRICKS WEIGHING OVER 20 POUNDS WERE HELD TOGETHER BY AN ALMOST WHITE MORTAR MADE FROM STICKY RICE.
IS RICE STRONG?
STRONGER THAN MODERN MORTAR! JUST ONE OF THE AMAZING THINGS THE CHINESE INVENTED.

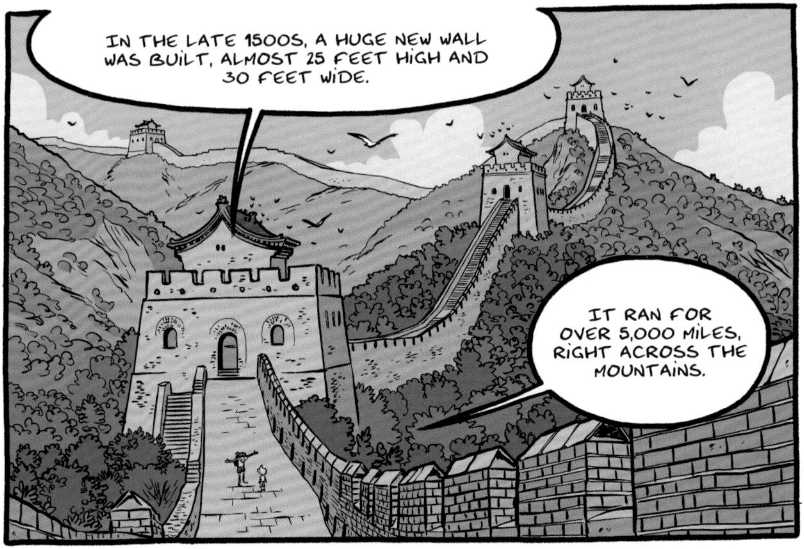
IN THE LATE 1500S, A HUGE NEW WALL WAS BUILT, ALMOST 25 FEET HIGH AND 30 FEET WIDE.
IT RAN FOR OVER 5,000 MILES, RIGHT ACROSS THE MOUNTAINS.

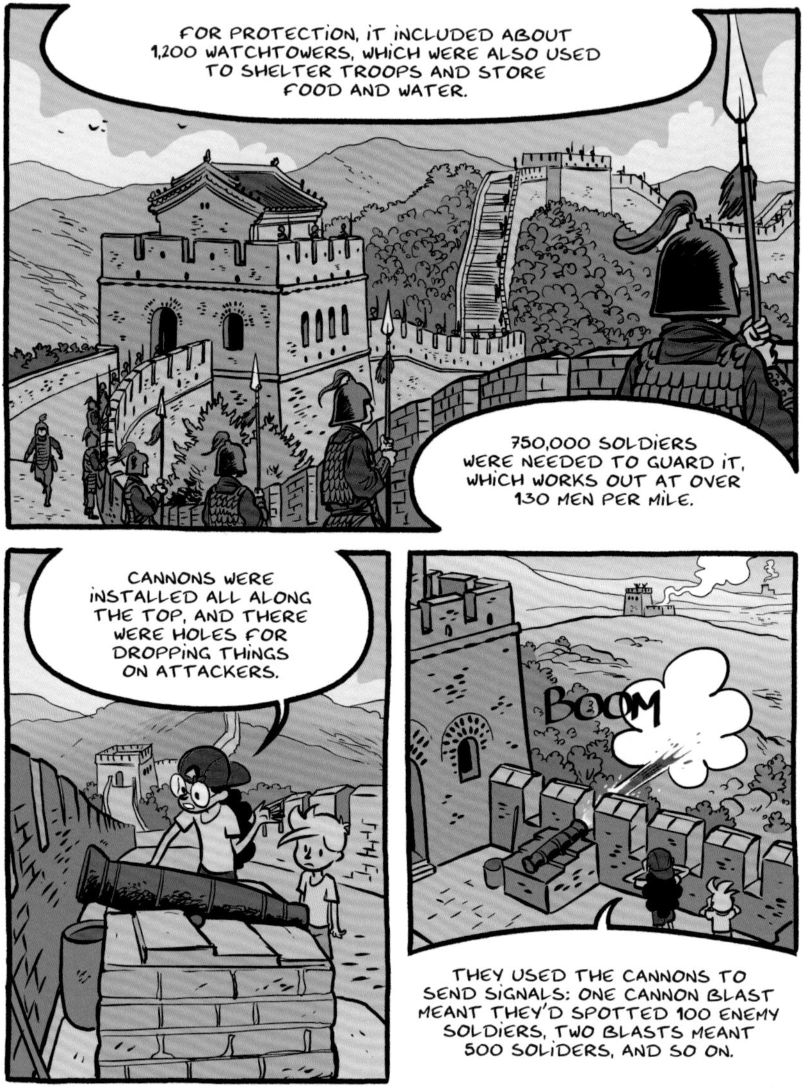
FOR PROTECTION, IT INCLUDED ABOUT 1,200 WATCHTOWERS, WHICH WERE ALSO USED TO SHELTER TROOPS AND STORE FOOD AND WATER.
750,000 SOLDIERS WERE NEEDED TO GUARD IT, WHICH WORKS OUT AT OVER 130 MEN PER MILE.
CANNONS WERE INSTALLED ALL ALONG THE TOP, AND THERE WERE HOLES FOR DROPPING THINGS ON ATTACKERS.
BOOM
THEY USED THE CANNONS TO SEND SIGNALS: ONE CANNON BLAST MEANT THEY'D SPOTTED 100 ENEMY SOLDIERS, TWO BLASTS MEANT 500 SOLIDERS, AND SO ON.

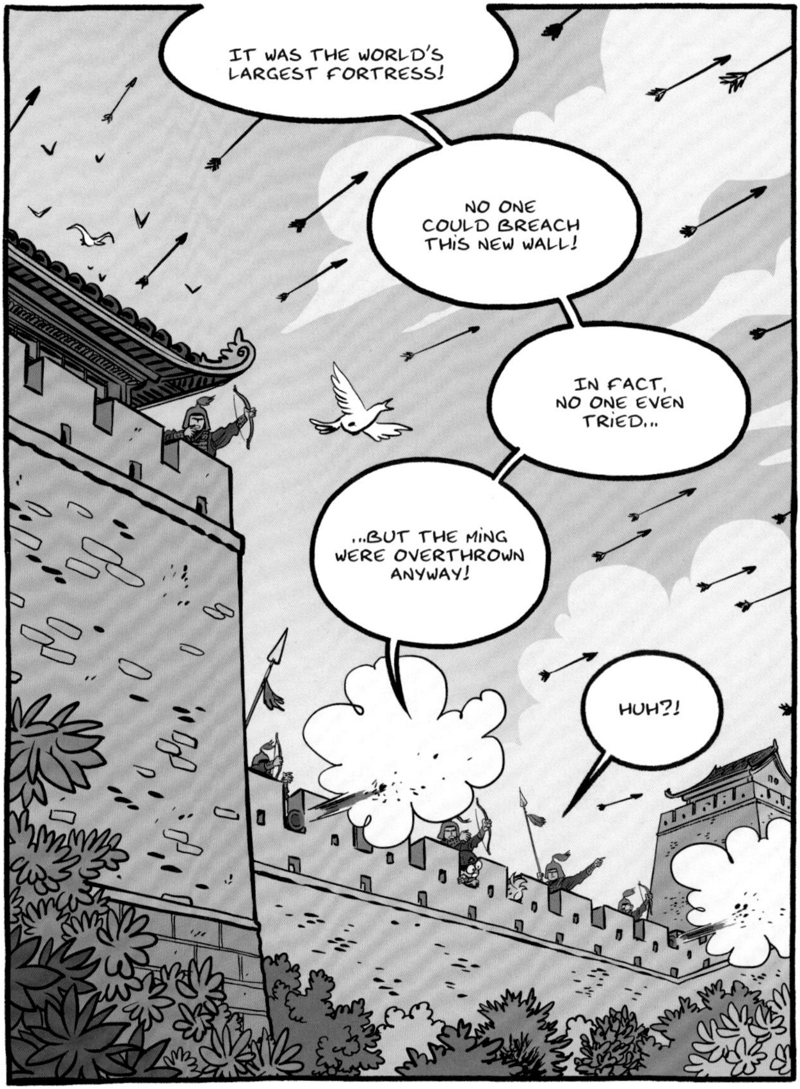
IT WAS THE WORLD'S LARGEST FORTRESS!
NO ONE COULD BREACH THIS NEW WALL!
IN FACT, NO ONE EVEN TRIED...
...BUT THE MING WERE OVERTHROWN ANYWAY!
HUH?!

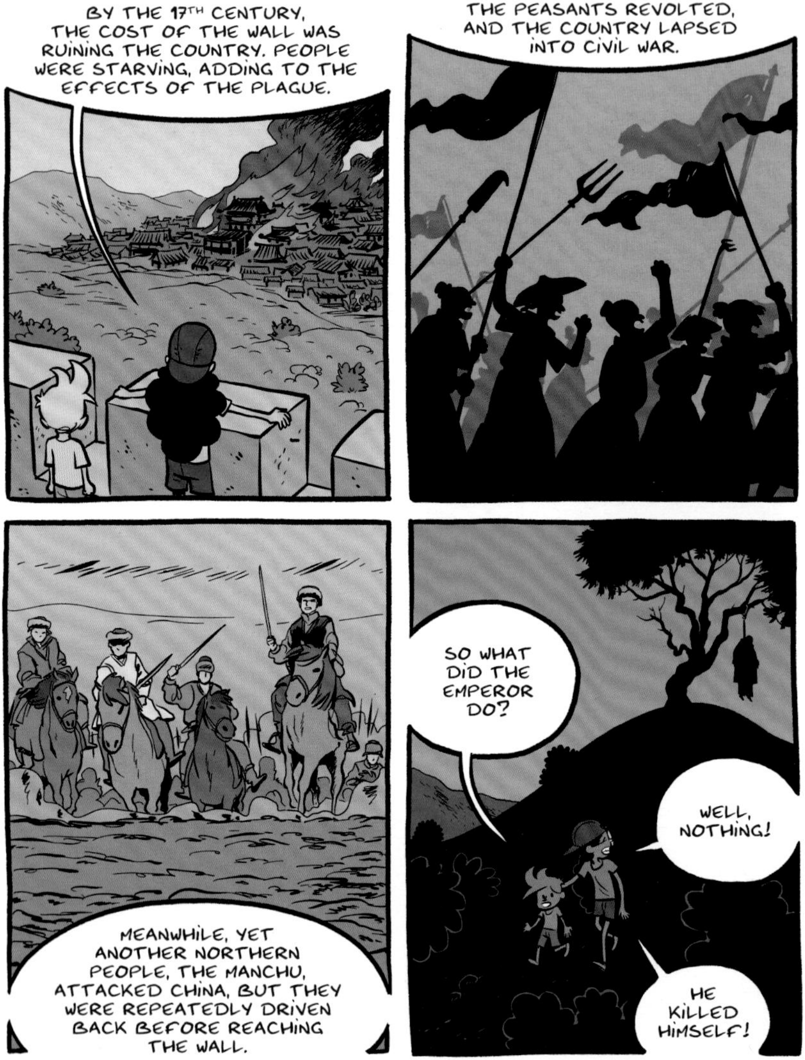
BY THE 17TH CENTURY, THE COST OF THE WALL WAS RUINING THE COUNTRY. PEOPLE WERE STARVING, ADDING TO THE EFFECTS OF THE PLAGUE.
THE PEASANTS REVOLTED, AND THE COUNTRY LAPSED INTO CIVIL WAR.
MEANWHILE, YET ANOTHER NORTHERN PEOPLE, THE MANCHU, ATTACKED CHINA, BUT THEY WERE REPEATEDLY DRIVEN BACK BEFORE REACHING THE WALL.
SO WHAT DID THE EMPEROR DO?
WELL, NOTHING!
HE KILLED HIMSELF!

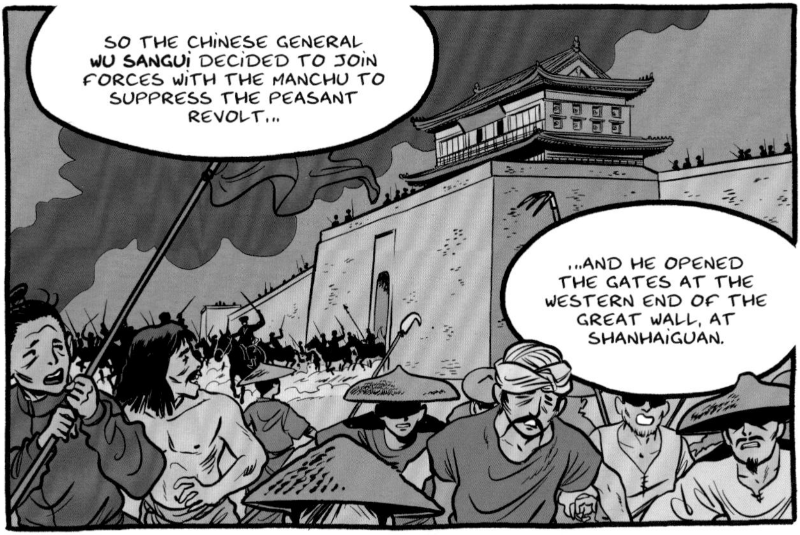
SO THE CHINESE GENERAL **WU SANGUI** DECIDED TO JOIN FORCES WITH THE MANCHU TO SUPPRESS THE PEASANT REVOLT...
...AND HE OPENED THE GATES AT THE WESTERN END OF THE GREAT WALL, AT SHANHAIGUAN.

THE MANCHU FLOODED IN AND SET UP A NEW DYNASTY, THE QING, WHICH WOULD BE THE LAST FAMILY TO RULE OVER CHINA.

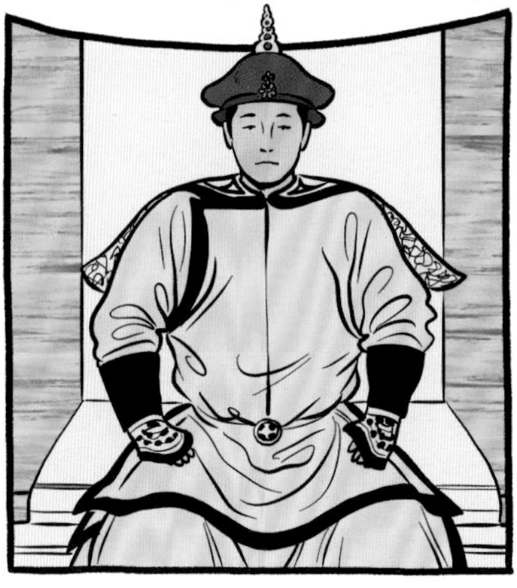

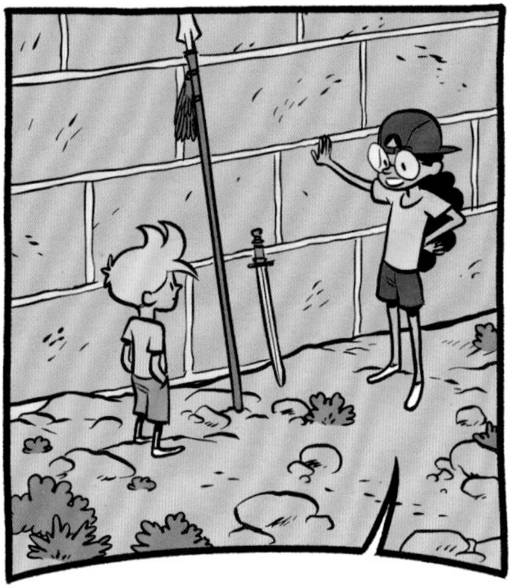

DURING THE QING DYNASTY, THE WALL NO LONGER HAD A USE AS A DEFENSIVE BARRIER.

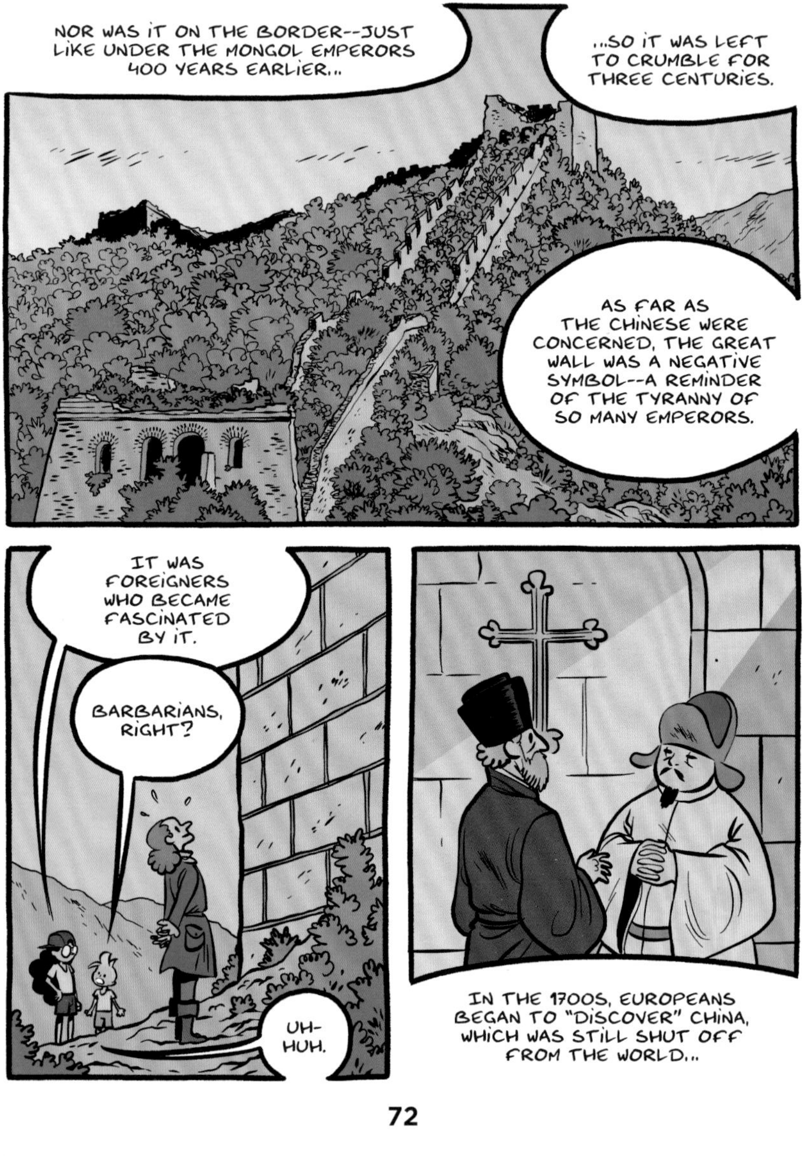
NOR WAS IT ON THE BORDER--JUST LIKE UNDER THE MONGOL EMPERORS 400 YEARS EARLIER...
...SO IT WAS LEFT TO CRUMBLE FOR THREE CENTURIES.
AS FAR AS THE CHINESE WERE CONCERNED, THE GREAT WALL WAS A NEGATIVE SYMBOL--A REMINDER OF THE TYRANNY OF SO MANY EMPERORS.
IT WAS FOREIGNERS WHO BECAME FASCINATED BY IT.
BARBARIANS, RIGHT?
UH-HUH.
IN THE 1700S, EUROPEANS BEGAN TO "DISCOVER" CHINA, WHICH WAS STILL SHUT OFF FROM THE WORLD...

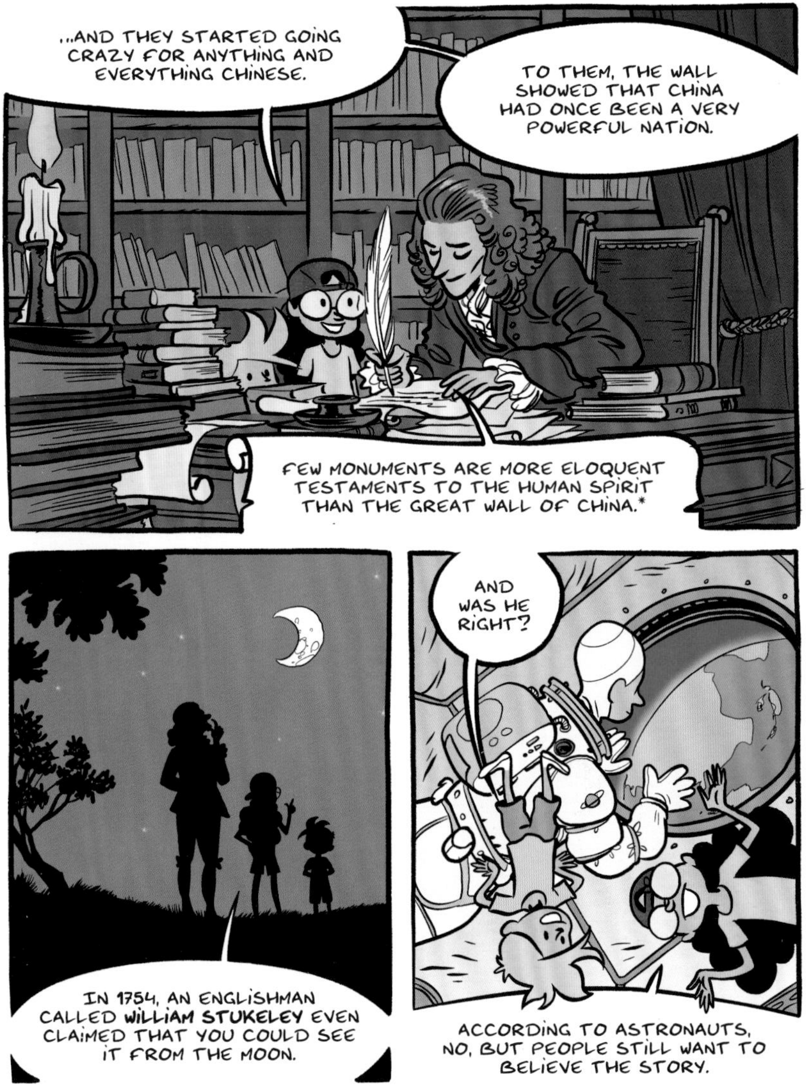
...AND THEY STARTED GOING CRAZY FOR ANYTHING AND EVERYTHING CHINESE.
TO THEM, THE WALL SHOWED THAT CHINA HAD ONCE BEEN A VERY POWERFUL NATION.
FEW MONUMENTS ARE MORE ELOQUENT TESTAMENTS TO THE HUMAN SPIRIT THAN THE GREAT WALL OF CHINA.*
IN 1754, AN ENGLISHMAN CALLED **WILLIAM STUKELEY** EVEN CLAIMED THAT YOU COULD SEE IT FROM THE MOON.
AND WAS HE RIGHT?
ACCORDING TO ASTRONAUTS, NO, BUT PEOPLE STILL WANT TO BELIEVE THE STORY.

*FROM L'ORPHELIN DE LA CHINE BY VOLTAIRE.

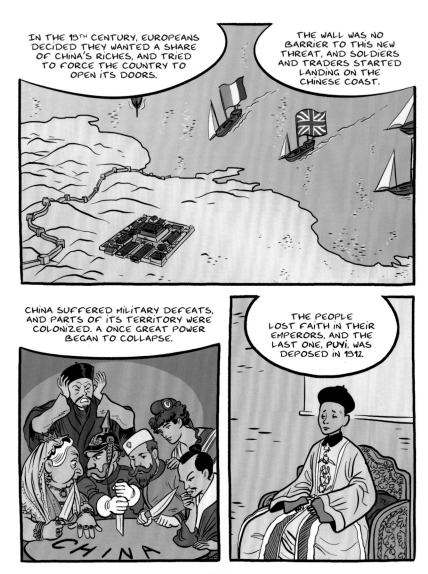

IN THE 19TH CENTURY, EUROPEANS DECIDED THEY WANTED A SHARE OF CHINA'S RICHES, AND TRIED TO FORCE THE COUNTRY TO OPEN ITS DOORS.

THE WALL WAS NO BARRIER TO THIS NEW THREAT, AND SOLDIERS AND TRADERS STARTED LANDING ON THE CHINESE COAST.

CHINA SUFFERED MILITARY DEFEATS, AND PARTS OF ITS TERRITORY WERE COLONIZED. A ONCE GREAT POWER BEGAN TO COLLAPSE.

CHINA

THE PEOPLE LOST FAITH IN THEIR EMPERORS, AND THE LAST ONE, PUYI, WAS DEPOSED IN 1912.

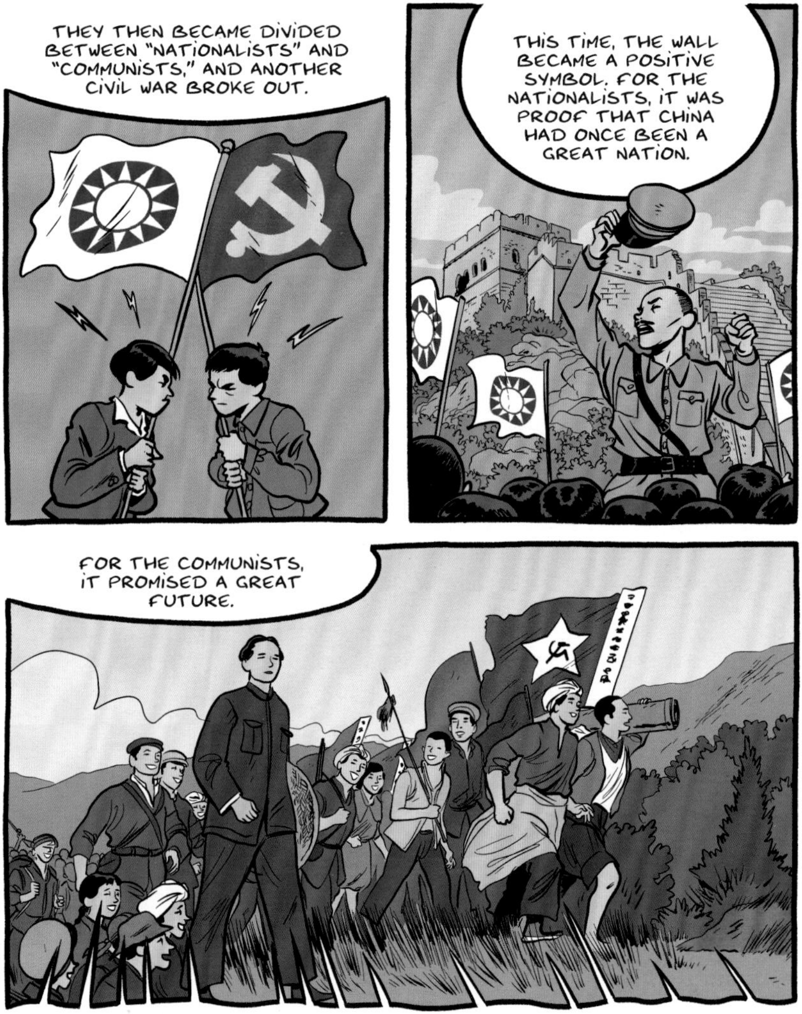
THEY THEN BECAME DIVIDED BETWEEN "NATIONALISTS" AND "COMMUNISTS," AND ANOTHER CIVIL WAR BROKE OUT.
THIS TIME, THE WALL BECAME A POSITIVE SYMBOL. FOR THE NATIONALISTS, IT WAS PROOF THAT CHINA HAD ONCE BEEN A GREAT NATION.
FOR THE COMMUNISTS, IT PROMISED A GREAT FUTURE.

ARISE! LET US PUT AN END TO SLAVERY! LET US BUILD A NEW GREAT WALL FOR OURSELVES, WITH OUR OWN FLESH AND BLOOD!*

*FROM THE COMMUNIST ANTHEM "MARCH OF THE VOLUNTEERS" (1934)

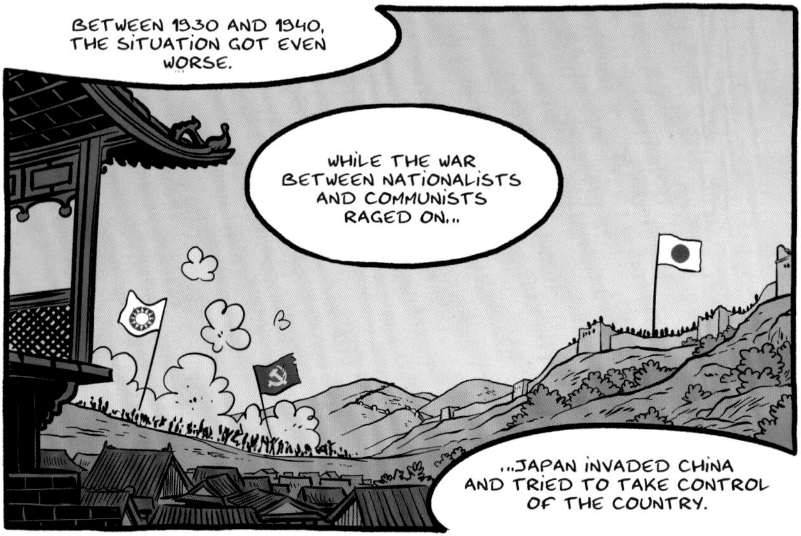
BETWEEN 1930 AND 1940, THE SITUATION GOT EVEN WORSE.
WHILE THE WAR BETWEEN NATIONALISTS AND COMMUNISTS RAGED ON...
...JAPAN INVADED CHINA AND TRIED TO TAKE CONTROL OF THE COUNTRY.

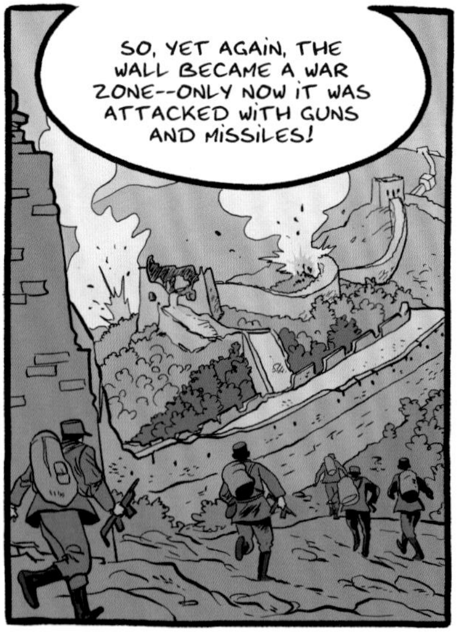
SO, YET AGAIN, THE WALL BECAME A WAR ZONE--ONLY NOW IT WAS ATTACKED WITH GUNS AND MISSILES!

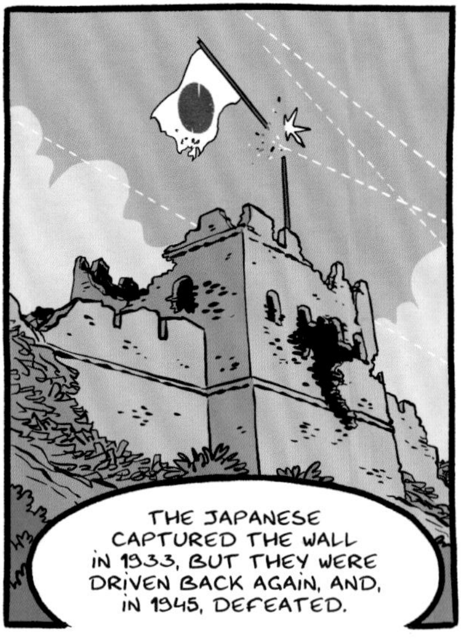
THE JAPANESE CAPTURED THE WALL IN 1933, BUT THEY WERE DRIVEN BACK AGAIN, AND, IN 1945, DEFEATED.

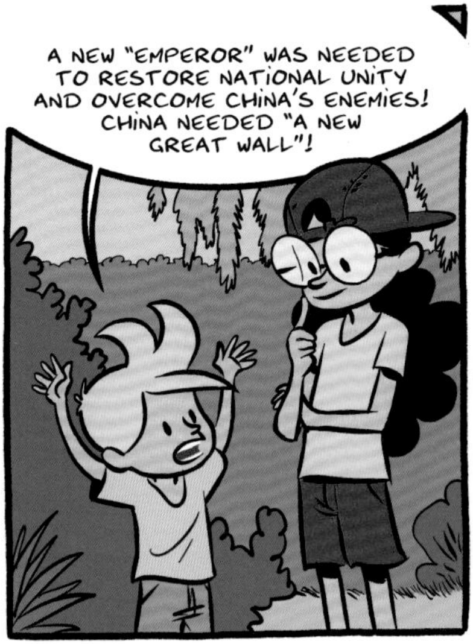
A NEW "EMPEROR" WAS NEEDED TO RESTORE NATIONAL UNITY AND OVERCOME CHINA'S ENEMIES! CHINA NEEDED "A NEW GREAT WALL"!

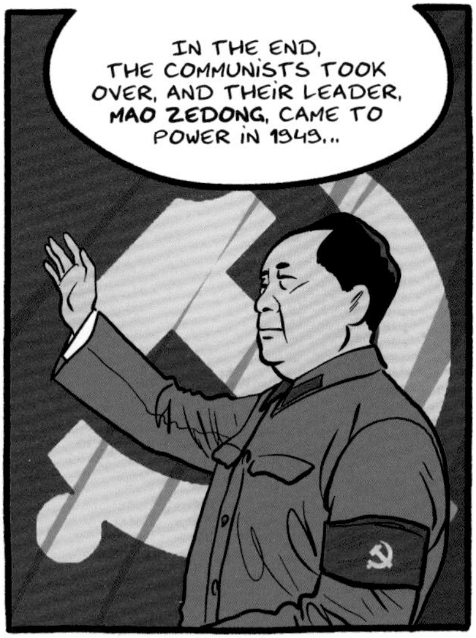
IN THE END, THE COMMUNISTS TOOK OVER, AND THEIR LEADER, **MAO ZEDONG**, CAME TO POWER IN 1949...

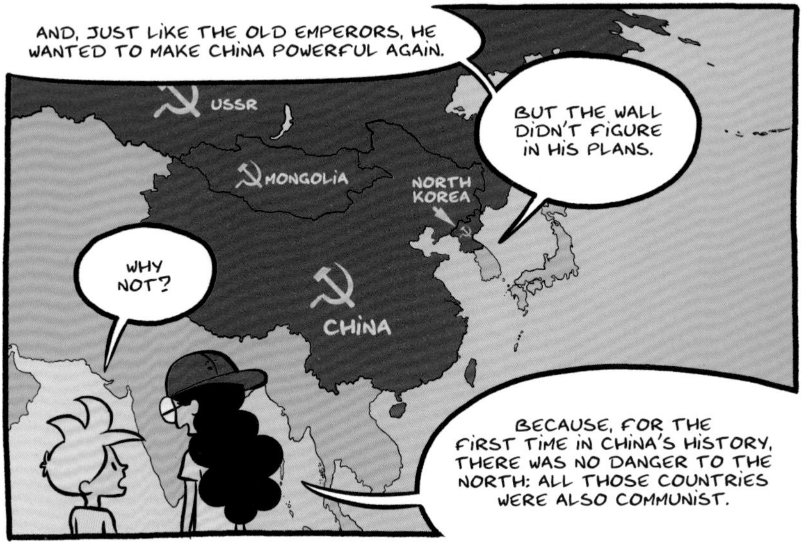
AND, JUST LIKE THE OLD EMPERORS, HE WANTED TO MAKE CHINA POWERFUL AGAIN.
BUT THE WALL DIDN'T FIGURE IN HIS PLANS.
USSR
MONGOLIA
NORTH KOREA
CHINA
WHY NOT?
BECAUSE, FOR THE FIRST TIME IN CHINA'S HISTORY, THERE WAS NO DANGER TO THE NORTH: ALL THOSE COUNTRIES WERE ALSO COMMUNIST.

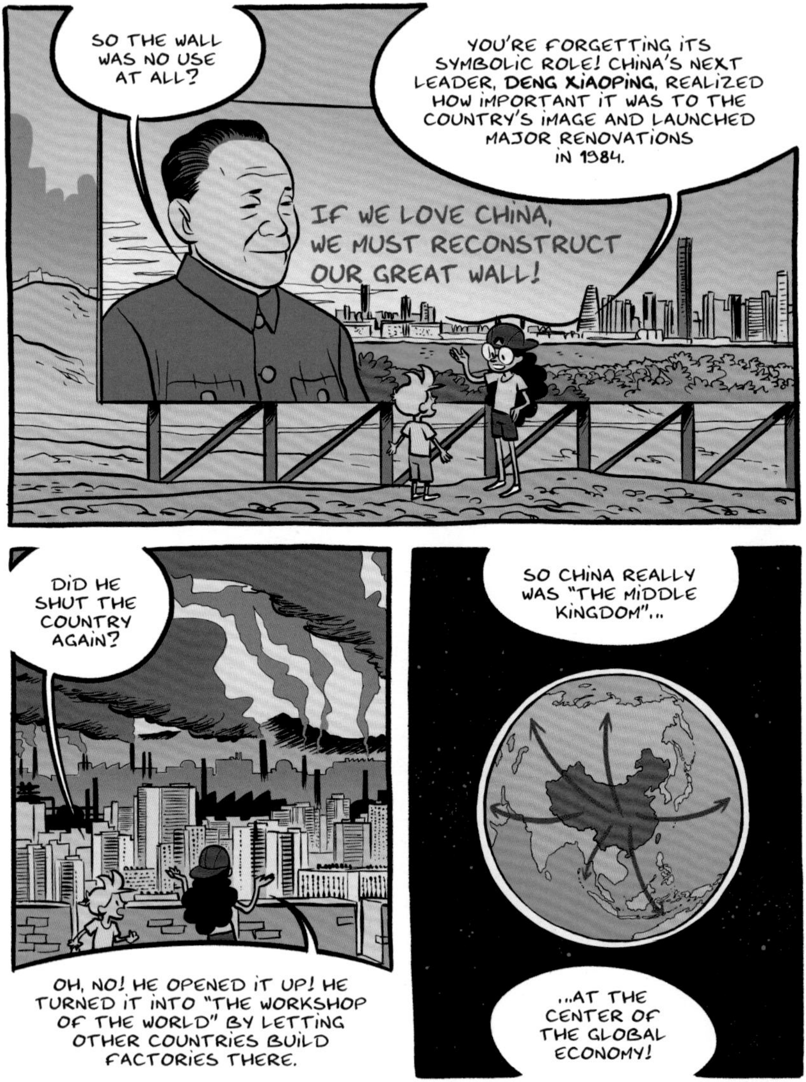

SO THE WALL WAS NO USE AT ALL?
YOU'RE FORGETTING ITS SYMBOLIC ROLE! CHINA'S NEXT LEADER, DENG XIAOPING, REALIZED HOW IMPORTANT IT WAS TO THE COUNTRY'S IMAGE AND LAUNCHED MAJOR RENOVATIONS IN 1984.
IF WE LOVE CHINA, WE MUST RECONSTRUCT OUR GREAT WALL!
DID HE SHUT THE COUNTRY AGAIN?
OH, NO! HE OPENED IT UP! HE TURNED IT INTO "THE WORKSHOP OF THE WORLD" BY LETTING OTHER COUNTRIES BUILD FACTORIES THERE.
SO CHINA REALLY WAS "THE MIDDLE KINGDOM"...
...AT THE CENTER OF THE GLOBAL ECONOMY!

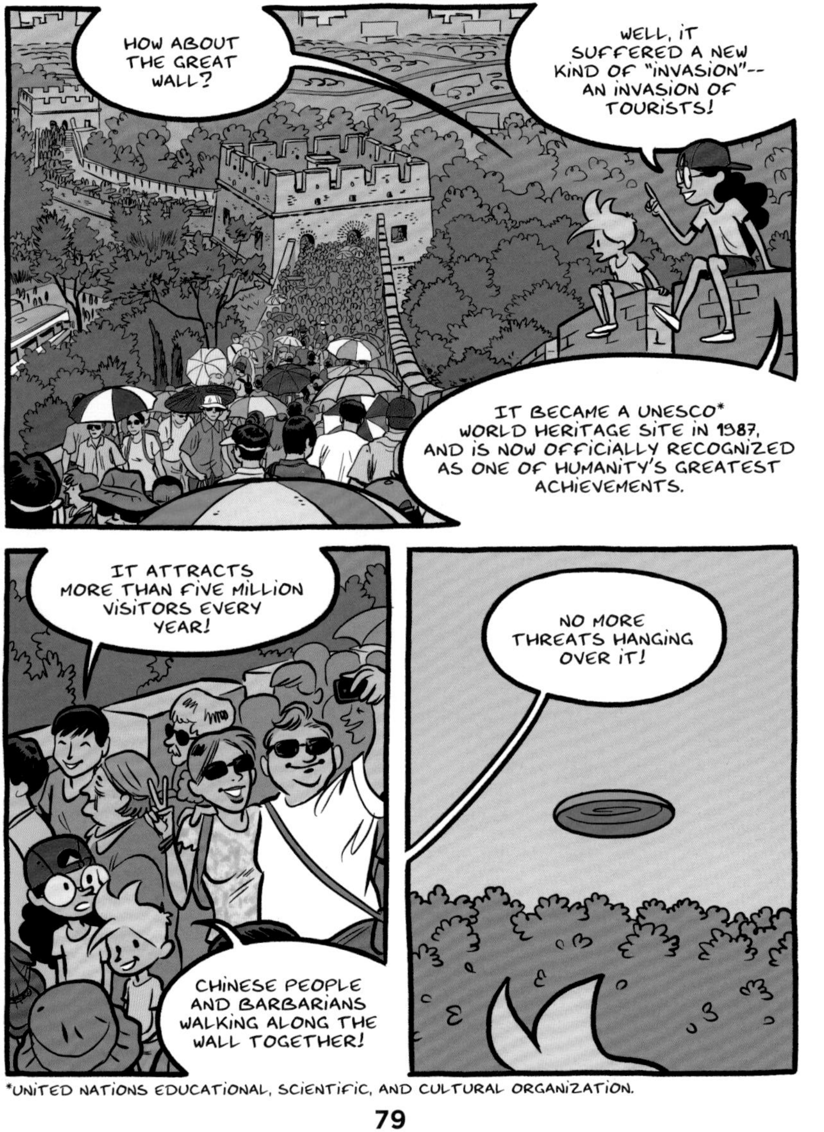
HOW ABOUT THE GREAT WALL?
WELL, IT SUFFERED A NEW KIND OF "INVASION"-- AN INVASION OF TOURISTS!
IT BECAME A UNESCO* WORLD HERITAGE SITE IN 1987, AND IS NOW OFFICIALLY RECOGNIZED AS ONE OF HUMANITY'S GREATEST ACHIEVEMENTS.
IT ATTRACTS MORE THAN FIVE MILLION VISITORS EVERY YEAR!
CHINESE PEOPLE AND BARBARIANS WALKING ALONG THE WALL TOGETHER!
NO MORE THREATS HANGING OVER IT!

*UNITED NATIONS EDUCATIONAL, SCIENTIFIC, AND CULTURAL ORGANIZATION.

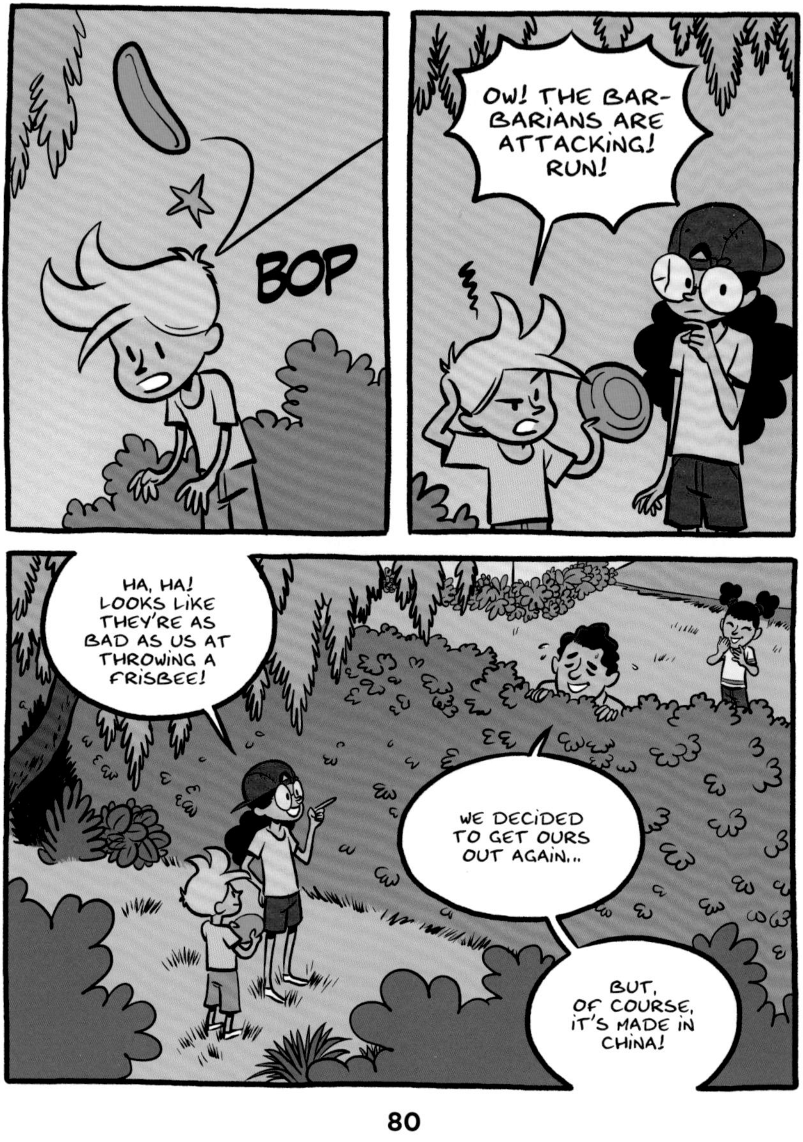
BOP
OW! THE BAR-BARIANS ARE ATTACKING! RUN!
HA, HA! LOOKS LIKE THEY'RE AS BAD AS US AT THROWING A FRISBEE!
WE DECIDED TO GET OURS OUT AGAIN...
BUT, OF COURSE, IT'S MADE IN CHINA!

And there's more...

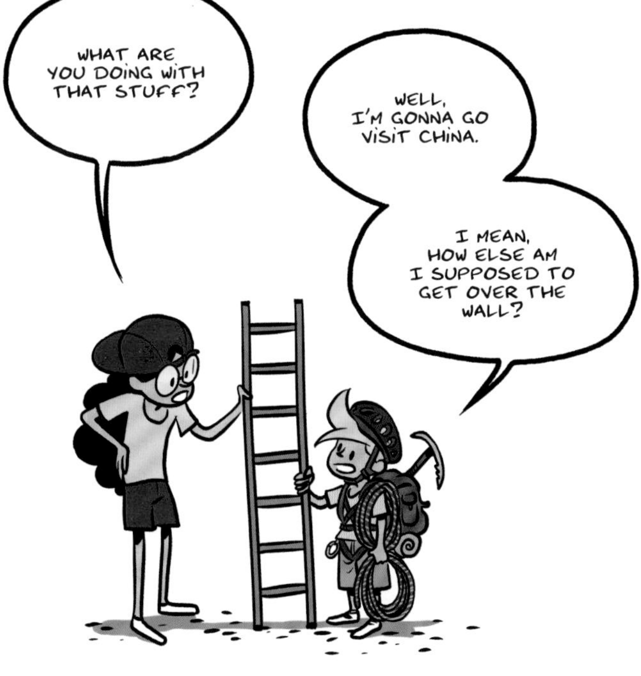
WHAT ARE YOU DOING WITH THAT STUFF?
WELL, I'M GONNA GO VISIT CHINA.
I MEAN, HOW ELSE AM I SUPPOSED TO GET OVER THE WALL?

Some people who made history

Qin Shi Huang
(259–210 B.C.)

His real name was Zhao Zheng, but at the age of 12 he became King of Qin, one of the early warring states. After defeating all the others, he unified China and was called Shi Huang, which means "first Emperor." As well as founding the Chinese state, he created the Great Wall by building the first part of it. He was a dictator—a pretty cruel one at that—and insisted on being buried with his entire army: 7,000 soldiers and horses—all made of terra cotta.

Meng Tian
(died in 210 B.C.)

Meng Tian was a Chinese general who helped Qin Shi Huang unify the country. The Emperor then sent him to fight the Xiongnu and instructed him to extend the Wall to the north. Later, Meng Tian regretted doing this. He believed he had "cut into the arteries of the land" by building the Wall. He saw it as a crime against Nature and took his own life by drinking poison.

Genghis Khan
(c. 1160–1227)

Leader of the Mongols and a military genius, Genghis Khan is one of the few men to have broken through the Great Wall. He did so in 1215, using a clever deception, which enabled him to take control of China. But he didn't stop there! He went on to conquer the whole of Asia and create the greatest empire in history. His grandson, Kublai, became Emperor of China and was the first of the Yuan dynasty.

Wu Sangui
(1612–1678)

Wu Sangui was a Chinese general who was responsible for guarding the Shanhai Pass in the Great Wall. When the peasants rose up against the Chongzhen Emperor in 1644, Wu Sangui opened the Pass to Manchu warriors, who then took control of China. Afterwards, Wu Sangui tried to defeat the Manchu army, but was defeated and killed.

The Design of the Ming Wall

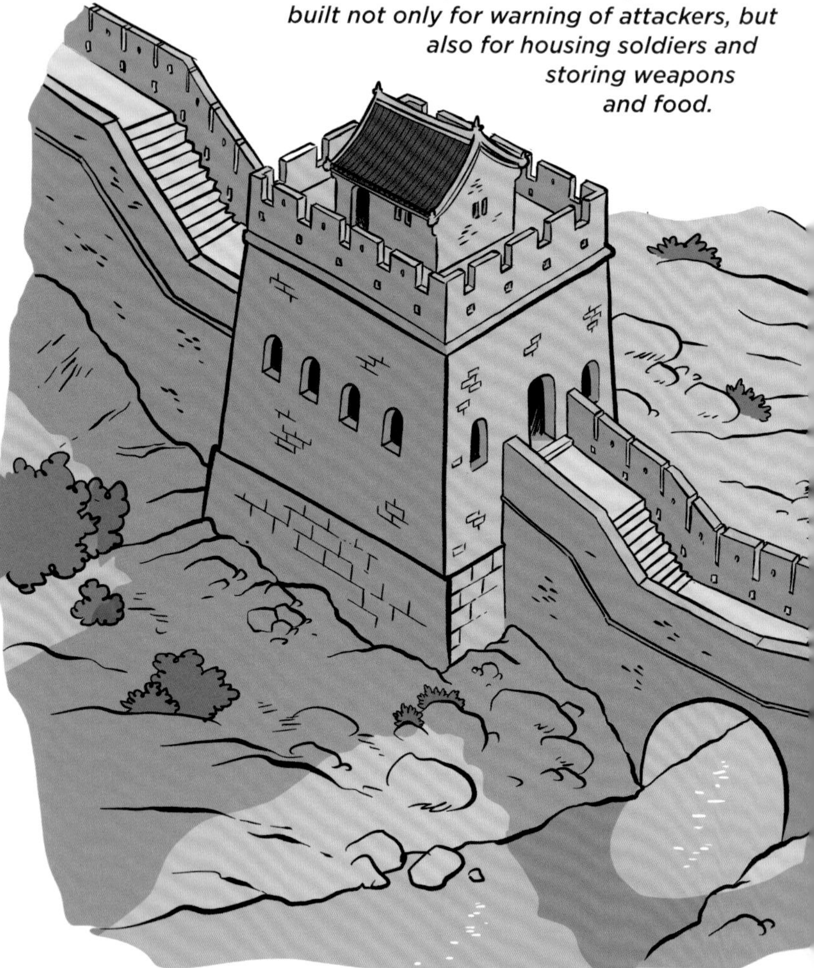
Watchtowers: *One every 250 feet or so, these were built not only for warning of attackers, but also for housing soldiers and storing weapons and food.*

Gates: *Gates at regular intervals along the Wall allowed troops to cross the border and traders to exchange goods. The major gates, called "passes," were heavily guarded.*

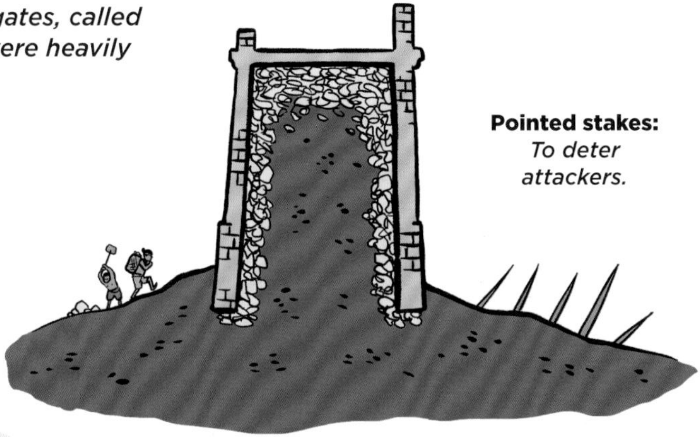

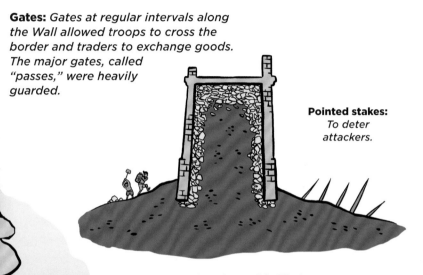

Pointed stakes: *To deter attackers.*

Interior: **The Wall is filled with earth and stones.**

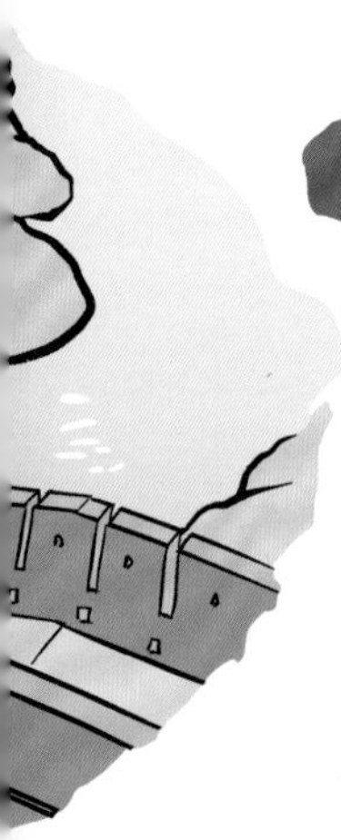

Top: *The Wall is 23 feet wide on average, allowing troops to patrol along the top or get from one part of the Wall to another.*

Walls: *The Ming Wall is made of 3.8 billion bricks. Huge ovens measuring 10 feet by 15 feet were built to fire the bricks, and it took millions of workers to make them and construct the walls.*

Great Wall Stories

There are few official records of how the Wall was built, but there are a lot of stories about how hard the work was—especially at the time of the first Emperor, Qin Shi Huang.

The Story of Meng Jiangnu is one of the most popular of all Chinese legends, and there are several versions of it. It tells of a young woman called Meng Jiangnu, whose husband, Fan Xiliang, was forced to build the first part of the Great Wall.

When she went to the site to find him, she was told by the other workers that he had died and been entombed inside the Wall. Meng Jiangnu cried so much that her tears brought the Wall down, revealing her husband's body, which she then buried. Then the Emperor Qin Shi Huang fell in love with her and asked her to marry him. Meng Jiangnu agreed, but then she denounced him as a murderer and committed suicide either by running head-first into the Wall (which collapsed again) or, according to another version of the story, by throwing herself off the Wall into the sea. Meng Jiangnu was later buried and a temple was dedicated to her.

According to another legend, *the ruthless Qin Shi Huang became very frustrated by how long it was taking to finish the Great Wall because so many peasants chose to work in their fields rather than build walls. Overcome by anger, he went up to Heaven to find a tree that would freeze the earth. When he shook its branches, all the peasants' crops froze, which forced them to leave the land and join the workers building the Great Wall.*

A third legend *explains why the Wall was never finished. It tells of a dragon—a mythical and sacred creature in Chinese culture—that goes to talk to the peasants who have been forced to work on the Wall. They explain to the dragon that Emperor Qin Shi Huang has a magical whip, which he threatens to lash them with. The dragon decides to help them by asking his wife (who has a human body and is very beautiful) to come down to earth, seduce the Emperor, and steal his whip. She succeeds, and so it is because of the dragon's wife that the Great Wall was never finished.*

Timeline

The "warring states" build the first defensive walls in northern China.

▼

500–300 B.C.

Qin Shi Huang unifies China, and construction of the Great Wall begins.

▼

221 B.C.

1644

▲

The Chinese general Wu Sangui opens gates in the Wall to let in Manchu warriors.

1368–1644

▲

The Ming Emperors build the parts of the Great Wall we can see today.

1644–1912

▲

Under the Qing dynasty, the Wall is left to fall apart.

1933–1945

▲

The Chinese and Japanese fight over the Great Wall.

ANTIQUITY | MIDDLE AGES | RENAISSANCE | MODERN TIMES

206 B.C.–220 A.D.

The Han dynasty fortifies the Wall and extends it as far as the Gobi Desert.

618–907

The Tang dynasty makes the Wall a defensive frontier as well as a marketplace for traders.

1215

Genghis Khan breaks through the Wall and takes control of the Chinese capital, Zhongdu (Beijing).

1279–1368

Under the Yuan dynasty, the Wall no longer runs along the border.

1984

The Chinese leader Deng Xiaoping decides to restore the Wall.

1987

The Great Wall becomes a World Heritage Site and a major tourist attraction.

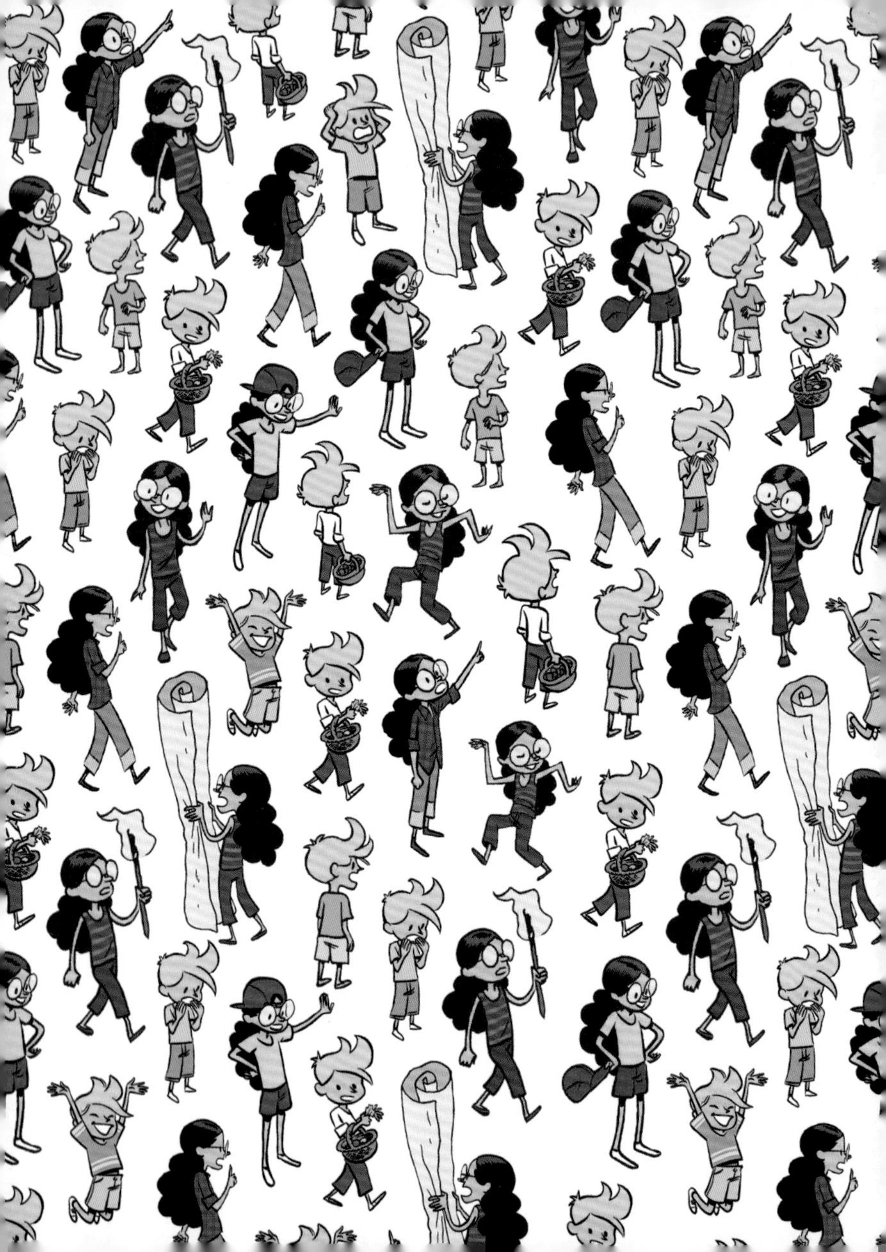

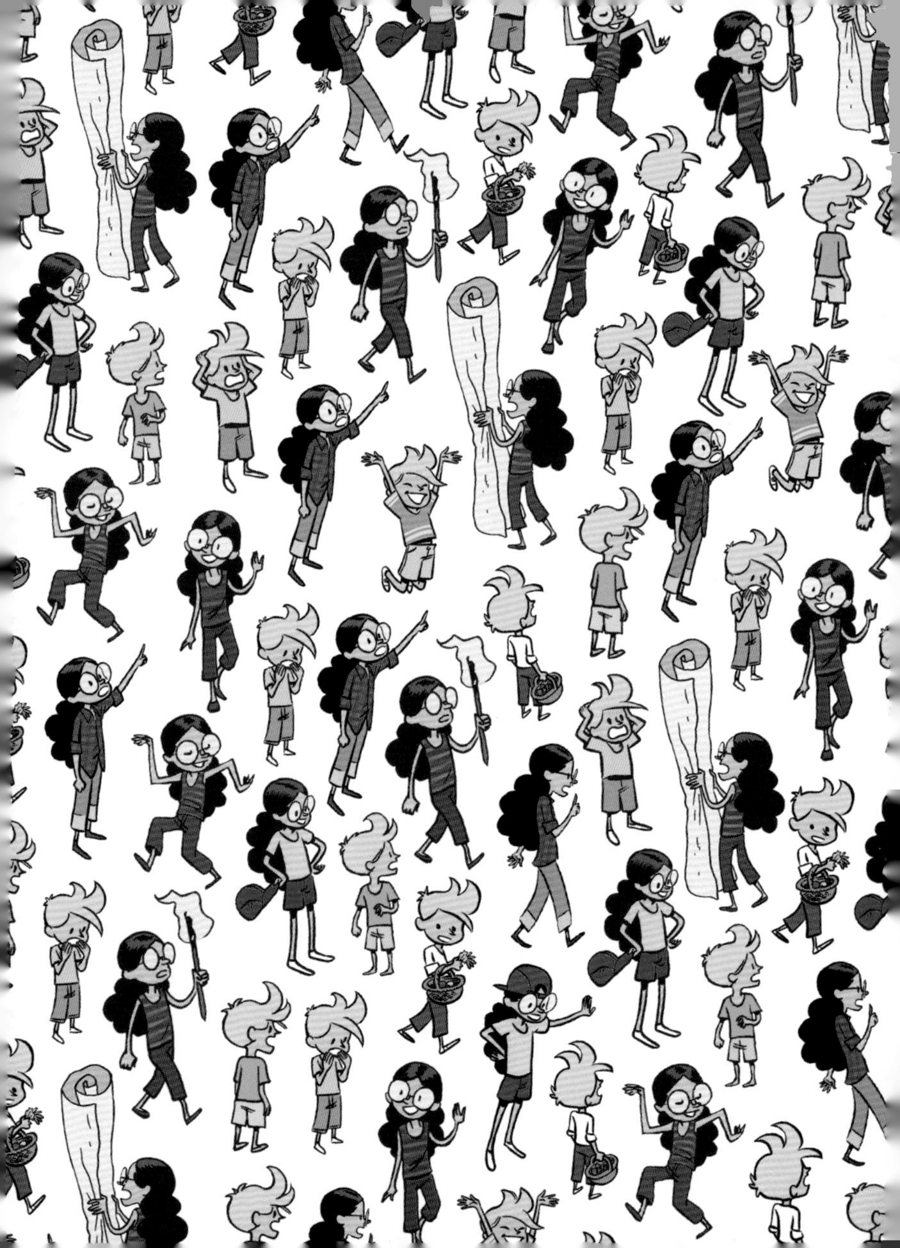

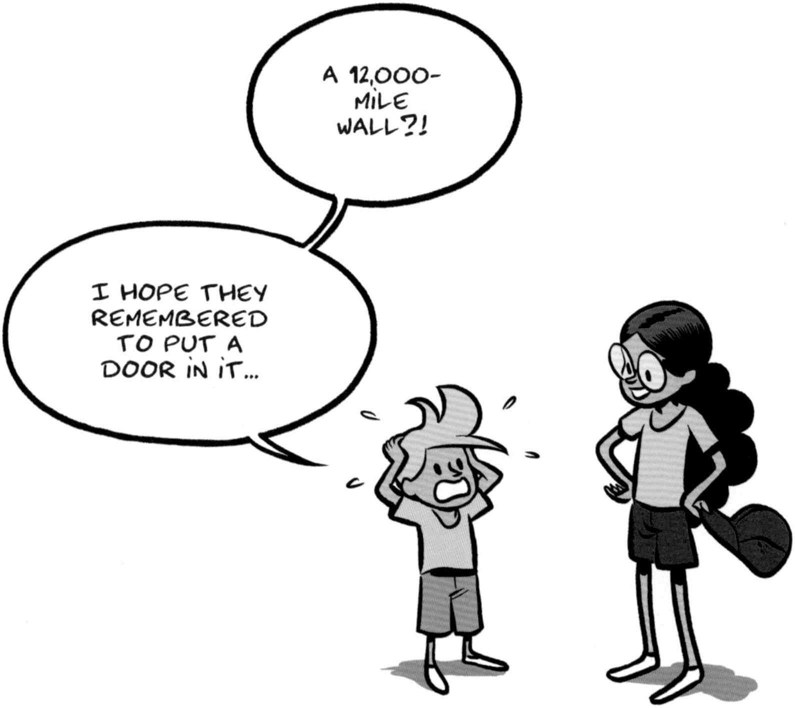
A 12,000-MILE WALL?!
I HOPE THEY REMEMBERED TO PUT A DOOR IN IT...

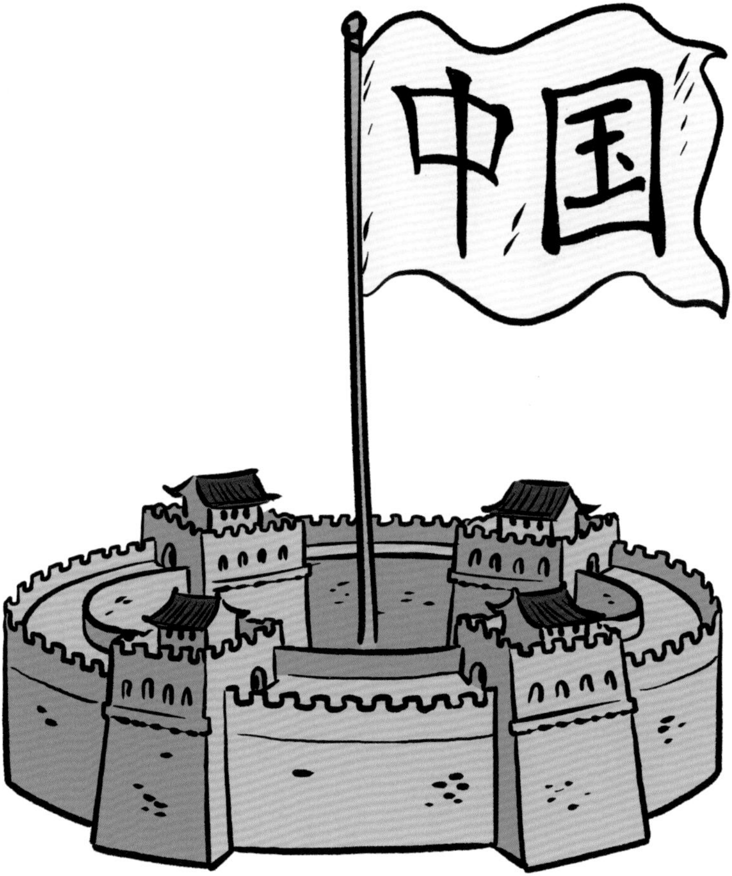
中国

FABRICE ERRE SYLVAIN SAVOIA

Magical History Tour

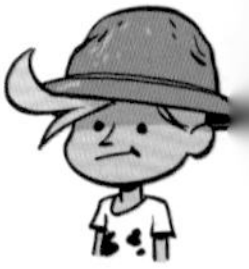
NICO

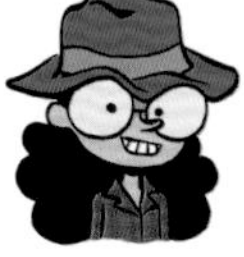
ANNIE

Hidden Oil

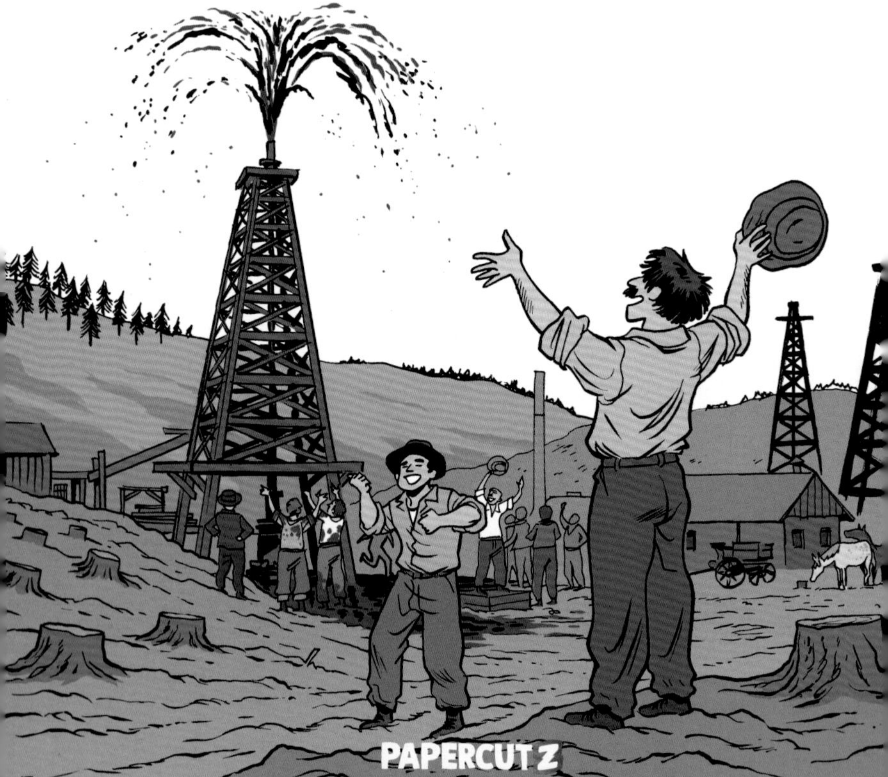

PAPERCUTZ

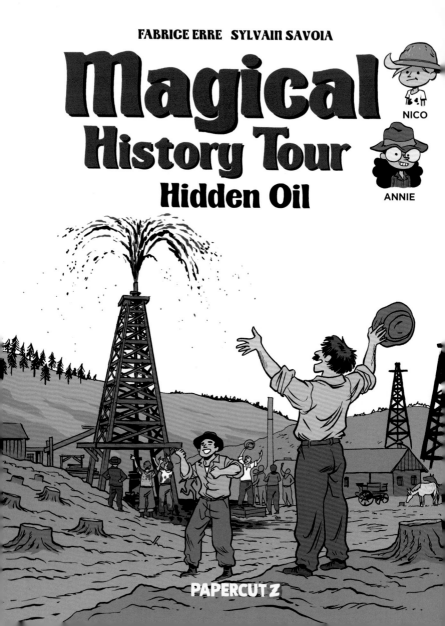

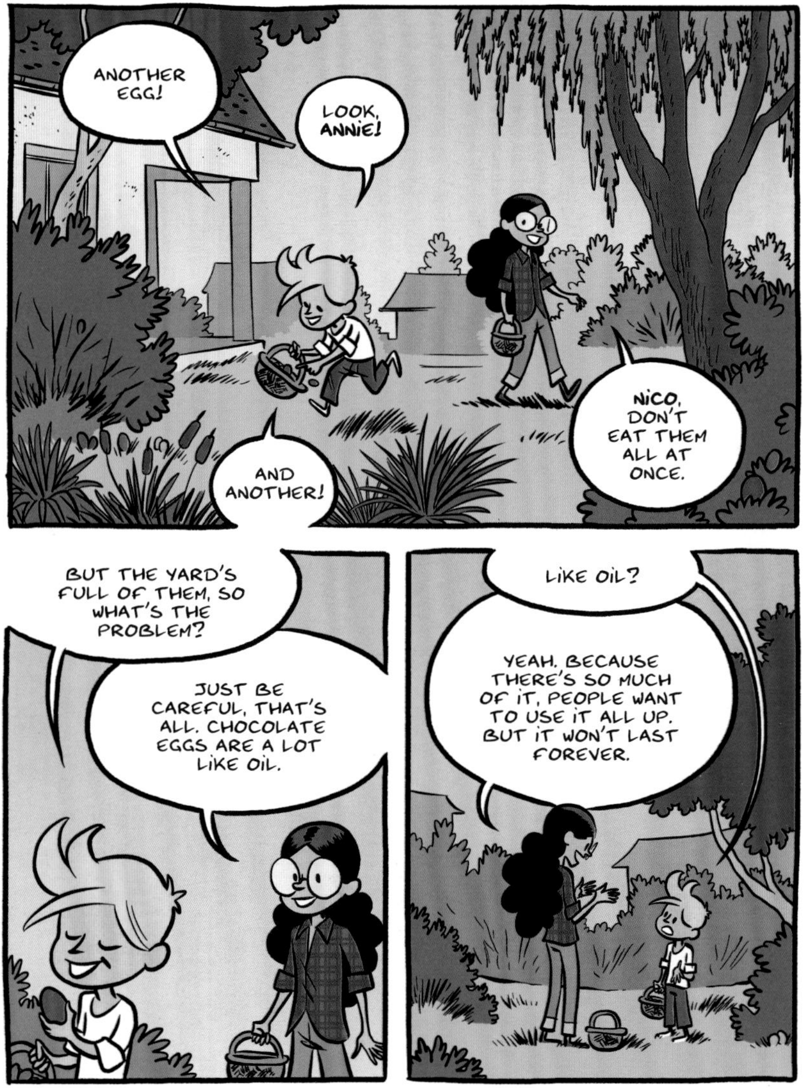

ANOTHER EGG!
LOOK, ANNIE!
AND ANOTHER!
NICO, DON'T EAT THEM ALL AT ONCE.
BUT THE YARD'S FULL OF THEM, SO WHAT'S THE PROBLEM?
JUST BE CAREFUL, THAT'S ALL. CHOCOLATE EGGS ARE A LOT LIKE OIL.
LIKE OIL?
YEAH. BECAUSE THERE'S SO MUCH OF IT, PEOPLE WANT TO USE IT ALL UP. BUT IT WON'T LAST FOREVER.

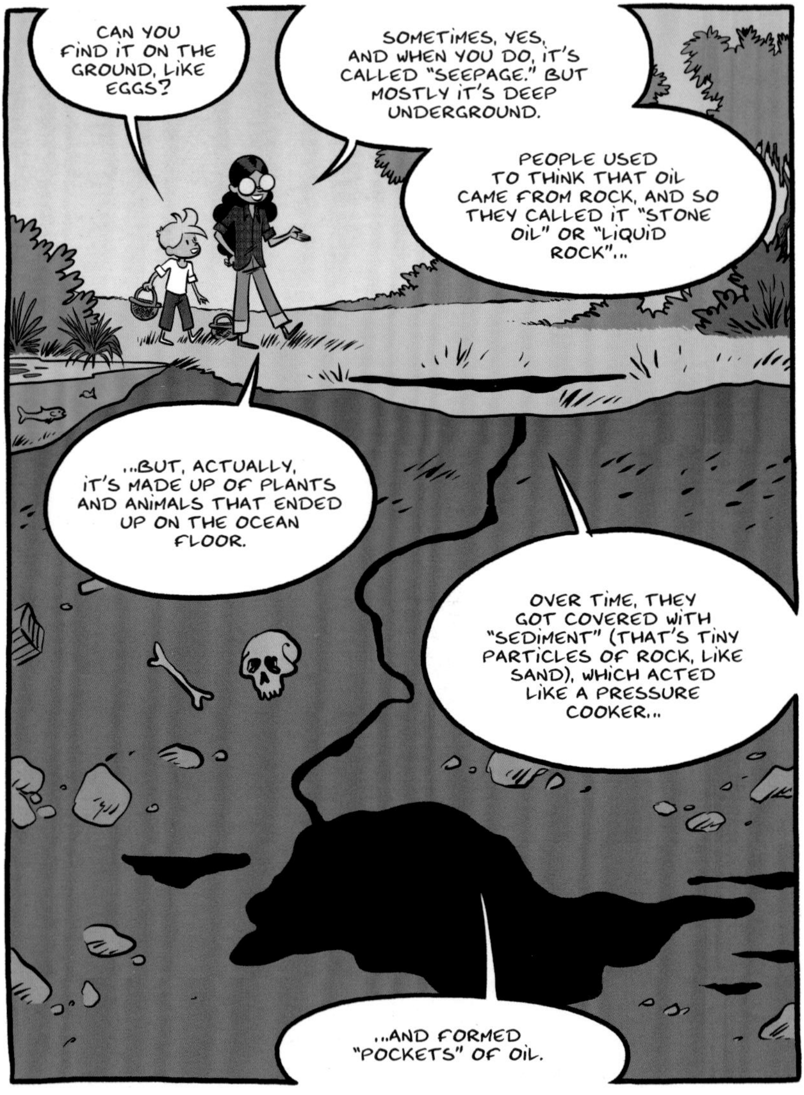
CAN YOU FIND IT ON THE GROUND, LIKE EGGS?
SOMETIMES, YES, AND WHEN YOU DO, IT'S CALLED "SEEPAGE." BUT MOSTLY IT'S DEEP UNDERGROUND.
PEOPLE USED TO THINK THAT OIL CAME FROM ROCK, AND SO THEY CALLED IT "STONE OIL" OR "LIQUID ROCK"...
...BUT, ACTUALLY, IT'S MADE UP OF PLANTS AND ANIMALS THAT ENDED UP ON THE OCEAN FLOOR.
OVER TIME, THEY GOT COVERED WITH "SEDIMENT" (THAT'S TINY PARTICLES OF ROCK, LIKE SAND), WHICH ACTED LIKE A PRESSURE COOKER...
...AND FORMED "POCKETS" OF OIL.

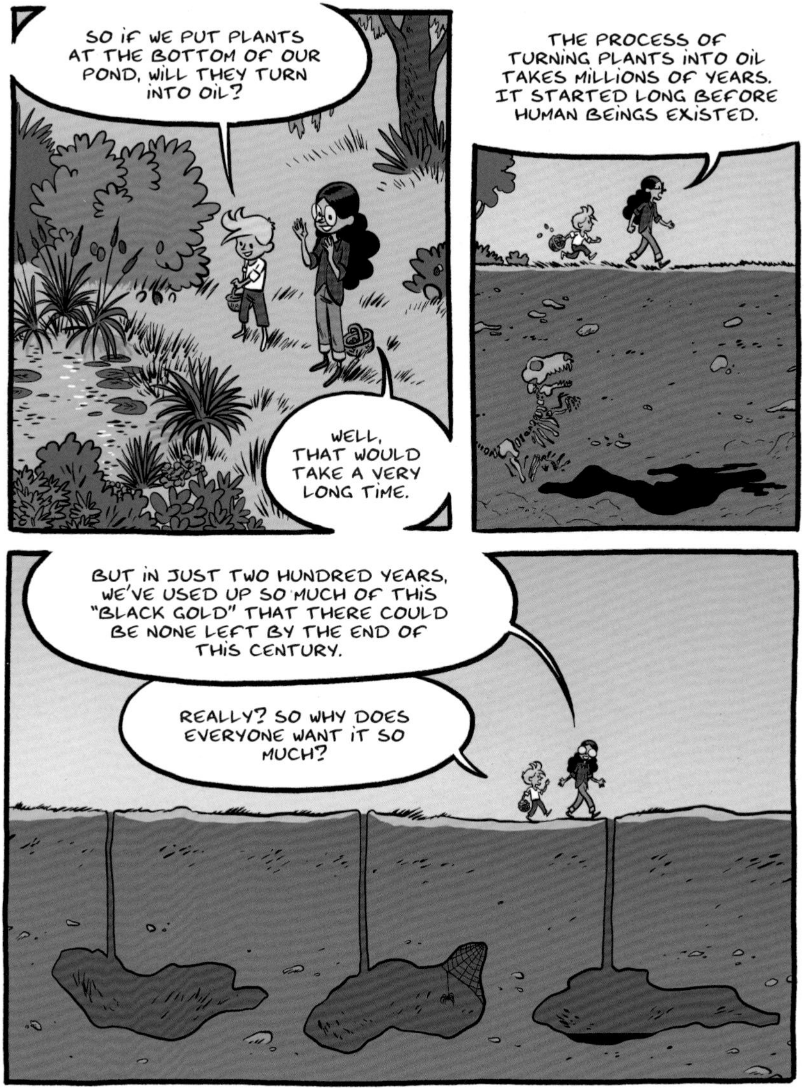
SO IF WE PUT PLANTS AT THE BOTTOM OF OUR POND, WILL THEY TURN INTO OIL?
WELL, THAT WOULD TAKE A VERY LONG TIME.
THE PROCESS OF TURNING PLANTS INTO OIL TAKES MILLIONS OF YEARS. IT STARTED LONG BEFORE HUMAN BEINGS EXISTED.
BUT IN JUST TWO HUNDRED YEARS, WE'VE USED UP SO MUCH OF THIS "BLACK GOLD" THAT THERE COULD BE NONE LEFT BY THE END OF THIS CENTURY.
REALLY? SO WHY DOES EVERYONE WANT IT SO MUCH?

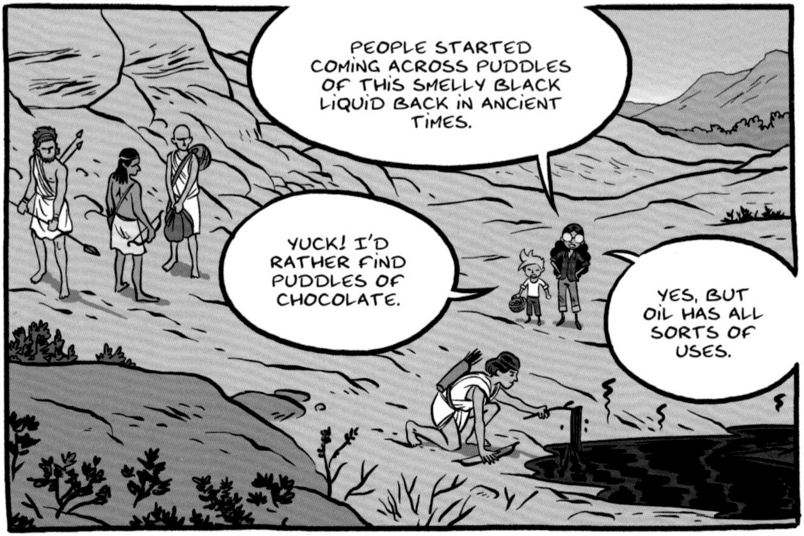
PEOPLE STARTED COMING ACROSS PUDDLES OF THIS SMELLY BLACK LIQUID BACK IN ANCIENT TIMES.
YUCK! I'D RATHER FIND PUDDLES OF CHOCOLATE.
YES, BUT OIL HAS ALL SORTS OF USES.

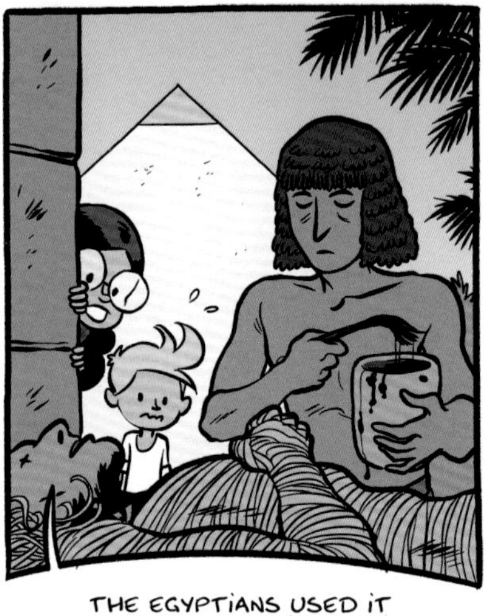

THE EGYPTIANS USED IT TO PRESERVE THEIR MUMMIES.

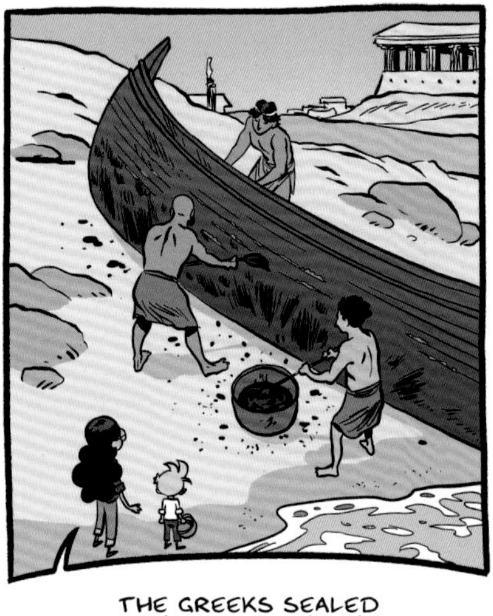

THE GREEKS SEALED THEIR BOATS WITH IT.

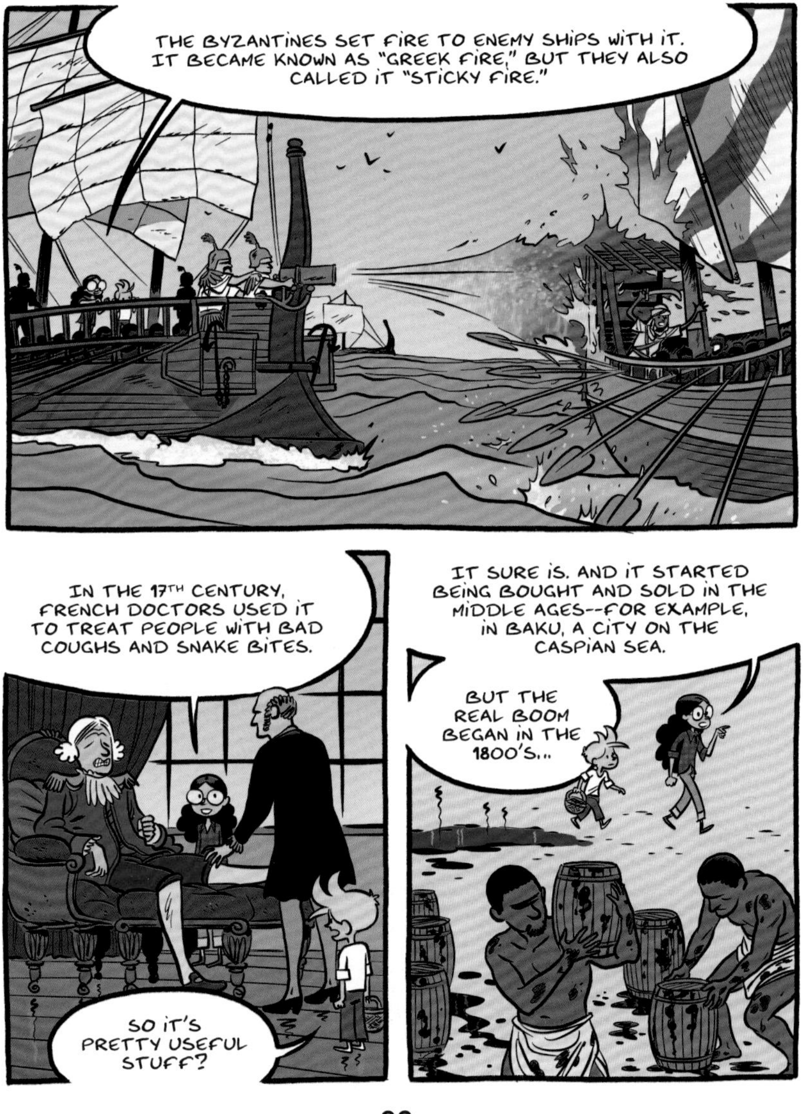
THE BYZANTINES SET FIRE TO ENEMY SHIPS WITH IT. IT BECAME KNOWN AS "GREEK FIRE," BUT THEY ALSO CALLED IT "STICKY FIRE."
IN THE 17TH CENTURY, FRENCH DOCTORS USED IT TO TREAT PEOPLE WITH BAD COUGHS AND SNAKE BITES.
SO IT'S PRETTY USEFUL STUFF?
IT SURE IS. AND IT STARTED BEING BOUGHT AND SOLD IN THE MIDDLE AGES--FOR EXAMPLE, IN BAKU, A CITY ON THE CASPIAN SEA.
BUT THE REAL BOOM BEGAN IN THE 1800'S...

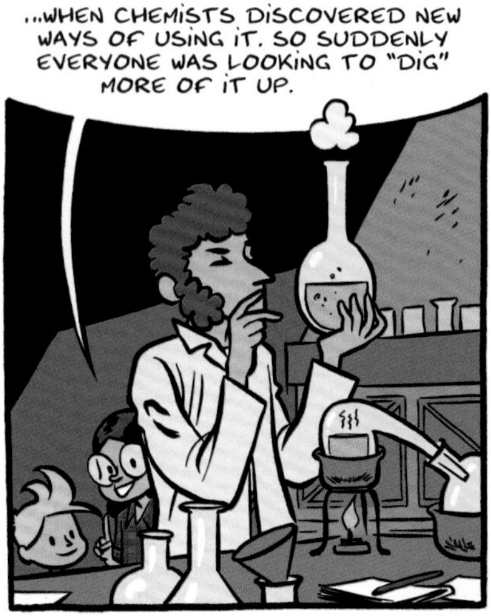
...WHEN CHEMISTS DISCOVERED NEW WAYS OF USING IT. SO SUDDENLY EVERYONE WAS LOOKING TO "DIG" MORE OF IT UP.

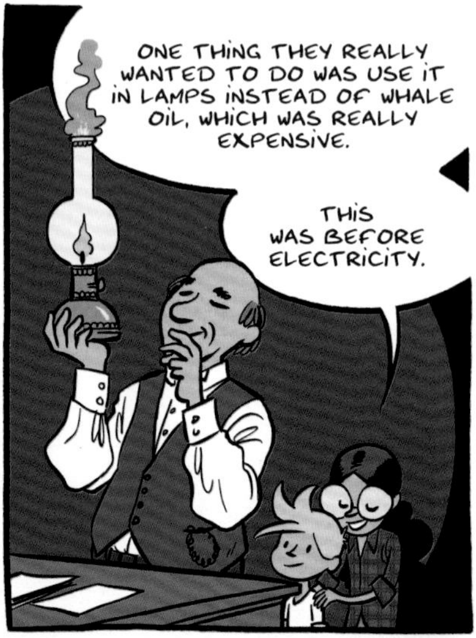
ONE THING THEY REALLY WANTED TO DO WAS USE IT IN LAMPS INSTEAD OF WHALE OIL, WHICH WAS REALLY EXPENSIVE.
THIS WAS BEFORE ELECTRICITY.

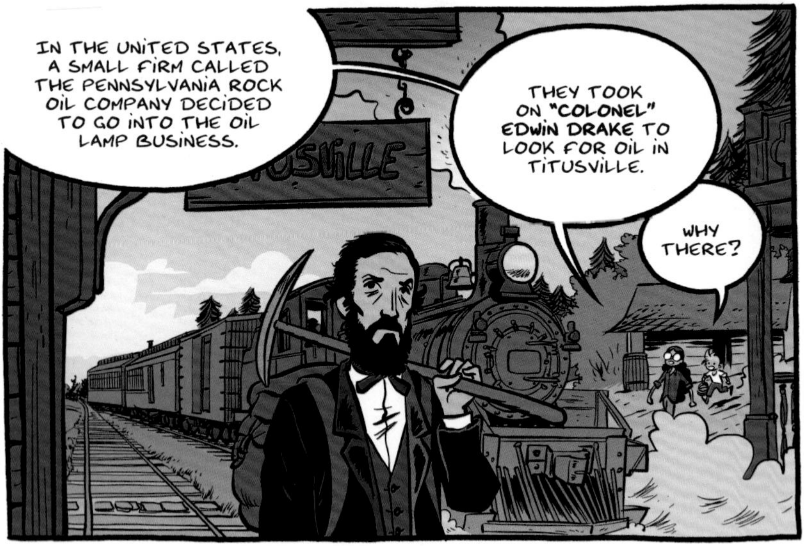
IN THE UNITED STATES, A SMALL FIRM CALLED THE PENNSYLVANIA ROCK OIL COMPANY DECIDED TO GO INTO THE OIL LAMP BUSINESS.
THEY TOOK ON **"COLONEL" EDWIN DRAKE** TO LOOK FOR OIL IN TITUSVILLE.
WHY THERE?

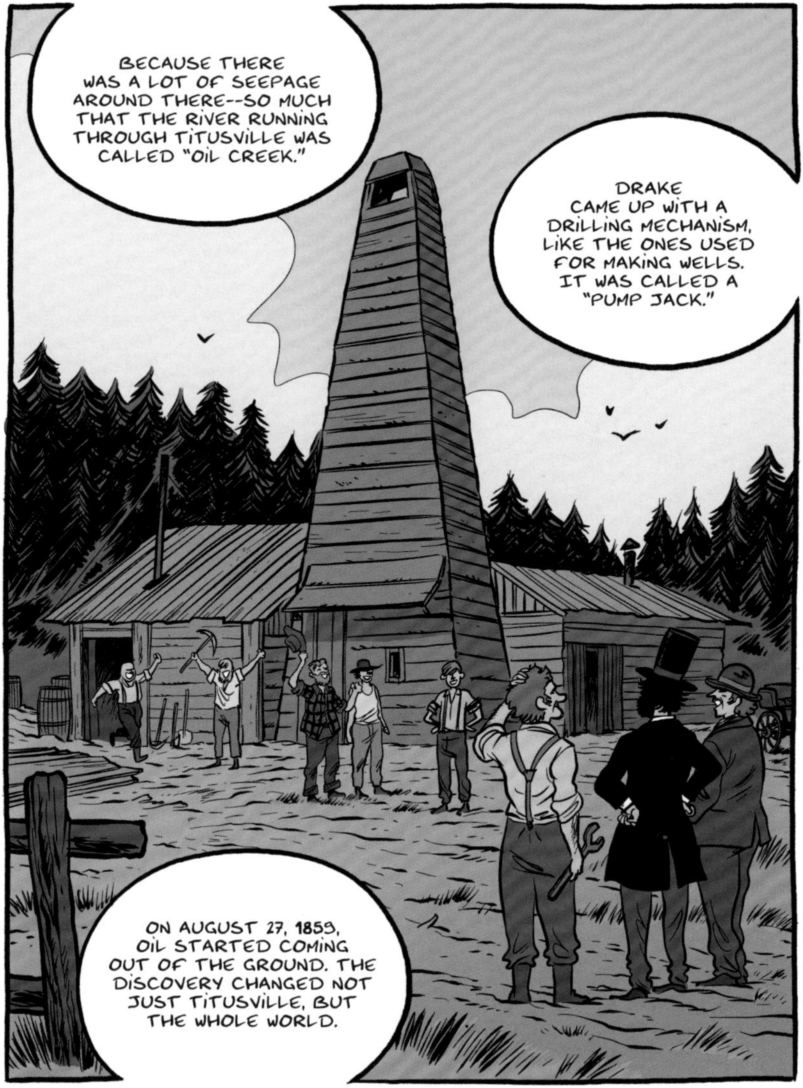
BECAUSE THERE WAS A LOT OF SEEPAGE AROUND THERE--SO MUCH THAT THE RIVER RUNNING THROUGH TITUSVILLE WAS CALLED "OIL CREEK."
DRAKE CAME UP WITH A DRILLING MECHANISM, LIKE THE ONES USED FOR MAKING WELLS. IT WAS CALLED A "PUMP JACK."
ON AUGUST 27, 1859, OIL STARTED COMING OUT OF THE GROUND. THE DISCOVERY CHANGED NOT JUST TITUSVILLE, BUT THE WHOLE WORLD.

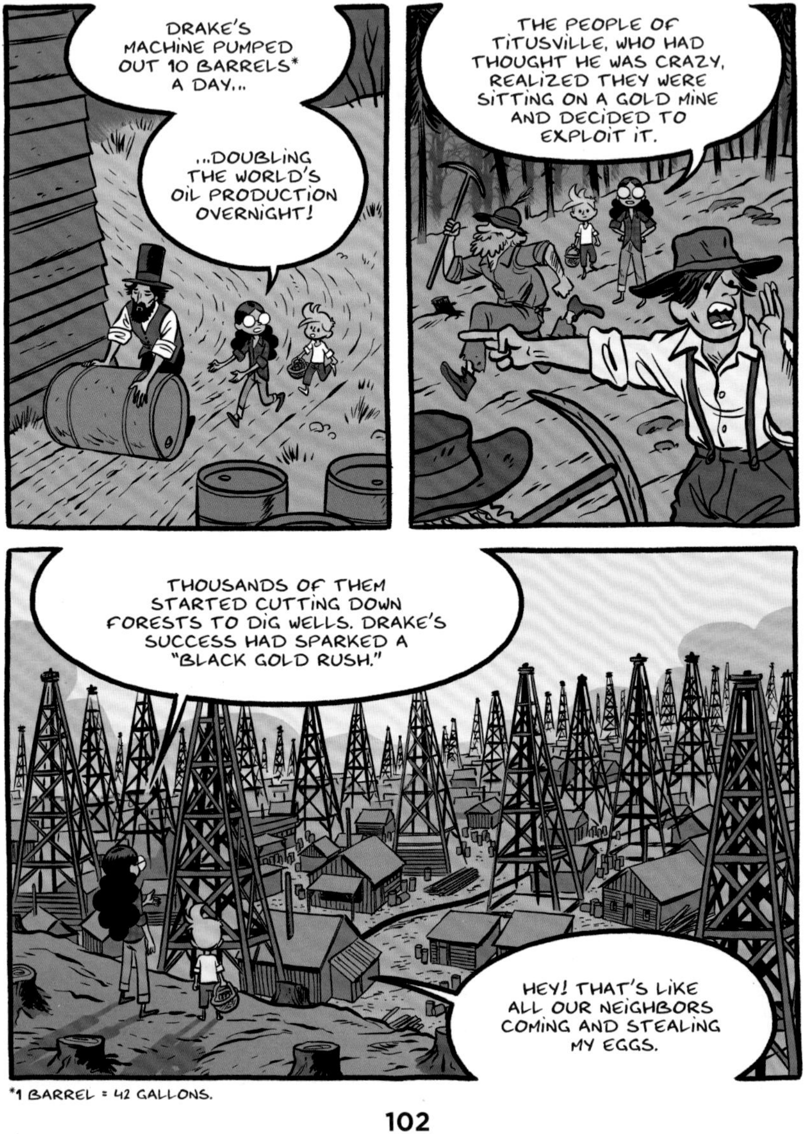
DRAKE'S MACHINE PUMPED OUT 10 BARRELS* A DAY...
...DOUBLING THE WORLD'S OIL PRODUCTION OVERNIGHT!
THE PEOPLE OF TITUSVILLE, WHO HAD THOUGHT HE WAS CRAZY, REALIZED THEY WERE SITTING ON A GOLD MINE AND DECIDED TO EXPLOIT IT.
THOUSANDS OF THEM STARTED CUTTING DOWN FORESTS TO DIG WELLS. DRAKE'S SUCCESS HAD SPARKED A "BLACK GOLD RUSH."
HEY! THAT'S LIKE ALL OUR NEIGHBORS COMING AND STEALING MY EGGS.

*1 BARREL = 42 GALLONS.

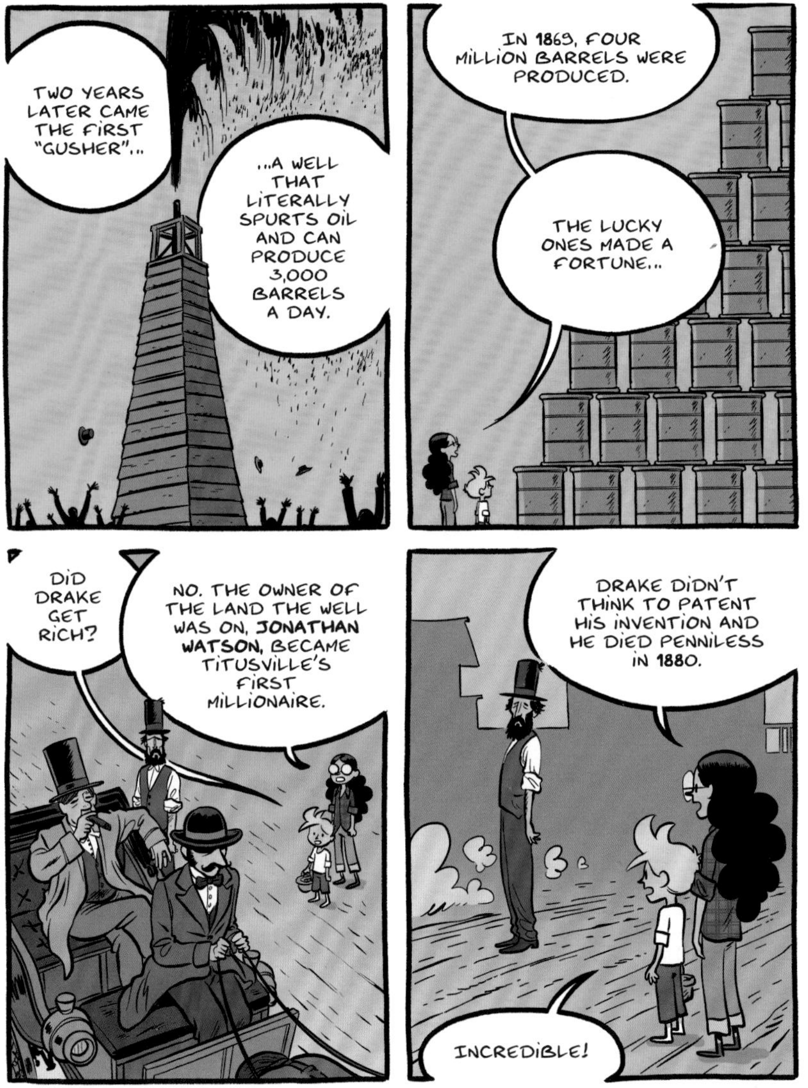
TWO YEARS LATER CAME THE FIRST "GUSHER"...
...A WELL THAT LITERALLY SPURTS OIL AND CAN PRODUCE 3,000 BARRELS A DAY.
IN 1869, FOUR MILLION BARRELS WERE PRODUCED.
THE LUCKY ONES MADE A FORTUNE...
DID DRAKE GET RICH?
NO. THE OWNER OF THE LAND THE WELL WAS ON, **JONATHAN WATSON**, BECAME TITUSVILLE'S FIRST MILLIONAIRE.
DRAKE DIDN'T THINK TO PATENT HIS INVENTION AND HE DIED PENNILESS IN 1880.
INCREDIBLE!

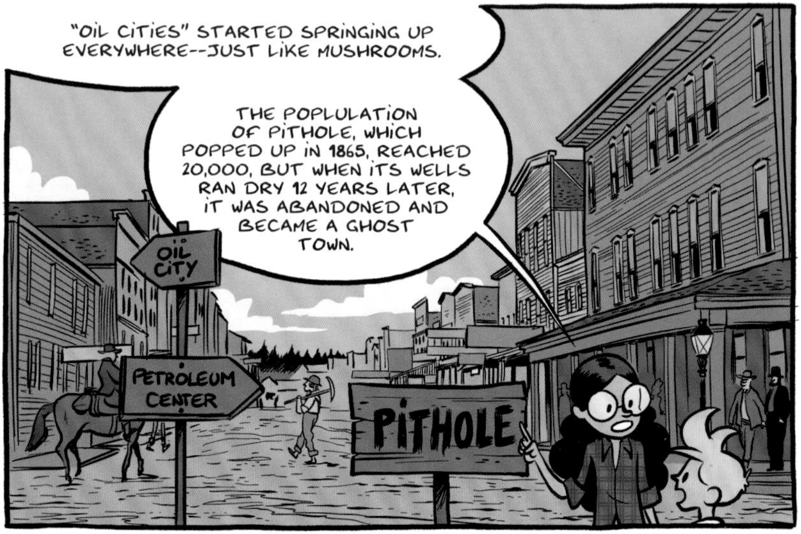
"OIL CITIES" STARTED SPRINGING UP EVERYWHERE--JUST LIKE MUSHROOMS.
THE POPLULATION OF PITHOLE, WHICH POPPED UP IN 1865, REACHED 20,000, BUT WHEN ITS WELLS RAN DRY 12 YEARS LATER, IT WAS ABANDONED AND BECAME A GHOST TOWN.
OIL CITY
PETROLEUM CENTER
PITHOLE

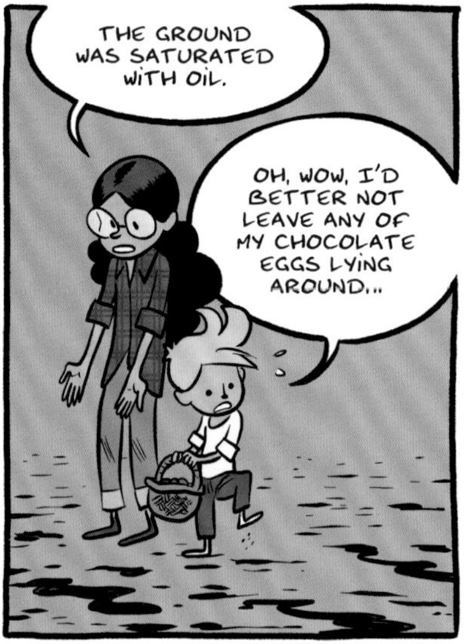
THE GROUND WAS SATURATED WITH OIL.
OH, WOW, I'D BETTER NOT LEAVE ANY OF MY CHOCOLATE EGGS LYING AROUND...

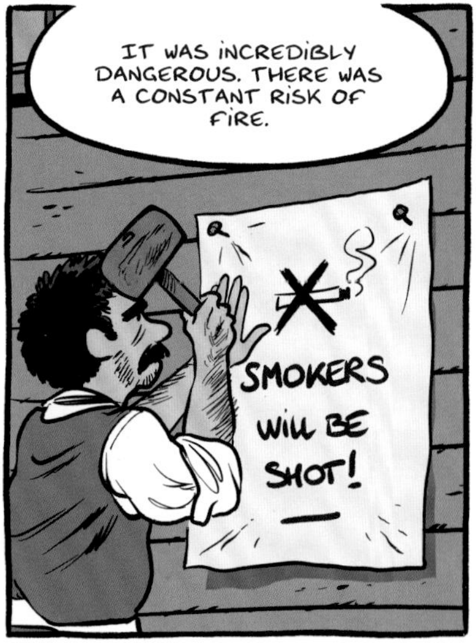
IT WAS INCREDIBLY DANGEROUS. THERE WAS A CONSTANT RISK OF FIRE.
SMOKERS WILL BE SHOT!

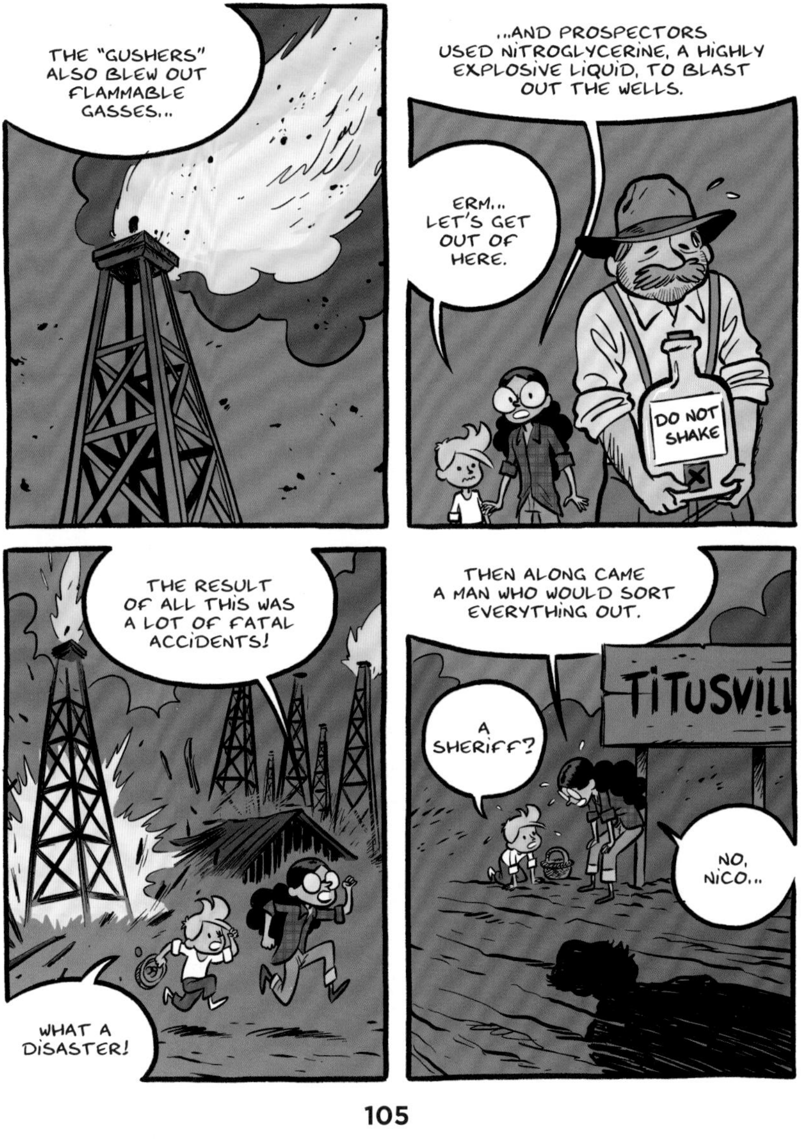
THE "GUSHERS" ALSO BLEW OUT FLAMMABLE GASSES...
...AND PROSPECTORS USED NITROGLYCERINE, A HIGHLY EXPLOSIVE LIQUID, TO BLAST OUT THE WELLS.
ERM... LET'S GET OUT OF HERE.
DO NOT SHAKE
THE RESULT OF ALL THIS WAS A LOT OF FATAL ACCIDENTS!
WHAT A DISASTER!
THEN ALONG CAME A MAN WHO WOULD SORT EVERYTHING OUT.
TITUSVILL
A SHERIFF?
NO, NICO...

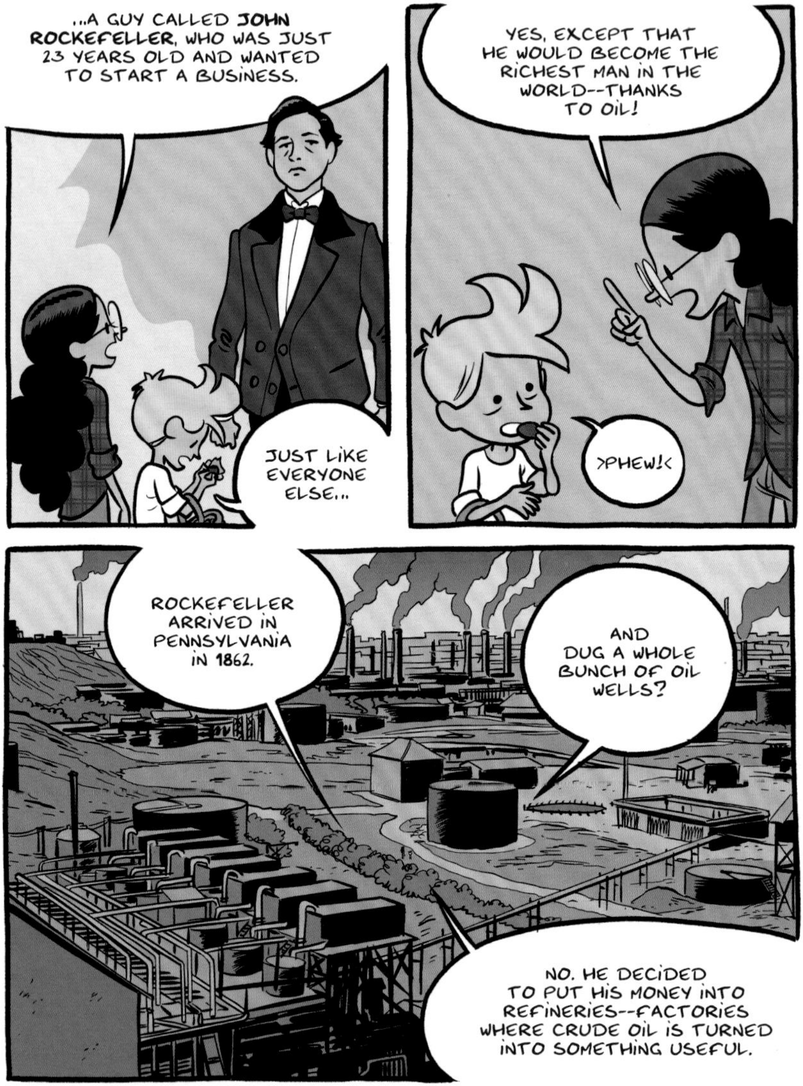
...A GUY CALLED **JOHN ROCKEFELLER**, WHO WAS JUST 23 YEARS OLD AND WANTED TO START A BUSINESS.
JUST LIKE EVERYONE ELSE...
YES, EXCEPT THAT HE WOULD BECOME THE RICHEST MAN IN THE WORLD--THANKS TO OIL!
>PHEW!<
ROCKEFELLER ARRIVED IN PENNSYLVANIA IN 1862.
AND DUG A WHOLE BUNCH OF OIL WELLS?
NO. HE DECIDED TO PUT HIS MONEY INTO REFINERIES--FACTORIES WHERE CRUDE OIL IS TURNED INTO SOMETHING USEFUL.

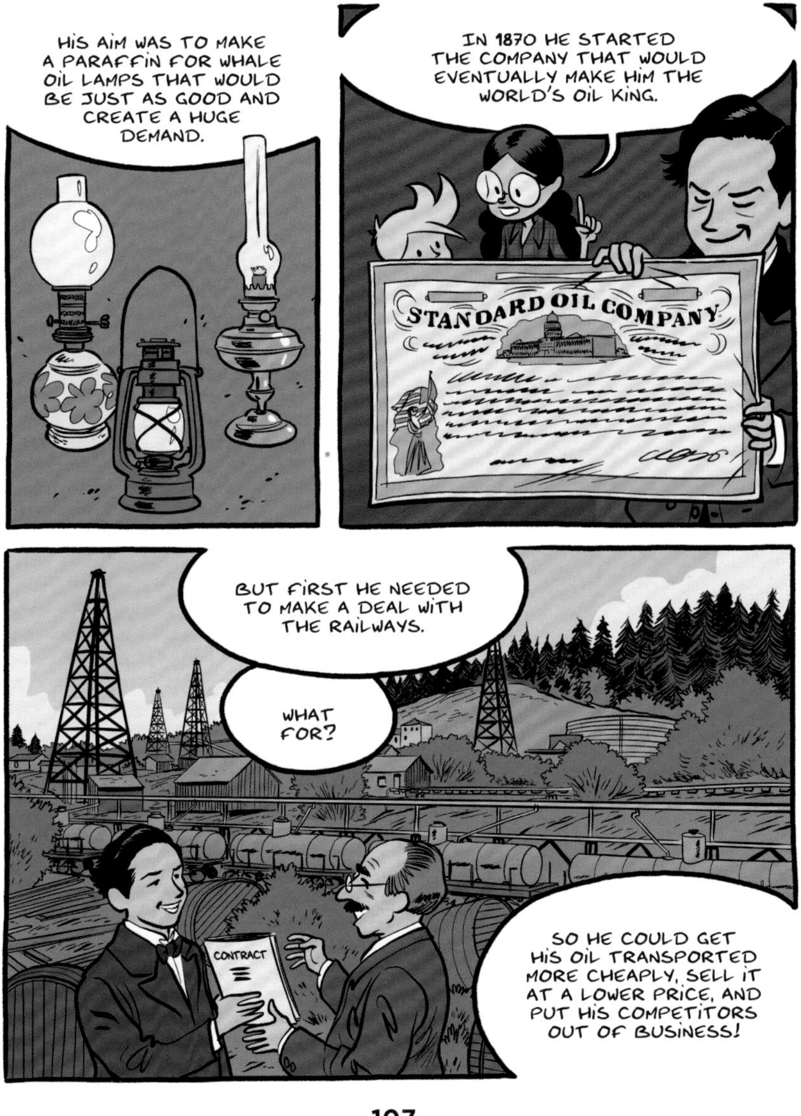
HIS AIM WAS TO MAKE A PARAFFIN FOR WHALE OIL LAMPS THAT WOULD BE JUST AS GOOD AND CREATE A HUGE DEMAND.
IN 1870 HE STARTED THE COMPANY THAT WOULD EVENTUALLY MAKE HIM THE WORLD'S OIL KING.
STANDARD OIL COMPANY
BUT FIRST HE NEEDED TO MAKE A DEAL WITH THE RAILWAYS.
WHAT FOR?
CONTRACT
SO HE COULD GET HIS OIL TRANSPORTED MORE CHEAPLY, SELL IT AT A LOWER PRICE, AND PUT HIS COMPETITORS OUT OF BUSINESS!

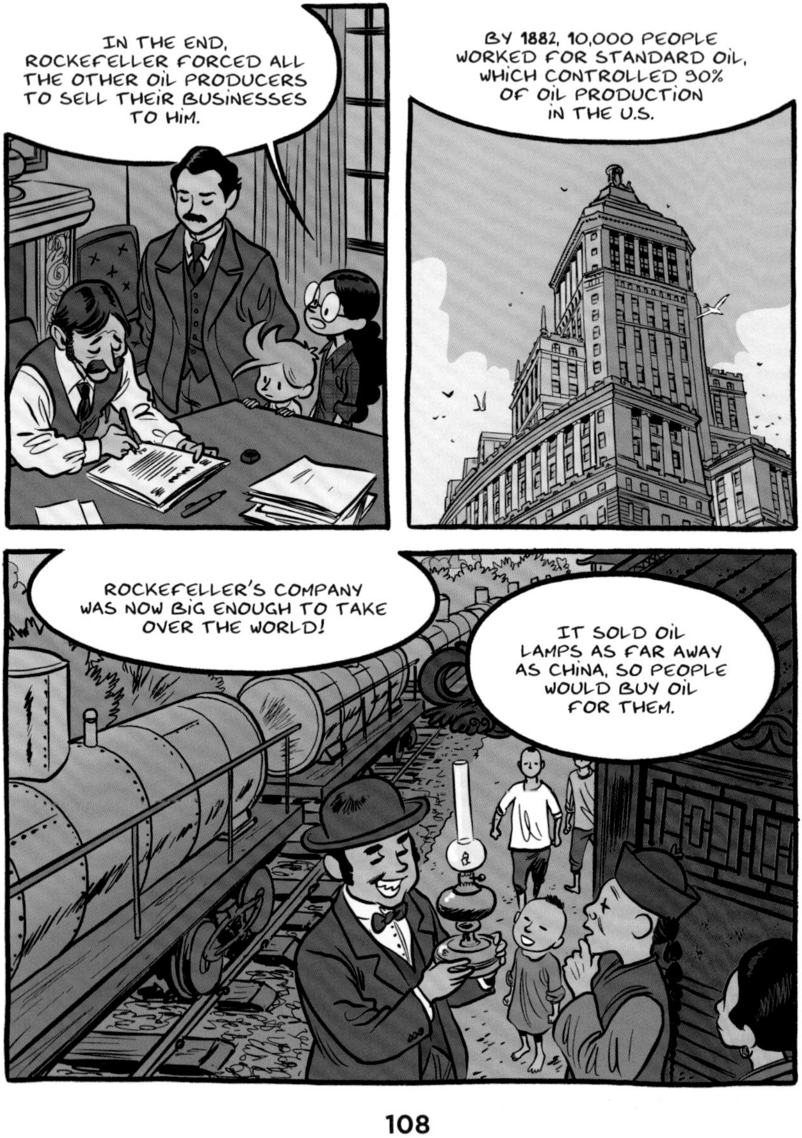
IN THE END, ROCKEFELLER FORCED ALL THE OTHER OIL PRODUCERS TO SELL THEIR BUSINESSES TO HIM.
BY 1882, 10,000 PEOPLE WORKED FOR STANDARD OIL, WHICH CONTROLLED 90% OF OIL PRODUCTION IN THE U.S.
ROCKEFELLER'S COMPANY WAS NOW BIG ENOUGH TO TAKE OVER THE WORLD!
IT SOLD OIL LAMPS AS FAR AWAY AS CHINA, SO PEOPLE WOULD BUY OIL FOR THEM.

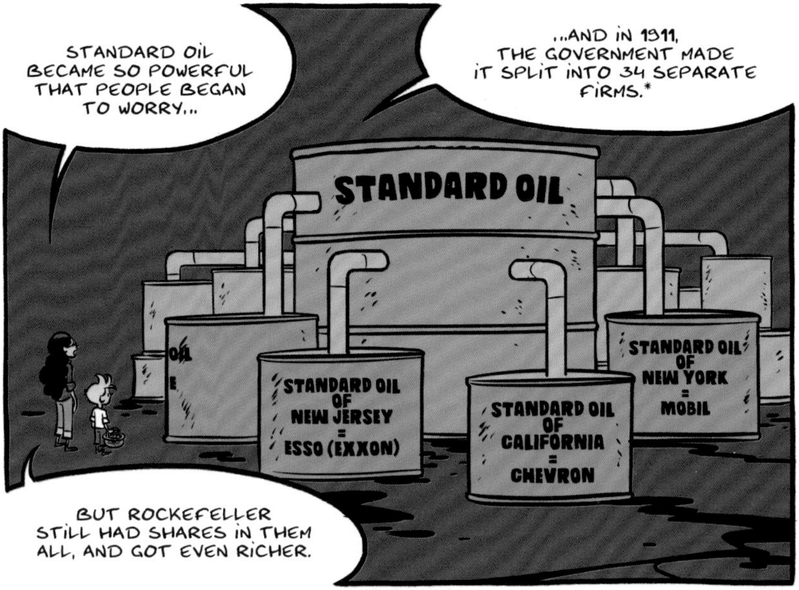

STANDARD OIL BECAME SO POWERFUL THAT PEOPLE BEGAN TO WORRY...
...AND IN 1911, THE GOVERNMENT MADE IT SPLIT INTO 34 SEPARATE FIRMS.*
STANDARD OIL
STANDARD OIL OF NEW JERSEY = ESSO (EXXON)
STANDARD OIL OF CALIFORNIA = CHEVRON
STANDARD OIL OF NEW YORK = MOBIL
BUT ROCKEFELLER STILL HAD SHARES IN THEM ALL, AND GOT EVEN RICHER.

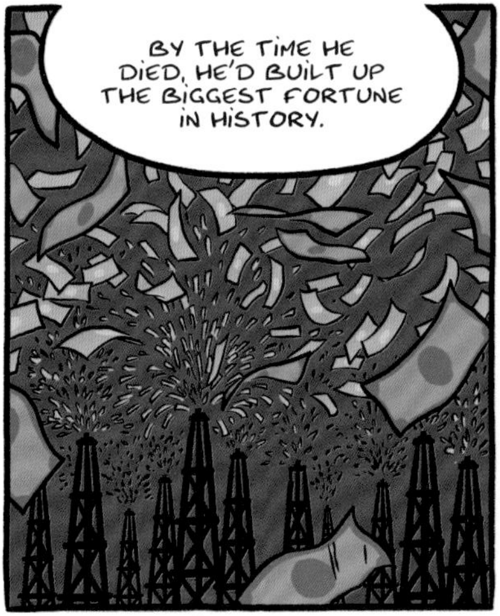

BY THE TIME HE DIED, HE'D BUILT UP THE BIGGEST FORTUNE IN HISTORY.

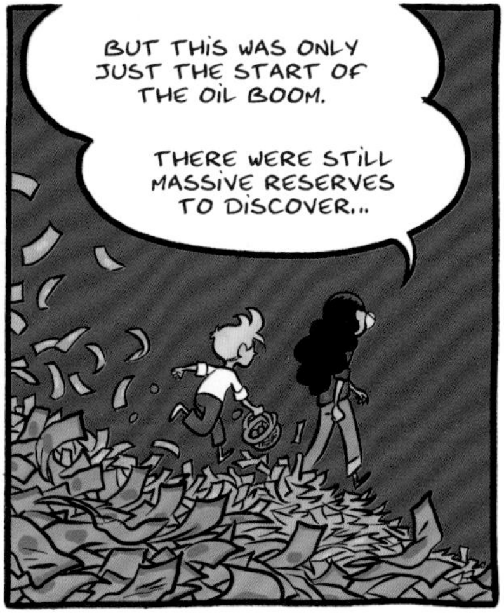

BUT THIS WAS ONLY JUST THE START OF THE OIL BOOM.
THERE WERE STILL MASSIVE RESERVES TO DISCOVER...

*FOLLOWING THE SHERMAN ANTITRUST ACT OF 1890 WHICH LIMITED THE SIZE OF COMPANIES.

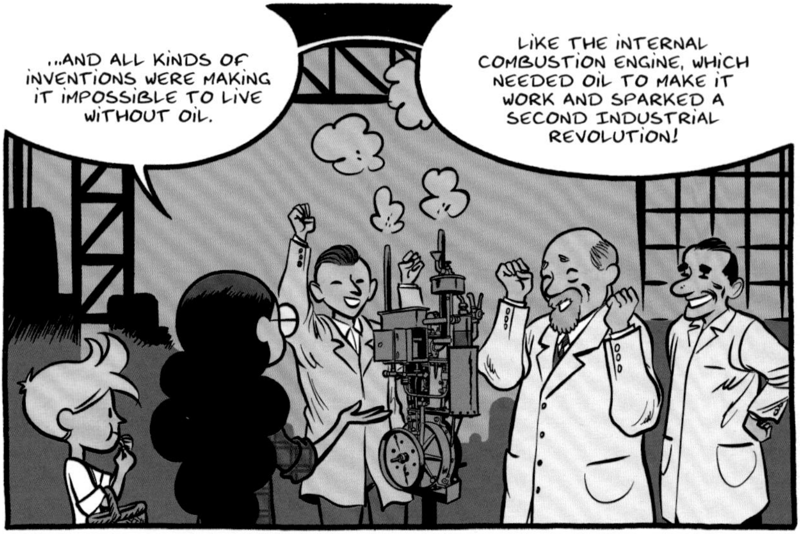
...AND ALL KINDS OF INVENTIONS WERE MAKING IT IMPOSSIBLE TO LIVE WITHOUT OIL.
LIKE THE INTERNAL COMBUSTION ENGINE, WHICH NEEDED OIL TO MAKE IT WORK AND SPARKED A SECOND INDUSTRIAL REVOLUTION!

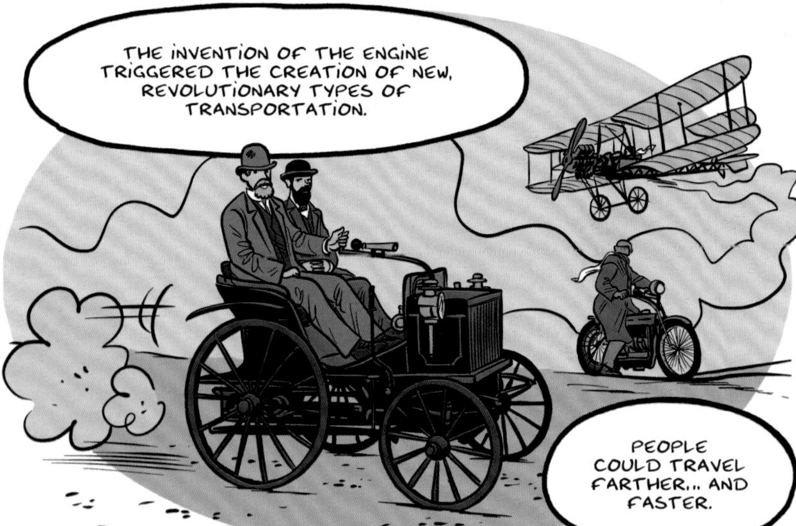
THE INVENTION OF THE ENGINE TRIGGERED THE CREATION OF NEW, REVOLUTIONARY TYPES OF TRANSPORTATION.
PEOPLE COULD TRAVEL FARTHER... AND FASTER.

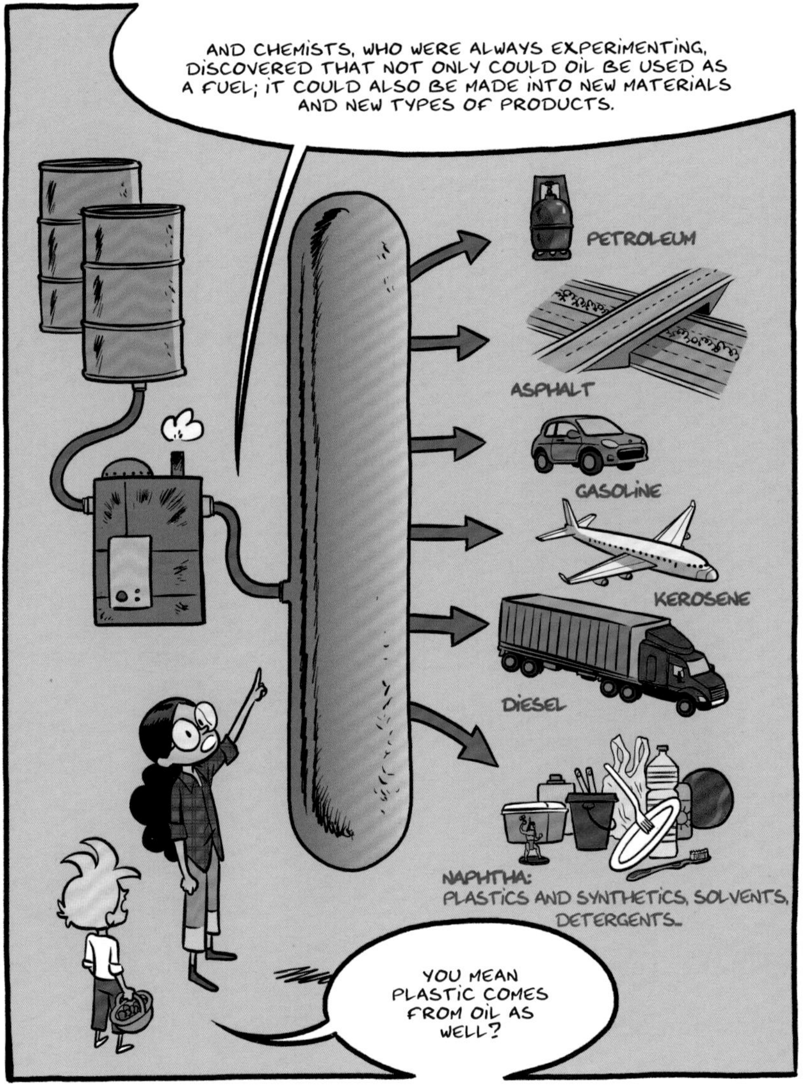
AND CHEMISTS, WHO WERE ALWAYS EXPERIMENTING, DISCOVERED THAT NOT ONLY COULD OIL BE USED AS A FUEL; IT COULD ALSO BE MADE INTO NEW MATERIALS AND NEW TYPES OF PRODUCTS.
PETROLEUM
ASPHALT
GASOLINE
KEROSENE
DIESEL
NAPHTHA:
PLASTICS AND SYNTHETICS, SOLVENTS, DETERGENTS...
YOU MEAN PLASTIC COMES FROM OIL AS WELL?

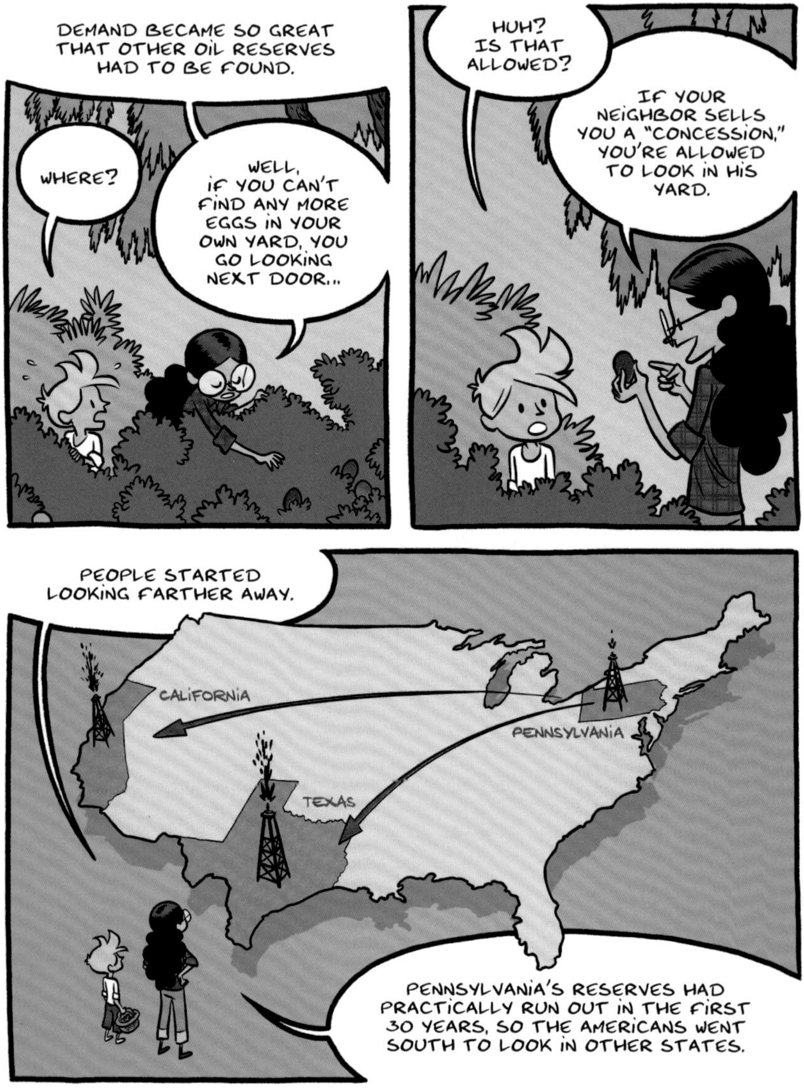
DEMAND BECAME SO GREAT THAT OTHER OIL RESERVES HAD TO BE FOUND.
WHERE?
WELL, IF YOU CAN'T FIND ANY MORE EGGS IN YOUR OWN YARD, YOU GO LOOKING NEXT DOOR...
HUH? IS THAT ALLOWED?
IF YOUR NEIGHBOR SELLS YOU A "CONCESSION," YOU'RE ALLOWED TO LOOK IN HIS YARD.
PEOPLE STARTED LOOKING FARTHER AWAY.
CALIFORNIA
PENNSYLVANIA
TEXAS
PENNSYLVANIA'S RESERVES HAD PRACTICALLY RUN OUT IN THE FIRST 30 YEARS, SO THE AMERICANS WENT SOUTH TO LOOK IN OTHER STATES.

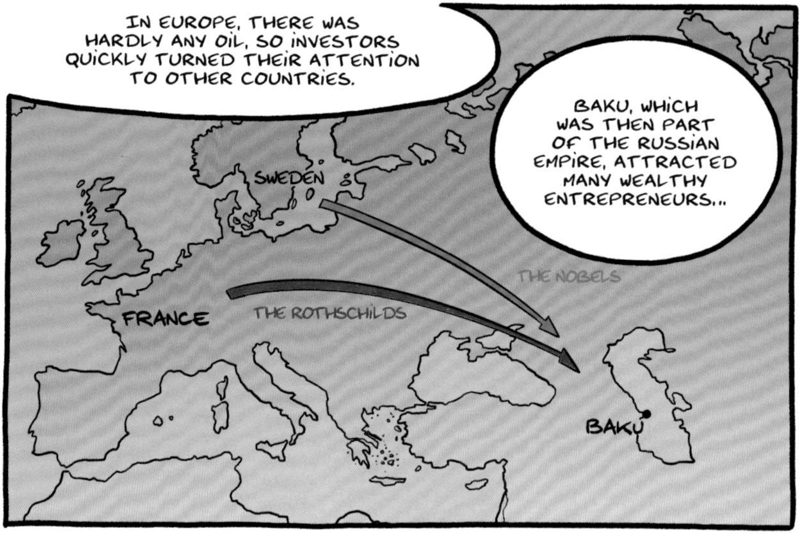
IN EUROPE, THERE WAS HARDLY ANY OIL, SO INVESTORS QUICKLY TURNED THEIR ATTENTION TO OTHER COUNTRIES.
BAKU, WHICH WAS THEN PART OF THE RUSSIAN EMPIRE, ATTRACTED MANY WEALTHY ENTREPRENEURS...
SWEDEN
THE NOBELS
FRANCE
THE ROTHSCHILDS
BAKU

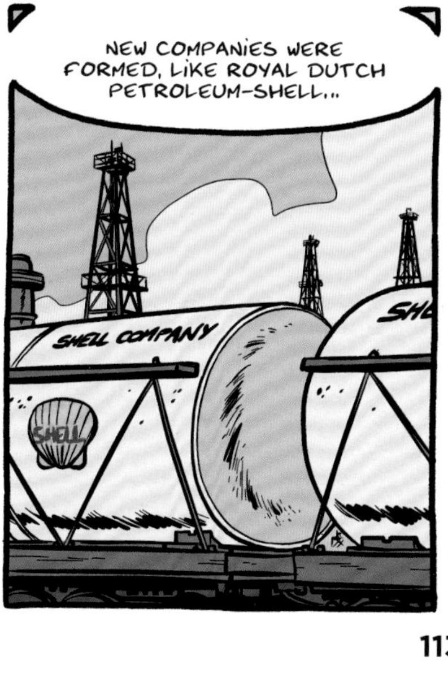
NEW COMPANIES WERE FORMED, LIKE ROYAL DUTCH PETROLEUM-SHELL...
SHELL COMPANY
SHELL

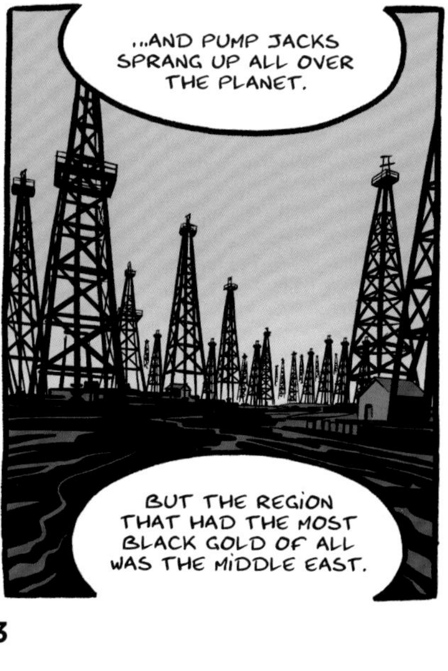
...AND PUMP JACKS SPRANG UP ALL OVER THE PLANET.
BUT THE REGION THAT HAD THE MOST BLACK GOLD OF ALL WAS THE MIDDLE EAST.

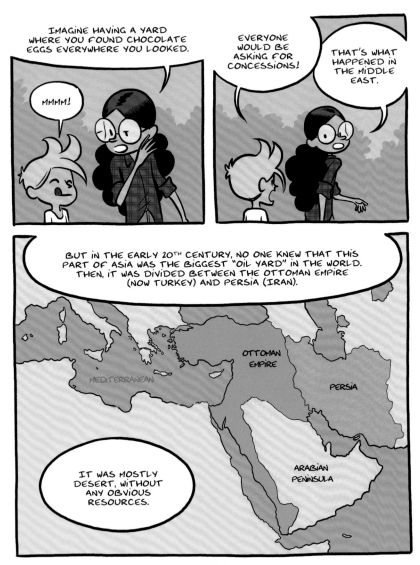

IMAGINE HAVING A YARD WHERE YOU FOUND CHOCOLATE EGGS EVERYWHERE YOU LOOKED.

MMMM!

EVERYONE WOULD BE ASKING FOR CONCESSIONS!

THAT'S WHAT HAPPENED IN THE MIDDLE EAST.

BUT IN THE EARLY 20TH CENTURY, NO ONE KNEW THAT THIS PART OF ASIA WAS THE BIGGEST "OIL YARD" IN THE WORLD. THEN, IT WAS DIVIDED BETWEEN THE OTTOMAN EMPIRE (NOW TURKEY) AND PERSIA (IRAN).

MEDITERRANEAN

OTTOMAN EMPIRE

PERSIA

ARABIAN PENINSULA

IT WAS MOSTLY DESERT, WITHOUT ANY OBVIOUS RESOURCES.

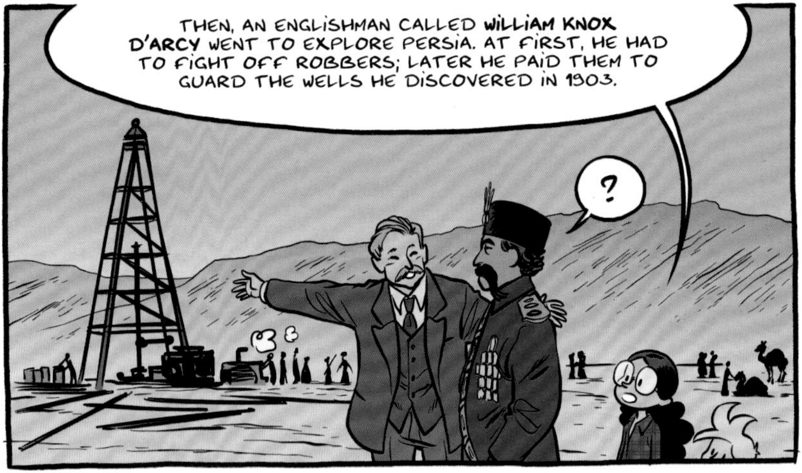
THEN, AN ENGLISHMAN CALLED **WILLIAM KNOX D'ARCY** WENT TO EXPLORE PERSIA. AT FIRST, HE HAD TO FIGHT OFF ROBBERS; LATER HE PAID THEM TO GUARD THE WELLS HE DISCOVERED IN 1903.
?

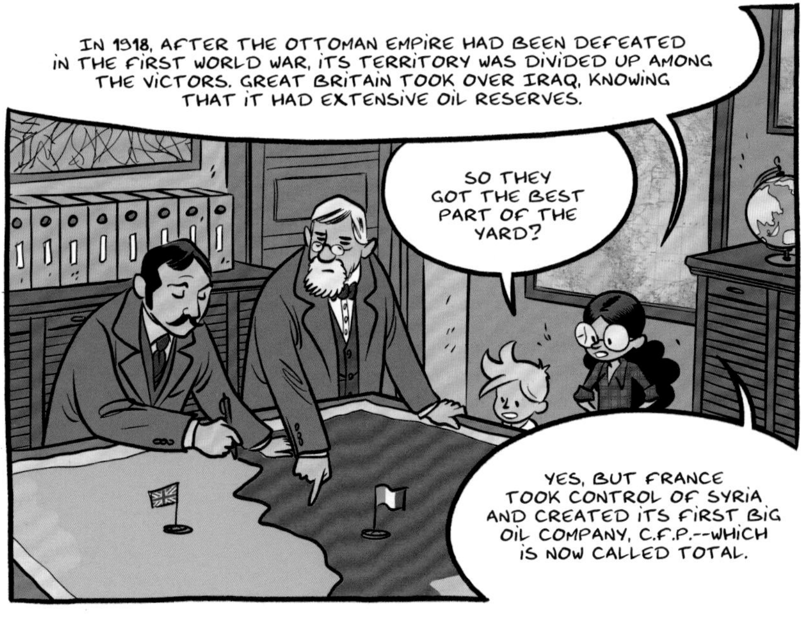
IN 1918, AFTER THE OTTOMAN EMPIRE HAD BEEN DEFEATED IN THE FIRST WORLD WAR, ITS TERRITORY WAS DIVIDED UP AMONG THE VICTORS. GREAT BRITAIN TOOK OVER IRAQ, KNOWING THAT IT HAD EXTENSIVE OIL RESERVES.
SO THEY GOT THE BEST PART OF THE YARD?
YES, BUT FRANCE TOOK CONTROL OF SYRIA AND CREATED ITS FIRST BIG OIL COMPANY, C.F.P.--WHICH IS NOW CALLED TOTAL.

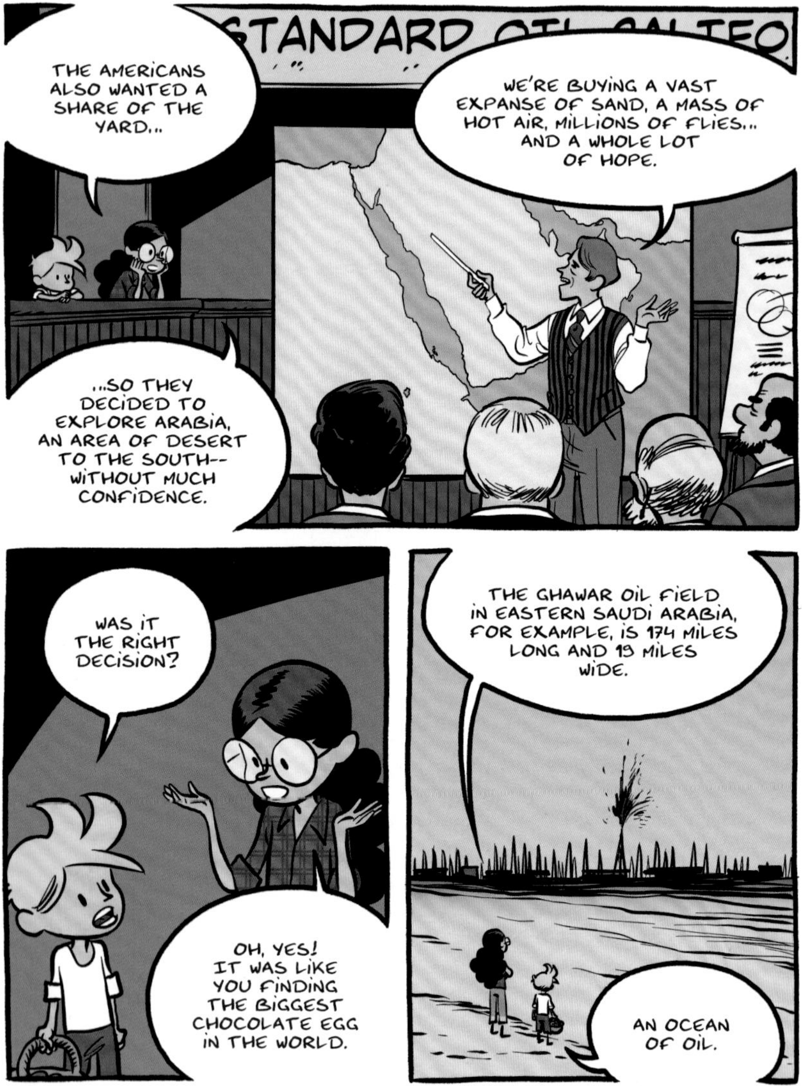
STANDARD OIL
THE AMERICANS ALSO WANTED A SHARE OF THE YARD...
WE'RE BUYING A VAST EXPANSE OF SAND, A MASS OF HOT AIR, MILLIONS OF FLIES... AND A WHOLE LOT OF HOPE.
...SO THEY DECIDED TO EXPLORE ARABIA, AN AREA OF DESERT TO THE SOUTH--WITHOUT MUCH CONFIDENCE.
WAS IT THE RIGHT DECISION?
OH, YES! IT WAS LIKE YOU FINDING THE BIGGEST CHOCOLATE EGG IN THE WORLD.
THE GHAWAR OIL FIELD IN EASTERN SAUDI ARABIA, FOR EXAMPLE, IS 174 MILES LONG AND 19 MILES WIDE.
AN OCEAN OF OIL.

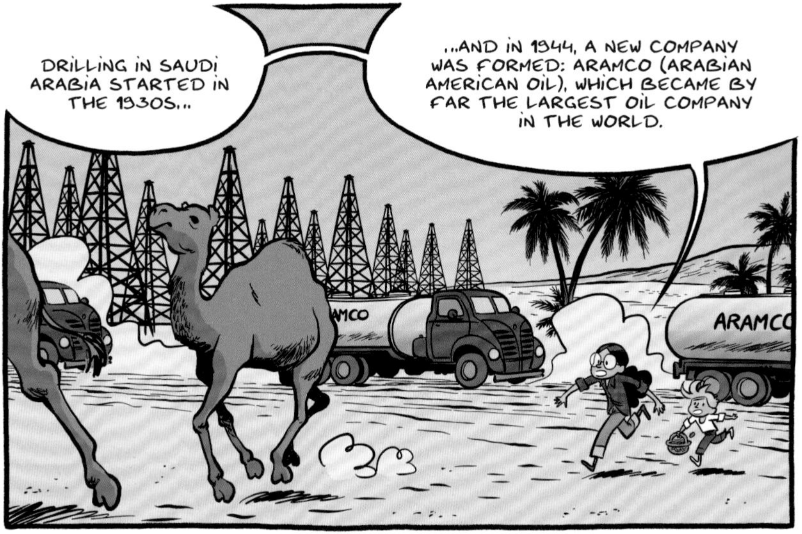
DRILLING IN SAUDI ARABIA STARTED IN THE 1930S...
...AND IN 1944, A NEW COMPANY WAS FORMED: ARAMCO (ARABIAN AMERICAN OIL), WHICH BECAME BY FAR THE LARGEST OIL COMPANY IN THE WORLD.
AMCO
ARAMCO

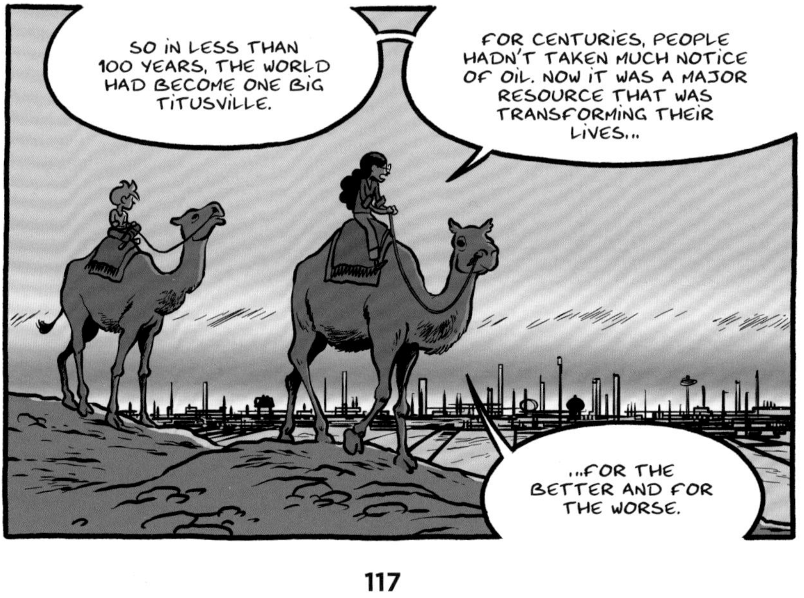
SO IN LESS THAN 100 YEARS, THE WORLD HAD BECOME ONE BIG TITUSVILLE.
FOR CENTURIES, PEOPLE HADN'T TAKEN MUCH NOTICE OF OIL. NOW IT WAS A MAJOR RESOURCE THAT WAS TRANSFORMING THEIR LIVES...
...FOR THE BETTER AND FOR THE WORSE.

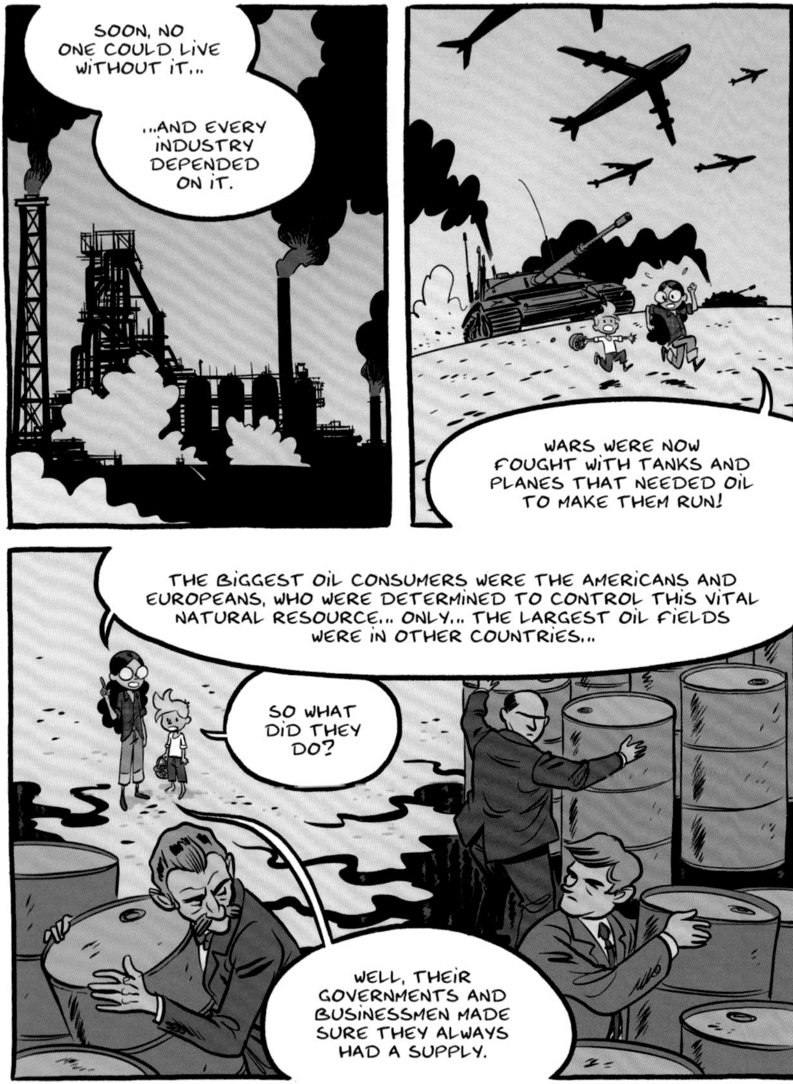
SOON, NO ONE COULD LIVE WITHOUT IT...
...AND EVERY INDUSTRY DEPENDED ON IT.
WARS WERE NOW FOUGHT WITH TANKS AND PLANES THAT NEEDED OIL TO MAKE THEM RUN!
THE BIGGEST OIL CONSUMERS WERE THE AMERICANS AND EUROPEANS, WHO WERE DETERMINED TO CONTROL THIS VITAL NATURAL RESOURCE... ONLY... THE LARGEST OIL FIELDS WERE IN OTHER COUNTRIES...
SO WHAT DID THEY DO?
WELL, THEIR GOVERNMENTS AND BUSINESSMEN MADE SURE THEY ALWAYS HAD A SUPPLY.

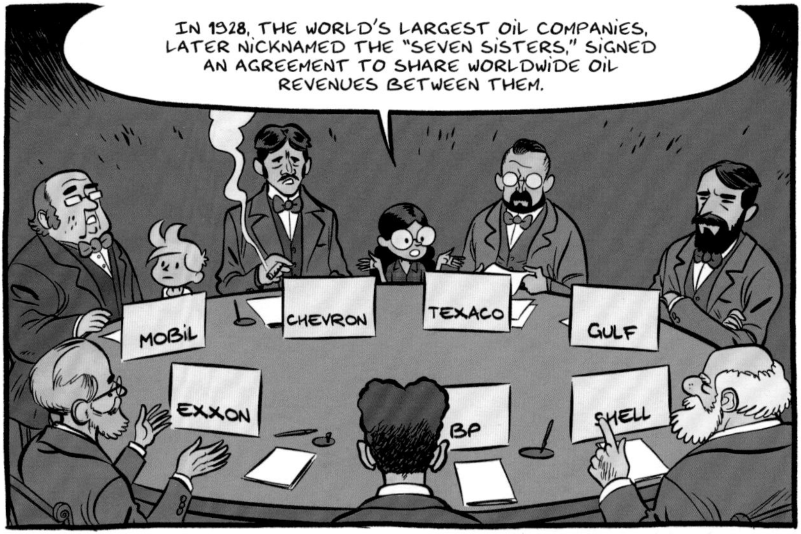
IN 1928, THE WORLD'S LARGEST OIL COMPANIES, LATER NICKNAMED THE "SEVEN SISTERS," SIGNED AN AGREEMENT TO SHARE WORLDWIDE OIL REVENUES BETWEEN THEM.
MOBIL
CHEVRON
TEXACO
GULF
EXXON
BP
SHELL

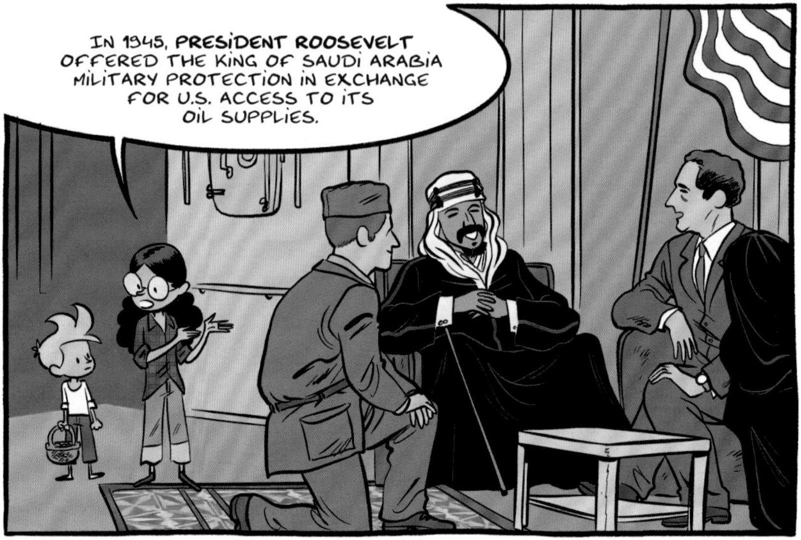
IN 1945, **PRESIDENT ROOSEVELT** OFFERED THE KING OF SAUDI ARABIA MILITARY PROTECTION IN EXCHANGE FOR U.S. ACCESS TO ITS OIL SUPPLIES.

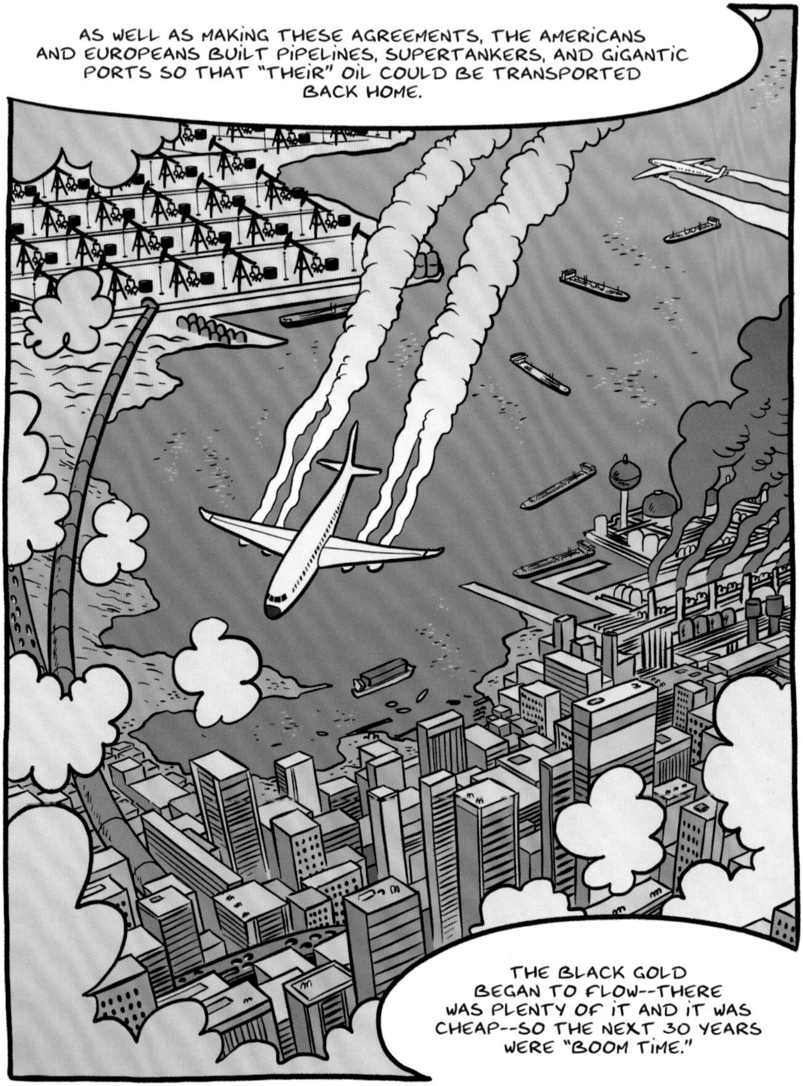
AS WELL AS MAKING THESE AGREEMENTS, THE AMERICANS AND EUROPEANS BUILT PIPELINES, SUPERTANKERS, AND GIGANTIC PORTS SO THAT "THEIR" OIL COULD BE TRANSPORTED BACK HOME.
THE BLACK GOLD BEGAN TO FLOW--THERE WAS PLENTY OF IT AND IT WAS CHEAP--SO THE NEXT 30 YEARS WERE "BOOM TIME."

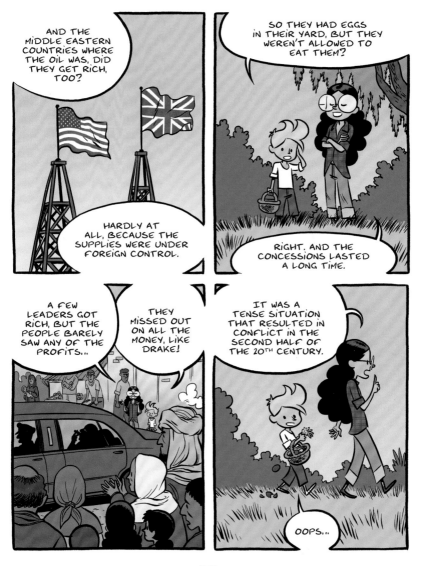

AND THE MIDDLE EASTERN COUNTRIES WHERE THE OIL WAS, DID THEY GET RICH, TOO?

HARDLY AT ALL, BECAUSE THE SUPPLIES WERE UNDER FOREIGN CONTROL.

SO THEY HAD EGGS IN THEIR YARD, BUT THEY WEREN'T ALLOWED TO EAT THEM?

RIGHT. AND THE CONCESSIONS LASTED A LONG TIME.

A FEW LEADERS GOT RICH, BUT THE PEOPLE BARELY SAW ANY OF THE PROFITS...

THEY MISSED OUT ON ALL THE MONEY, LIKE DRAKE!

IT WAS A TENSE SITUATION THAT RESULTED IN CONFLICT IN THE SECOND HALF OF THE 20TH CENTURY.

OOPS...

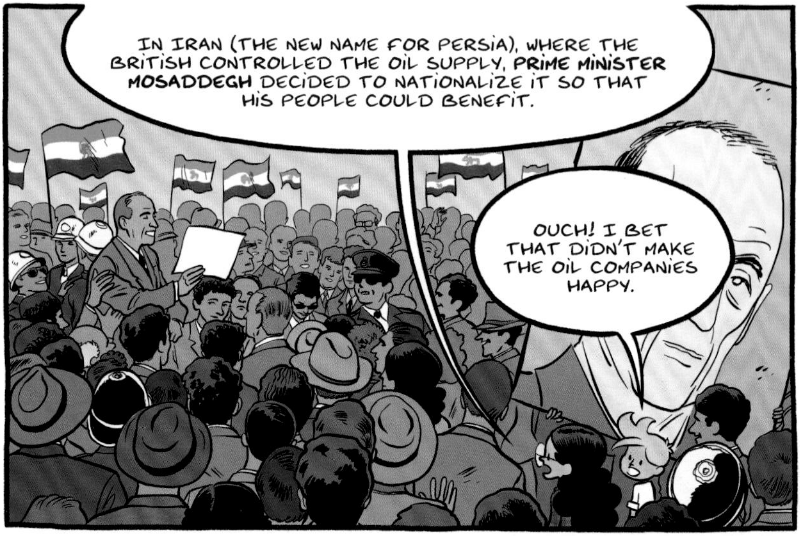
IN IRAN (THE NEW NAME FOR PERSIA), WHERE THE BRITISH CONTROLLED THE OIL SUPPLY, **PRIME MINISTER MOSADDEGH** DECIDED TO NATIONALIZE IT SO THAT HIS PEOPLE COULD BENEFIT.
OUCH! I BET THAT DIDN'T MAKE THE OIL COMPANIES HAPPY.

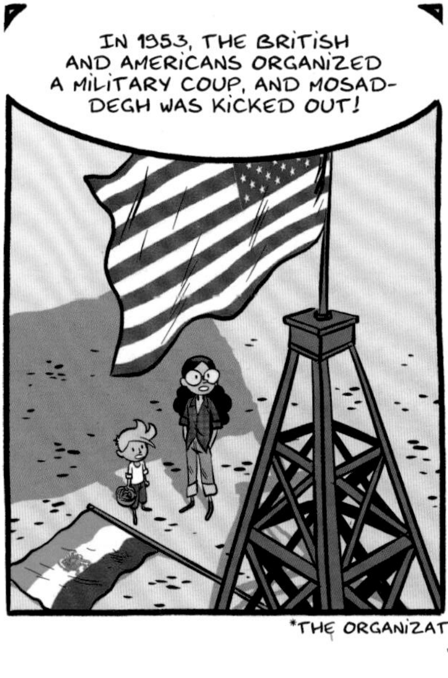
IN 1953, THE BRITISH AND AMERICANS ORGANIZED A MILITARY COUP, AND MOSAD-DEGH WAS KICKED OUT!

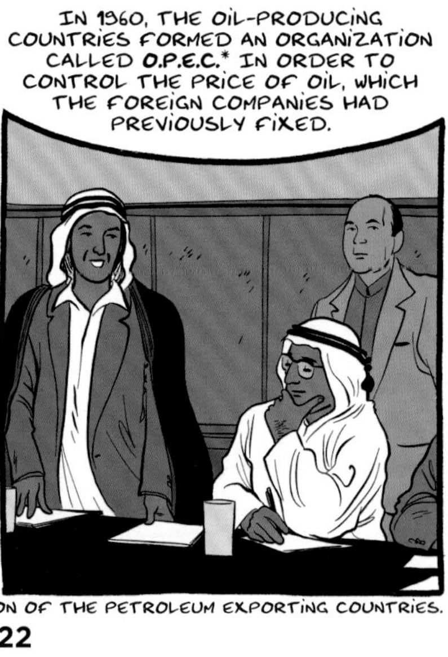
IN 1960, THE OIL-PRODUCING COUNTRIES FORMED AN ORGANIZATION CALLED **O.P.E.C.*** IN ORDER TO CONTROL THE PRICE OF OIL, WHICH THE FOREIGN COMPANIES HAD PREVIOUSLY FIXED.

*THE ORGANIZATION OF THE PETROLEUM EXPORTING COUNTRIES.

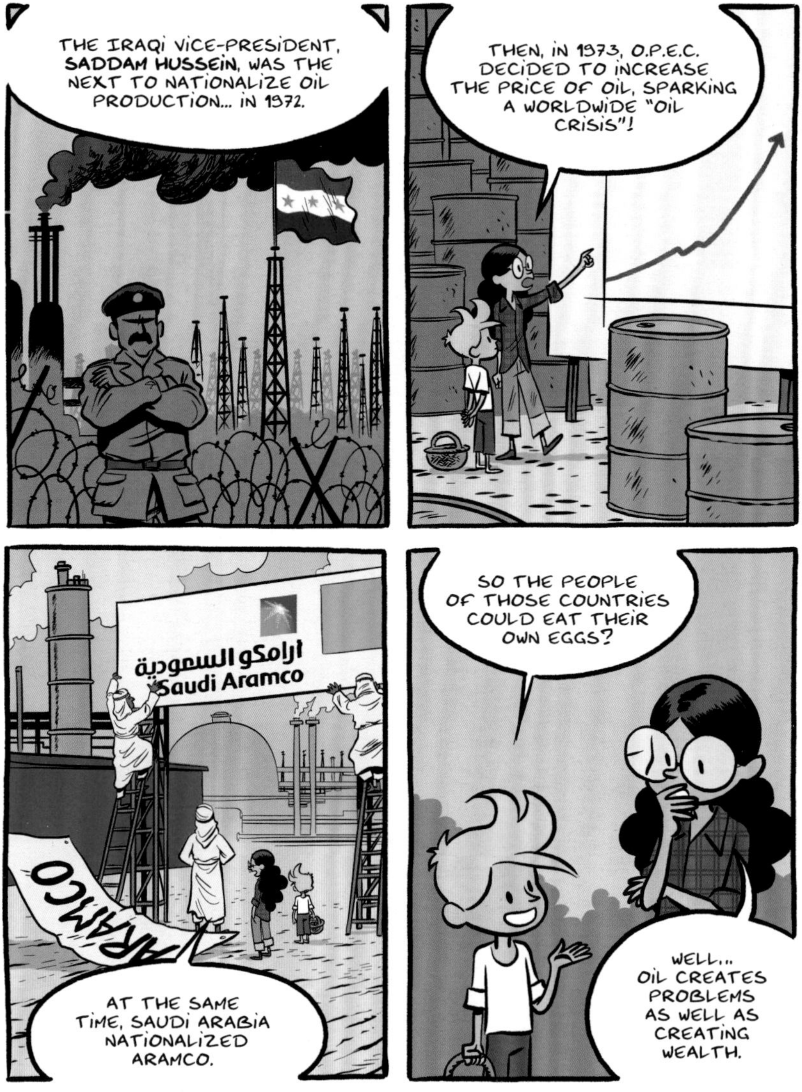
THE IRAQI VICE-PRESIDENT, SADDAM HUSSEIN, WAS THE NEXT TO NATIONALIZE OIL PRODUCTION... IN 1972.
THEN, IN 1973, O.P.E.C. DECIDED TO INCREASE THE PRICE OF OIL, SPARKING A WORLDWIDE "OIL CRISIS"!
ارامكو السعودية
Saudi Aramco
ARAMCO
AT THE SAME TIME, SAUDI ARABIA NATIONALIZED ARAMCO.
SO THE PEOPLE OF THOSE COUNTRIES COULD EAT THEIR OWN EGGS?
WELL... OIL CREATES PROBLEMS AS WELL AS CREATING WEALTH.

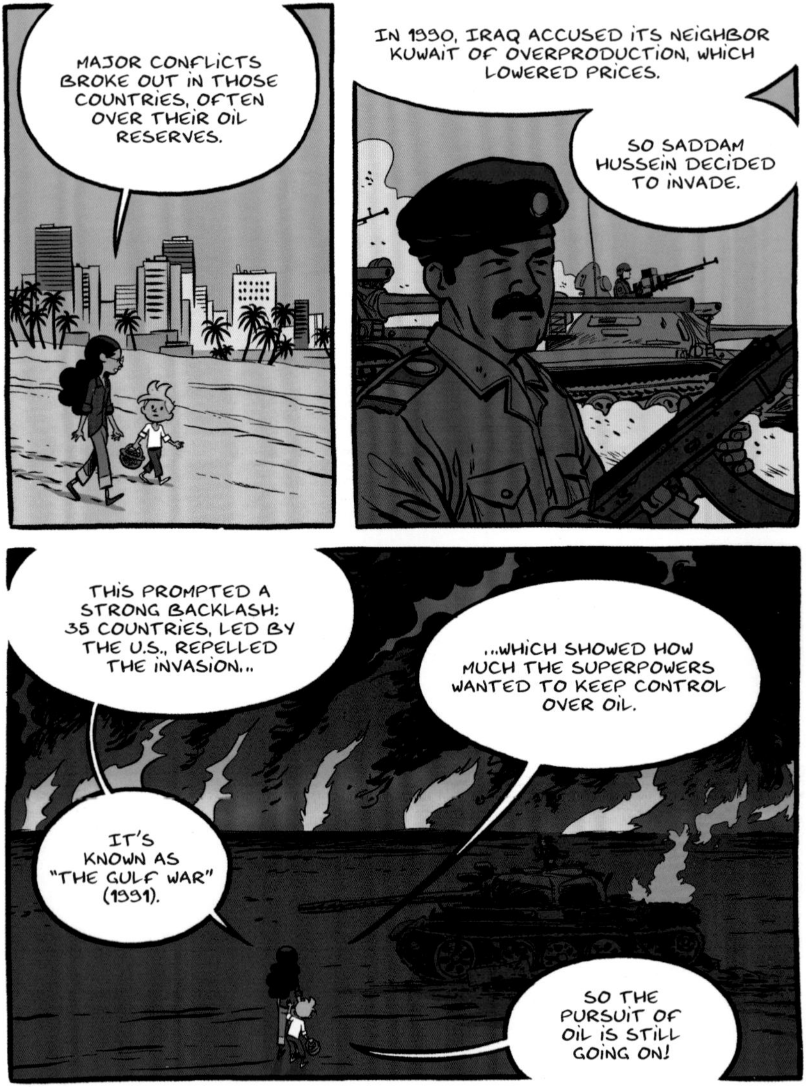
MAJOR CONFLICTS BROKE OUT IN THOSE COUNTRIES, OFTEN OVER THEIR OIL RESERVES.
IN 1990, IRAQ ACCUSED ITS NEIGHBOR KUWAIT OF OVERPRODUCTION, WHICH LOWERED PRICES.
SO SADDAM HUSSEIN DECIDED TO INVADE.
THIS PROMPTED A STRONG BACKLASH: 35 COUNTRIES, LED BY THE U.S., REPELLED THE INVASION...
...WHICH SHOWED HOW MUCH THE SUPERPOWERS WANTED TO KEEP CONTROL OVER OIL.
IT'S KNOWN AS "THE GULF WAR" (1991).
SO THE PURSUIT OF OIL IS STILL GOING ON!

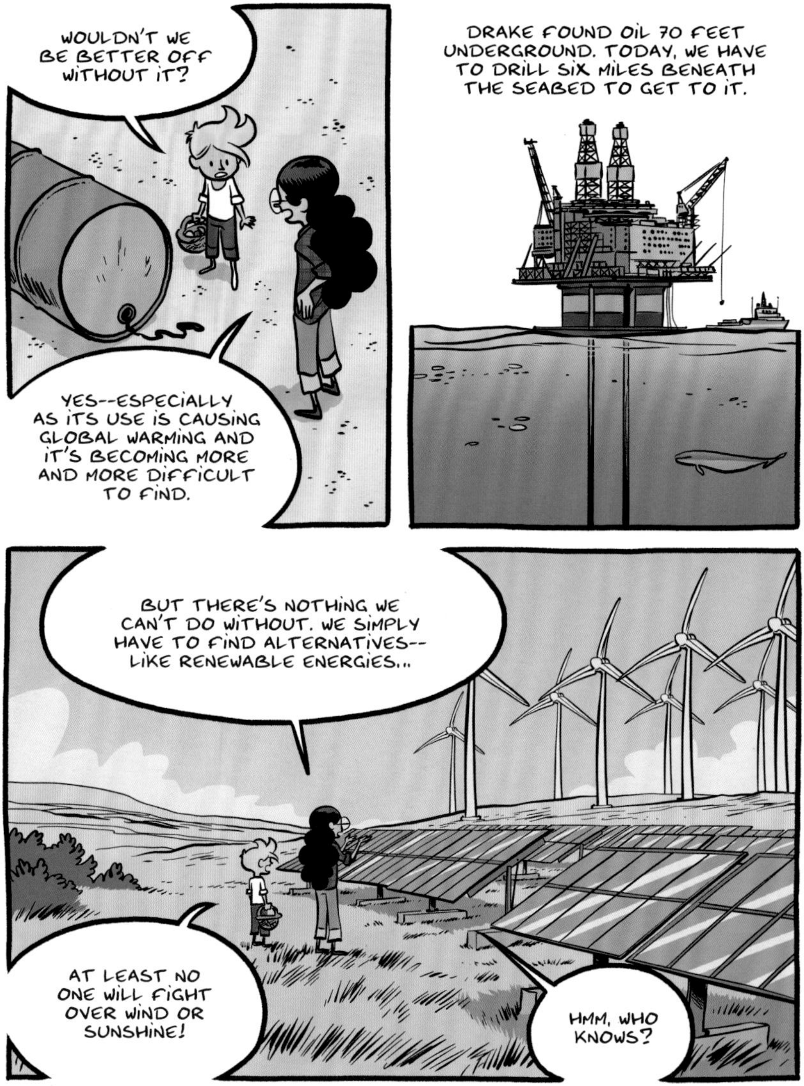
WOULDN'T WE BE BETTER OFF WITHOUT IT?
YES--ESPECIALLY AS ITS USE IS CAUSING GLOBAL WARMING AND IT'S BECOMING MORE AND MORE DIFFICULT TO FIND.
DRAKE FOUND OIL 70 FEET UNDERGROUND. TODAY, WE HAVE TO DRILL SIX MILES BENEATH THE SEABED TO GET TO IT.
BUT THERE'S NOTHING WE CAN'T DO WITHOUT. WE SIMPLY HAVE TO FIND ALTERNATIVES--LIKE RENEWABLE ENERGIES...
AT LEAST NO ONE WILL FIGHT OVER WIND OR SUNSHINE!
HMM, WHO KNOWS?

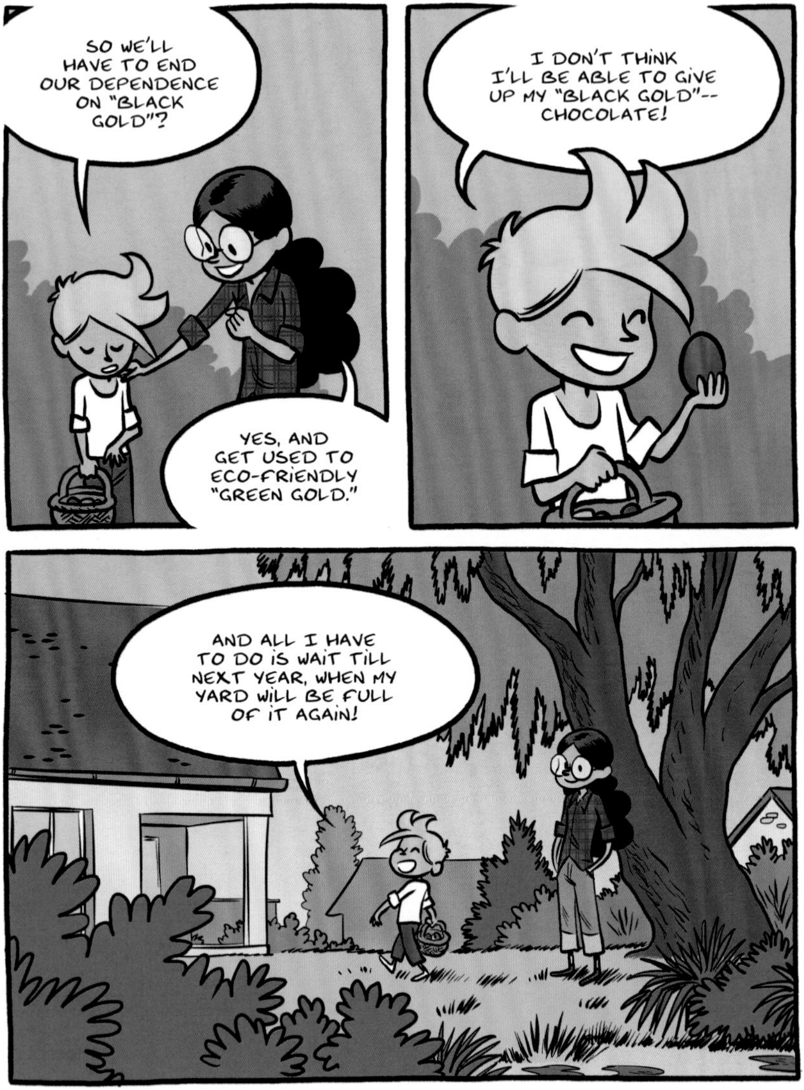
SO WE'LL HAVE TO END OUR DEPENDENCE ON "BLACK GOLD"?
YES, AND GET USED TO ECO-FRIENDLY "GREEN GOLD."
I DON'T THINK I'LL BE ABLE TO GIVE UP MY "BLACK GOLD"-- CHOCOLATE!
AND ALL I HAVE TO DO IS WAIT TILL NEXT YEAR, WHEN MY YARD WILL BE FULL OF IT AGAIN!

And there's more...

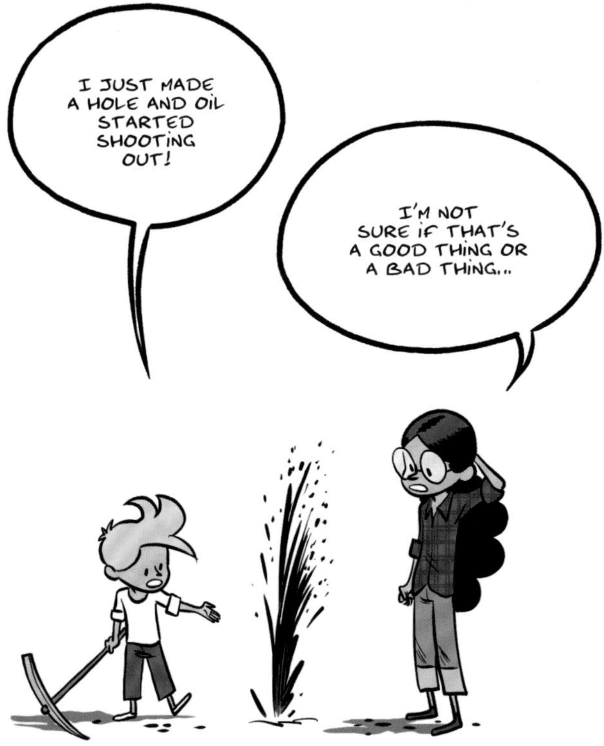
I JUST MADE A HOLE AND OIL STARTED SHOOTING OUT!
I'M NOT SURE IF THAT'S A GOOD THING OR A BAD THING...

Some people who made history

John D. Rockefeller
(1839-1937)

Rockefeller's father sold "miracle cures," and John started young in the business world. Attracted by the Pennsylvania "oil rush," he founded the Standard Oil Company, which by the end of the 19th century dominated the U.S. oil industry. In 1896, after becoming the richest man in the world, he left the company to his son and donated part of his fortune to various foundations—particularly for the creation of universities.

Henri Deterding
(1866-1939)

Born in Holland, Deterding went to work in Asia for the Dutch Petroleum Company, which he headed from 1899. Determined to compete with Standard Oil, he joined forces with the British company Shell Oil, forming what was then the world's largest oil-producing business. Nicknamed the "Napoleon of Oil," he managed wells all over the world. As a Nazi supporter, however, he went to live in Germany in 1936 and had to leave the company.

Calouste Gulbenkian

(1869-1955)

An Armenian financier, Gulbenkian was responsible for negotiating concessions with the Ottoman rulers on behalf of the European oil companies. Nicknamed "Mr. 5%" after gaining a 5% share in the Turkish Petroleum Company, he accumulated a vast fortune and a huge art collection. He spent his last years in Portugal and left his art collection to the government when he died.

Abdelaziz ben Abderrahmane Al Saoud

(ca. 1880-1953)

After 30 years of fighting, Al Saoud founded modern Saudi Arabia in 1932 and became its first King. The discovery of oil in 1938 made Saudi Arabia one of the world's major producers, and Al Saoud made an alliance with the Americans, who would manage the country's oil supplies and provide it with military protection—an agreement that continued after his death.

The Oil-rich United Arab Emirates

In the 1960s, huge reserves of oil and gas were discovered in a strip of land situated between the Persian Gulf and Saudi Arabia.

IRAQ
IRAN
AFGHANISTAN
KUWAIT
PAKISTAN
DUBAI
ABU DHABI
SAUDI ARABIA
UNITED ARAB EMIRATES

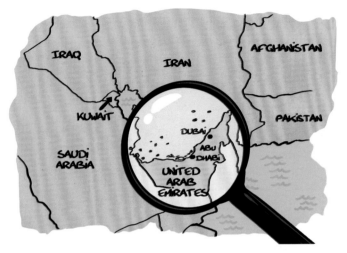

The **seven emirs** *(Arab tribal leaders) who then ruled over the area decided to join forces in order to exploit these resources, and they founded the* **United Arab Emirates** *in 1971.*

The country's founding President *is Zayed ben Sultan Al Nahyane, emir of Abu Dhabi (the country's capital), where the largest oil reserves can be found. Born in a village in the desert, Al Nahyane led the country until his death in 2004 and was responsible for the development of its oil industry, which made him one of the richest men in the world.*

Part of the wealth generated by the oil industry is distributed among the people of the UAE: **the state gives all citizens a house, as well as free education and health care**. But most (almost 85%) of the UAE's inhabitants are not citizens; they're foreigners, and they live and work in difficult conditions. Oil revenues have enabled the government to build ultra-modern cities, and, at over 2,700 feet, the **Burj Khalifa** tower in Dubai has been the world's tallest building since its construction in 2008.

The Burj Khalifa tower in Dubai has 163 stories.

But oil revenues will not last forever, and the Emirates are now looking to other sources of income, such as tourism. The **Louvre Abu Dhabi**, a museum of art and civilization, was opened by agreement with the French government in 2017.

The Louvre Abu Dhabi.

Oil and pollution

Deep drilling is needed to extract oil from the ground, and the gasses that escape from oil wells must be burned off. Both activities cause considerable pollution. The rivers near the wells at Khanty-Mansiysk in Siberia are so polluted that local people can no longer eat the fish, and the snow is no longer white, but gray!

Pump jacks in Siberia.

*Shipping accidents sometimes cause toxic "**oil slicks**," which can pollute coastlines and kill birds, coating their feathers with sticky oil. In 1999, the oil tanker "Erika" ran aground off the coast of Brittany, France, polluting 250 miles of shoreline; and in 2010, 11 people died when the "Deepwater Horizon" drilling platform in the Gulf of Mexico exploded, releasing 3 million barrels of oil into the sea and onto 1,250 miles of coastline.*

Oil slicks can kill tens of thousands of seabirds by gluing their feathers together.

*Oil is burned in engines and factories, which adds to the amount of carbon dioxide (CO_2) in the air. This leads to a "***greenhouse effect***," where the Earth's heat is "trapped" in the atmosphere—an effect that can have a negative impact on the planet's climate: for example, causing more frequent storms and turning more areas of land into desert.*

*Plastic, which is made from petroleum, is not bio-degradable, and growing "***plastic continents***," made up of millions of plastic objects that have been thrown away, can be seen floating on the Earth's oceans and drifting with the currents.*

NORTH ATLANTIC
NORTH PACIFIC
SOUTH PACIFIC
SOUTH ATLANTIC
INDIAN OCEAN

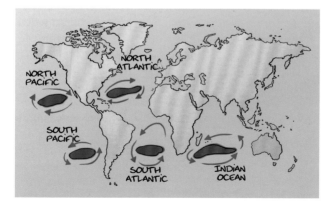

Timeline

The first oil wells
are dug in Baku
(Azerbaijan).

Edwin Drake designs
the first oil well in the
United States, starting
the "oil rush."

1847

1859

1935

1918-1922

Nylon, a synthetic
fiber made from oil,
is invented.

Britain and France
share the territory (and oil
reserves) of the former
Ottoman Empire.

1939-1941

1944

The control of oil
supplies helps the Allies
defeat the Nazis.

Aramco is founded, and
America takes control of
Saudi Arabia's oil supplies.

John Davison Rockefeller founds the Standard Oil Company.

▼

1870

The German Gottlieb Daimler invents the internal combustion engine.

▼

1885

1914 - 1918

▲

Oil becomes an international weapon during the First World War.

1903

▲

The first oil fields are discovered in Persia.

1945 - 1973

▲

The European and American economies enjoy an unprecedented boom thanks to oil.

1991

▲

Gulf War.

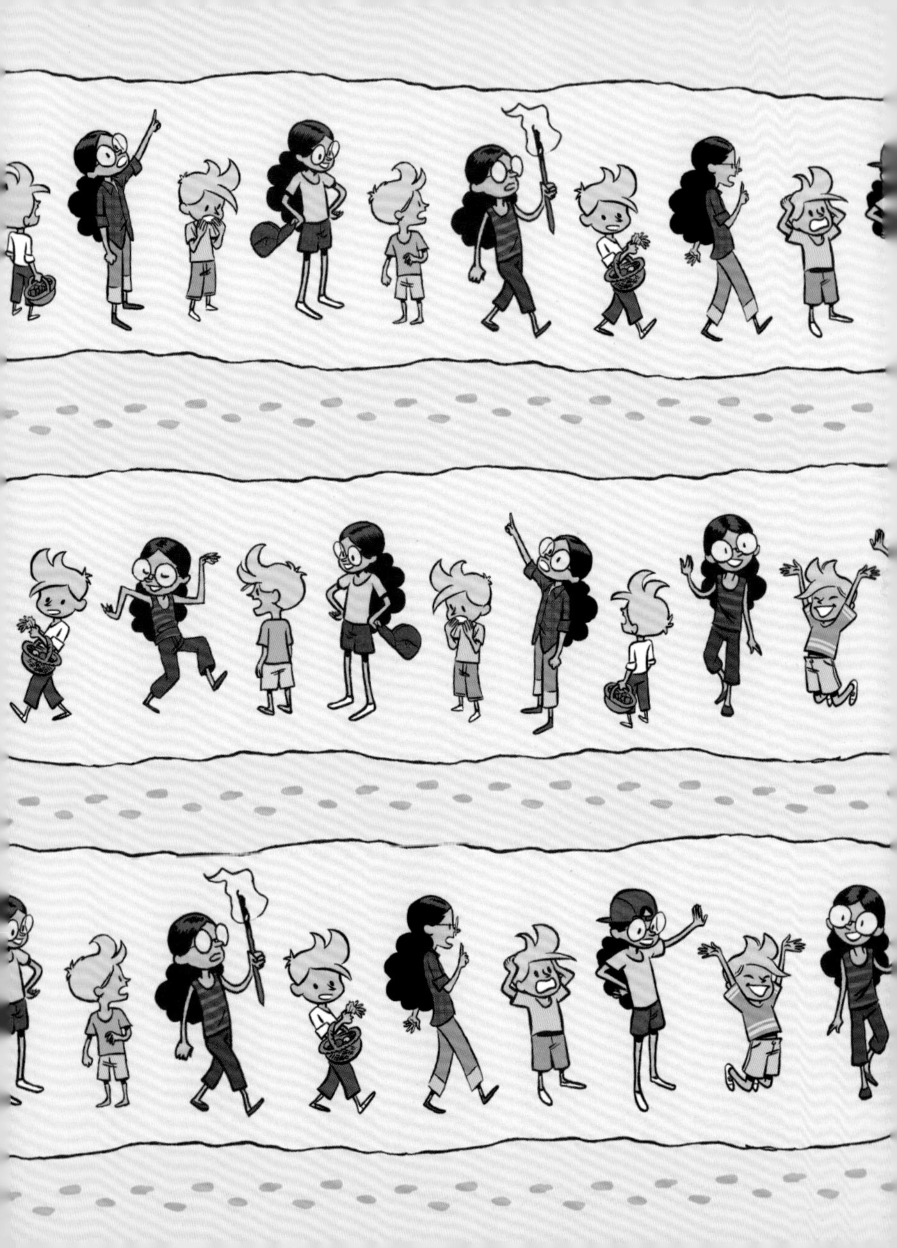

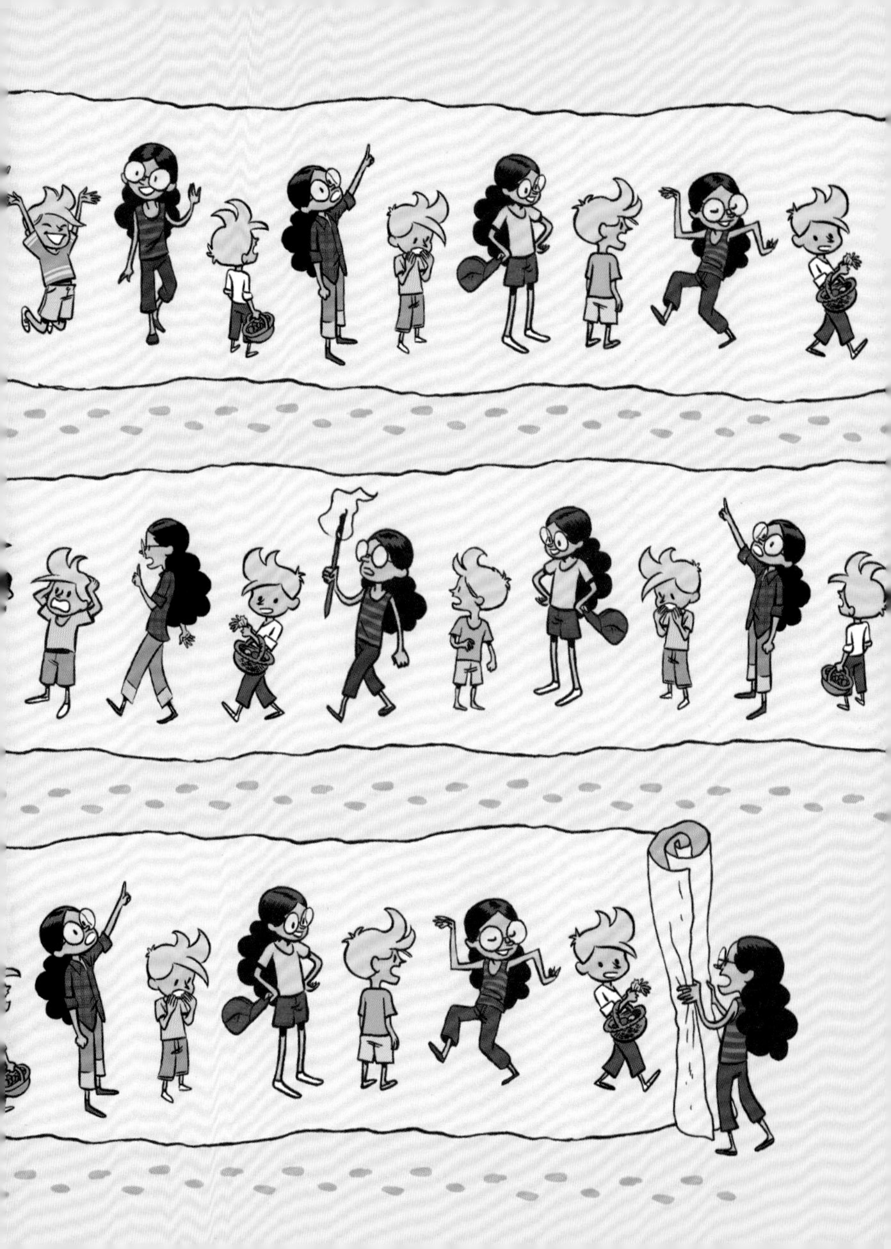

9781545806340

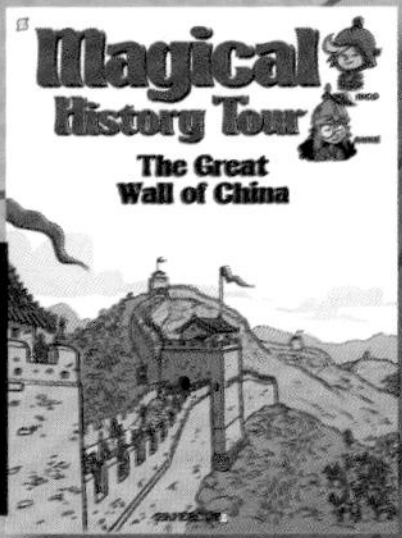
Magical
History Tour
The Great
Wall of China

9781545808948

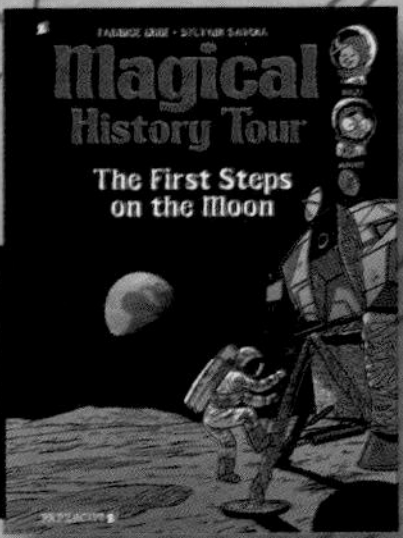
Magical
History Tour
The First Steps
on the Moon

9781545810347

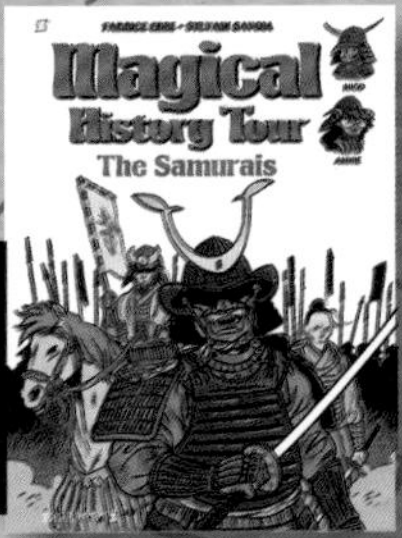
Magical
History Tour
The Samurais

9781545810057

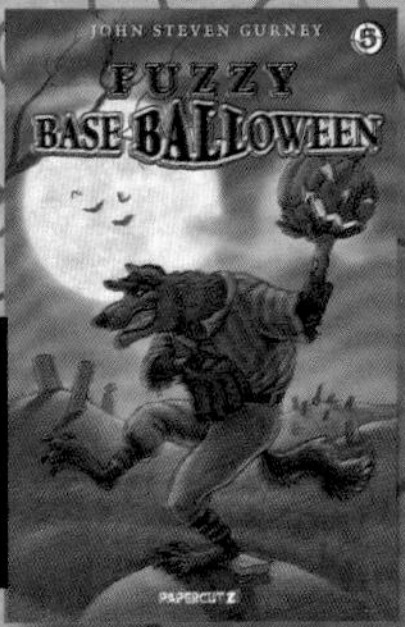
JOHN STEVEN GURNEY
FUZZY
BASE BALLOWEEN
PAPERCUTZ

9781545807217

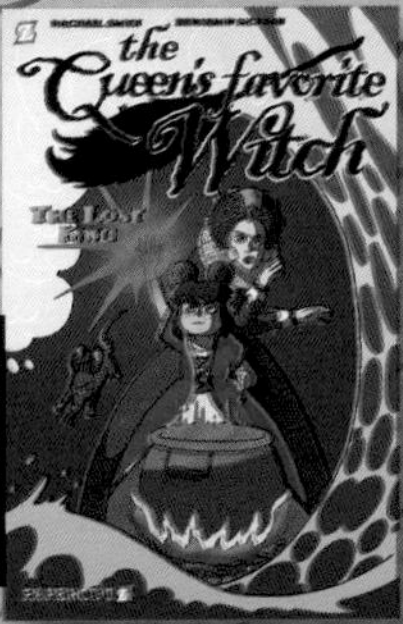
the Queen's favorite Witch

9781545809839

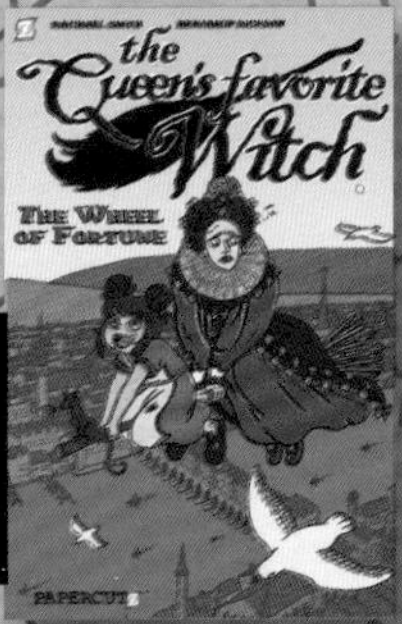
the Queen's favorite Witch
THE WHEEL
OF FORTUNE
PAPERCUTZ

9781545810217

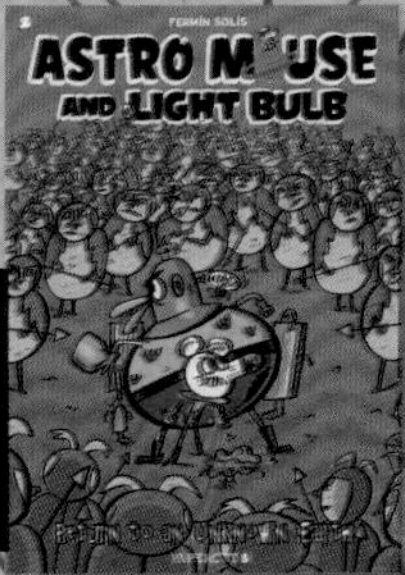
FERMÍN SOLÍS
ASTRO MOUSE
AND LIGHT BULB

9781545810194

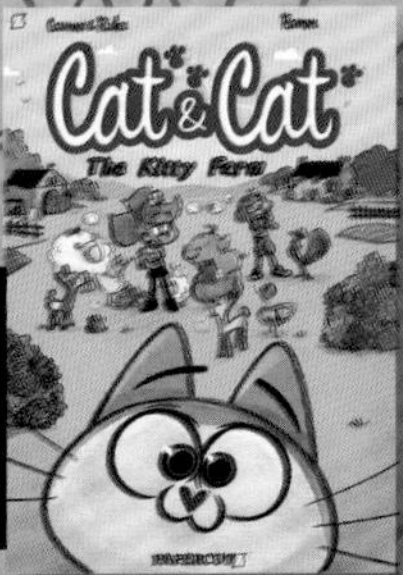
Cat & Cat
The Kitty Farm

9781545809730

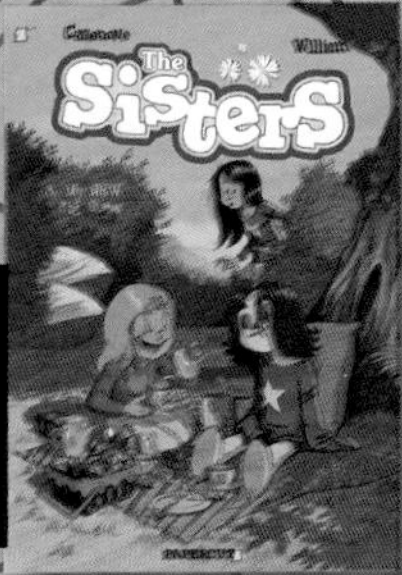
The
SisterS

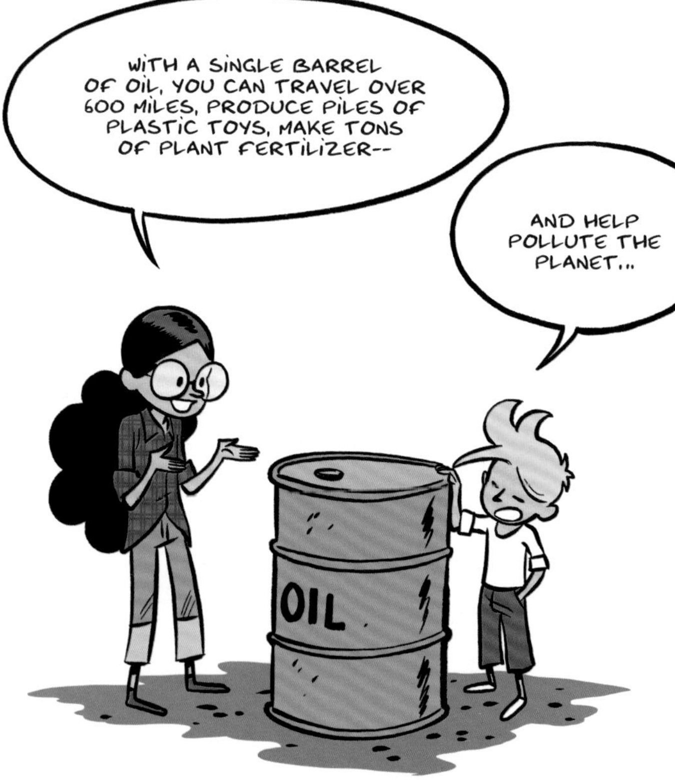
WITH A SINGLE BARREL OF OIL, YOU CAN TRAVEL OVER 600 MILES, PRODUCE PILES OF PLASTIC TOYS, MAKE TONS OF PLANT FERTILIZER--
AND HELP POLLUTE THE PLANET...
OIL

Fabrice Erre has a Ph.D. in History and teaches Geography and History at the Lycee Jean Jaures near Montpellier, France. He has written a thesis on the satirical press, writes the blog *Une annee au lycee (A Year in High School)* on the website of *Le Monde*, one of France's top national newspapers, and has published several comics.

Sylvain Savoia draws the *Marzi* series, which tells the history of Poland as seen through the eyes of a child. He has also drawn *Les esclaves oublies de Tromelin (The Forgotten Slaves of Tromelin)*, which won the *Academie de Marine de Paris* prize.

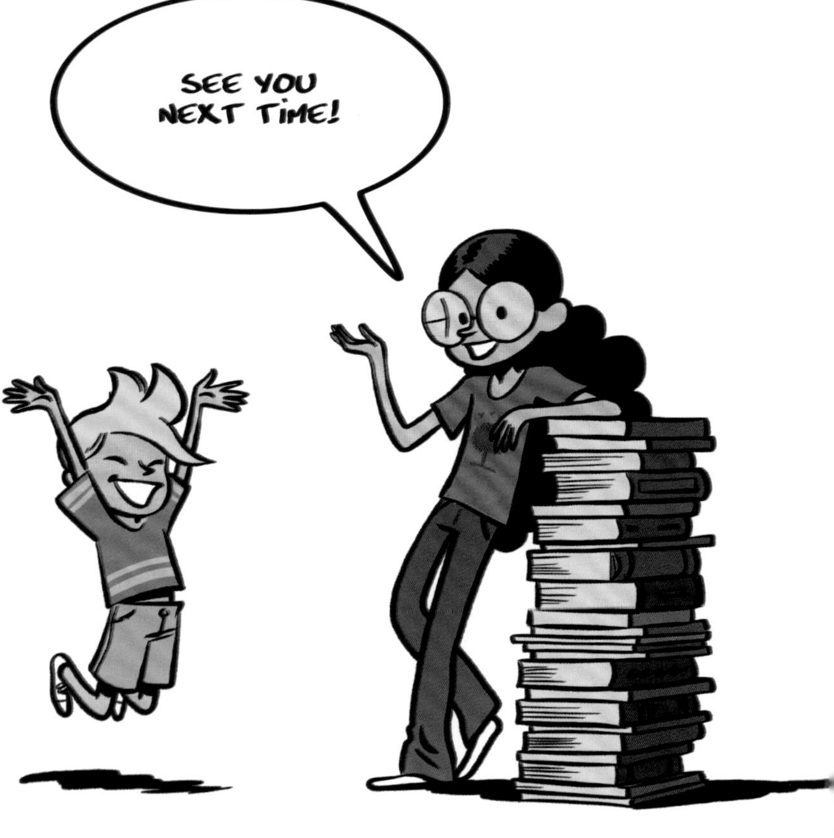
SEE YOU NEXT TIME!